# Enngonia Road

Richard Stanton

# Enngonia Road

## Death and deprivation
## in the Australian outback

G
P

## Publisher's note

Throughout *Enngonia Road*, material from original records has been quoted. No words have been changed, but some amendments to punctuation and paragraphing have been made in the interests of consistency and ease of reading.

*Enngonia Road: Death and deprivation in the Australian outback*
ISBN 978 1 76041 472 6
Copyright © Richard Stanton 2017

First published 2017 by
**GINNINDERRA PRESS**
PO Box 3461 Port Adelaide 5015
www.ginninderrapress.com.au

# Contents

# Foreword

On a lonely highway in the middle of the night, two teenage Aboriginal girls are killed in a crash. Like rag dolls, their bodies are thrown from the Toyota Hilux when it rolls at high speed. One suffers massive internal injuries. The other has her ear and scalp torn off. They bleed out in the dirt.

A drunk middle-aged white man crawls out of the crashed ute. It's after midnight. He spreads a green plastic sheet on the stony ground. He drags the dead fifteen-year-old onto the tarp and pulls her pants down. He pushes her top up, exposing her breasts. He tries to have sex with her. He stretches out with his arm across her breasts and goes to sleep.

The police charge him. He hires a criminal lawyer from the big end of town. An anonymous benefactor pays his expensive legal costs. The case drags on. Two years later, he fronts court. He walks.

This story is about the justice system that saw Alexander Ian Grant acquitted of killing Mona Lisa Smith and Jacinta Rose Smith and of a charge of indecently interfering with fifteen-year-old Jacinta when she was dead. It describes the sad events which led to their violent deaths. It analyses the police case, which was so fragmented that it failed to gain a conviction. It seeks to understand what caused the deaths of the girls, why the police got it so wrong and how the accused walked away from the crash without a scratch and away from the court a free man.

The tragic events occurred north of Bourke, New South Wales, in 1987. Cousins Mona and Jacinta – aged sixteen and fifteen – died violently in a motor vehicle crash in the middle of the night. Mona and Jacinta were passengers in a utility owned by Alexander Ian Grant, who was so drunk he could barely speak. There were no other vehicles involved. The ute was going flat out before it skidded and rolled. The driver's side of the roof was smashed in. As her body was flung through the busted windscreen onto the bitumen, Mona was scalped. She rolled into a drain and bled out in the dirt. Her left ear was missing and there was a large gaping wound from her left eye back to the base of her skull. Her blood soaked into the parched earth.

Jacinta (also known as Cindy) suffered massive internal injuries. She died slowly. Grant was uninjured. He was still so drunk the next morning, a few hours after the accident, that he could not recall what had transpired that night.

What did happen was that sometime between midnight and 4.30 a.m., Grant stripped fifteen-year-old Cindy's clothes off, laid her dead or dying body on a plastic sheet next to his busted ute, and attempted to have sex with her. He spent the next two years defending himself against causing the deaths of the girls and against the crime of 'offer indignity' – attempting to have sex with Cindy post-mortem.

The police took more than two years to build an acceptable prosecution case to take to trial. And then the case was badly managed from start to finish. The detective in charge appeared to be uninterested in obtaining a conviction. After all, it was only a couple of dead 'gins'. Other officers, some more senior, appear to have been similarly disposed towards the cultural divide in and around Bourke.

A few months before the incident, one of the officers on the case had been injured in a riot in the nearby town of Brewarrina. The riot was triggered by the death in police custody of an Aboriginal man named Lloyd Boney. There was plenty of bad blood between the police and the Aborigines.

Alexander Ian Grant was an itinerant worker who claimed to own a share in a small business. There was no solid evidence to support his pumped-up claim. He lived in a caravan park and owned nothing of value. His costly defence was financed by anonymous benefactors. To his wealthy silent partners, cost was no object. They engaged Sydney law firm Picone & Howes and leading Sydney crime barrister Anthony Quinlivan for more than two years.

This story is built on a forensic analysis of police and court transcripts, lawyer's notes, lawyer interviews, official records of interviews, ambulance logbooks, coroner's reports and author observations.

Times change and so it would be fair to say that Grant would not have got the same result had he been accused of killing Mona and Cindy today, almost thirty years later. On the other hand, he might still have escaped, given that Sydney's Lindt café killer Man Monis was free on bail for sex charges when he took and killed a hostage in December 2014. The coronial inquiry into the Lindt café siege that concluded in 2016 claimed to have been a careful factual analysis of what happened rather than a witch hunt. There was never any careful factual analysis of what happened in the dead of night on the Enngonia Road in 1987 – until now.

Mona and Cindy had lived their brief unremarkable lives in Bourke, a moribund violent town on the edge of the outback. This book is therefore also a representation of the hopeless despair that hangs over such towns where life and death are cheap and where the tradable currencies are sex and drugs and alcohol.

# Part One

# 1

# Introduction

On Saturday 5 December 1987, some time around 10 p.m., Mona and Cindy Smith took a ride in a Toyota Hilux with forty-year-old itinerant excavator operator Alex Grant. They drove north from Bourke, New South Wales, towards the Queensland border. They were near the village of Enngonia when the ute rolled and killed them.

The following morning before sunrise their bodies were found beside the wreckage of the ute. Mona had half her scalp torn off. As a result of being thrown violently through the front windscreen, her ear had been ripped off and she had sustained multiple internal injuries. Her younger cousin Cindy was found lying dead on a neatly arranged tarpaulin. Her tracksuit pants and underwear were around her ankles and her T-shirt was around her neck, exposing her breasts. Next to Cindy with his arm draped across her body lay Alex Grant, the owner of the vehicle.

Grant was so drunk he could not recount later what had occurred. He was taken to Bourke district hospital, where he was tested for blood alcohol content. While at the hospital, he gave a statement to police, followed later by another statement at Bourke police station. He then left town and travelled freely to Nyngan, more than two hundred kilometres away. A few days later, Bourke police drove to Nyngan, where they found Grant holed up in a sleazy motel still dressed in the clothes he had on at the time of the crash. He made no attempt to escape nor to resist. He was charged with two counts of 'wilful neglect or misconduct causing grievous bodily harm' and, even more bizarre, 'owner permit unlicensed driver'.

At a much later date, he was charged with interfering with a dead body, which was a polite way of saying he had attempted to have sex with a corpse. Based on the evidence available to the police, the initial charges were a denial of the facts.

It took more than two years for Alex Grant to be brought to trial. He was not arrested nor remanded in custody. He was free. There were no bail conditions and no financial sureties.

# 2

# The bodies are found

Very early on 6 December 1987, at precisely 4 a.m., two four-wheel drive utes carrying two drivers and four passengers rolled out of Bill Campbell's farm at North Bourke and headed towards Quilpie in Queensland. Quilpie was a small town 660 kilometres or nine hours' drive from Bourke. As the vehicles drove onto the Mitchell Highway, the radio in the lead ute announced the time. A passenger in the vehicle, Texter Johnson, remarked that they were getting away to a good start.

Tex, as he was known, was the foreman at Campbell's Ferguson Farm. He was in the truck with his wife Adele and the driver Michael Baty, who went by the nickname Joe. Michael's brother, Shane Baty, a seasonal worker, was driving the second ute, a 1984 Toyota Hilux, with passengers Shane Degenhart and James Kennedy.

It was a cloudless, dark morning. There was no traffic. The two vehicles travelled north at the speed limit. Both utes had bench seats, which meant a relatively tight squeeze for such a long drive. They had been driving steadily for half an hour or more when the lights from the lead vehicle picked out something unusual.

Michael Baty slowed to a stop on the shoulder of the highway. He turned his ute round and drove slowly back to examine what they had seen. He parked his vehicle on the wrong side of the road, shining his lights onto what they now saw was a vehicle on the left side of the roadway with its nose poking out onto the gravel near the scrub line of hop bushes. What they saw next was too shocking to contemplate.

Tex Johnson got out of the ute. He told his wife to stay in the truck. As he walked towards the vehicle in the scrub, he saw what appeared to be a human body lying on the gravel, face down, between the road and the vehicle. Tex knelt beside the body and checked it for signs of life. It was cold and purple and it seemed as though it had been dead for a fair while.

As Tex stood looking at the body on the ground, Shane Baty drove up in the second ute. When he saw his brother's ute stopped, he pulled up behind it. As he sat for a moment with the engine idling, Tex strode up the road shoulder, went round the side of the truck and spoke directly with Shane, who was sitting in the driver's seat. Shane then drove back into the road out and round his brother's ute. He parked so that his headlights shone down into the table drain and lit the scrub at the edge of the road. His headlights picked up something out of place near the scrub line about ten metres from the ute.

Adele called out to Tex, anxiety in her voice, that she could see other bodies. Tex walked gingerly towards the ute that was poking out of the scrub. A few metres beyond it and close to the scrub line, Tex saw two more bodies. Both appeared to be dead. Both were lying on a green tarpaulin spread neatly on the bone-dry red dirt in the table drain.

What Tex later said he saw was 'a body of a young Aboriginal girl lying on her back, she had her pants down around her ankles, but her legs were together. There was a fellow lying beside the dead girl on her right side, resting on his left side cuddling up to her with his right arm over her chest near about the centre.'

As Tex stood looking down at what appeared to be two dead bodies, Shane got out of his ute to have a closer look. He went towards the body lying nearer to the road. What he saw, he said later, was 'the person was laying [sic] face down and appeared to be dead. The person was dark skinned and appeared to be Aboriginal to me.'

Shane then went to where Tex was standing near the other two bodies. He knelt beside the body of the girl and felt for a pulse on the side of her neck. He found no sign of life. He then felt for a pulse under her armpit but, again, there was nothing. To Shane Baty's untrained eye, she also appeared dead and as he could find no pulse he assumed she was. He turned towards Tex and said as much. He also assumed the other person on the tarpaulin, a male, was also dead. But that was not the case.

As Shane felt for a pulse in the dead girl, the man on the ground began to come to. Shane was caught off-guard. He then did something unusual. He put the little finger of his right hand in the man's mouth to make sure his tongue was not obstructing his airways and that there was no vomit from which he might have choked. As he did so, the man lifted his head. He appeared to Shane to be 'very dopey in appearance'. He still had his left arm draped across the dead girl around her breasts.

Shane spoke to him directly. 'You've got two dead gins here, mate,' he said.

The man looked up. 'No, no,' he replied. 'They're all right. They've just had too much to drink.'

Shane looked at Tex then turned and spoke again to the man. 'Are you all right? How's your head and neck?' he asked.

The man did not reply. He lifted his head then lay back in a similar position to when he was first discovered, with his arm across the dead girl's breasts.

Shane went to his brother's ute, where he and Tex discussed what they should do. Then Shane went back to his ute, got in and pulled onto the highway. He drove to Enngonia, thirty-four kilometres north.

His brother Joe, still sitting in his ute, looked in his rear-view mirror. There was a large transport coming fast up the highway. He pushed the warning light button and his indicators began to flash on and off.

It was getting light as Shane drove to Enngonia but nonetheless his brother Joe, Tex and his wife Adele decided it would be best to stay at the scene until the authorities arrived. Tex said later they waited because he was concerned the crows would not distinguish between road kill and a dead human if they got hungry.

As Shane drove off, Tex walked back towards the ute and the tarpaulin. In the dirt at the foot of the tarpaulin was a half drunk bottle of beer.

As Tex stood nearby, the man on the tarpaulin lifted his head again and asked what was going on.

'We're all right, we're all right,' he said.

'That girl you're with is dead,' replied Tex.

'We're only resting,' the man responded in a slurred tone. He did not move from the tarp.

'That bloke up the bank is dead too,' Tex added.

'It's not a bloke. She's a girl. She's only resting too.'

Whatever it was that Tex had said, it triggered a violent response in the man lying on the tarpaulin.

As Tex later recounted, 'The bloke started getting very abusive and said something to me like "Fuck off. We're right."' This was over the top for Tex, given they had stopped to render assistance. 'We then left to Enngonia because since he was alive I figured the crows wouldn't get him. The fellow didn't get up at any stage and he was still lying down when I left. The guy was fully dressed when I saw him and although I didn't ask his name I did say, "Where are you from, mate?" and he said, "Bourke."'

Meanwhile, as dawn was breaking, Shane Baty and his mates had arrived in Enngonia.[1]

# 3

# The hot afternoon

When Alex Grant's excavator broke down on Saturday afternoon at around 12.30 p.m., Cindy was having lunch with her mother Iona. Earlier, around mid-morning, her sixteen-year-old cousin Mona was hanging around her Aunty June's house on the Reserve, not far out of Bourke on the Darling River. It was a warm day. Nothing much moved in Bourke in the summer months in the dry heat of the outback. Even short distances were travelled by car rather than walking.

The township of Bourke was dead flat. Away from the river, the streets were designed on a cross grid.[2] Between the river and the main highway, both of which take sweeping turns on the approaches to town, the streetscape was made up of commercial buildings and single-storey houses which were built for practicality rather than good design.[3] In 1987, the hotels dotted around town were also single-storey buildings, some constructed of timber, others of brick or stone. Most had small windows and large verandas to block the heat.

When his machine broke down, Grant removed the alternator and starter motor and put them in the utility tray and drove into town to try to have them repaired so he could continue working on the irrigation channels. It was not unusual for itinerant workers or contractors to operate seven days a week, given they were usually paid for the job rather than the time taken to complete it. The sooner the job was done, the better off they were financially. It is assumed that Grant was thinking along these lines when he travelled from North Bourke into town that Saturday afternoon. It was a fact that he was unable to find a repairer open after midday.

Unlike major towns and cities across Australia, service providers in small towns tend to stick to a cultural and religious routine that was favoured in the first half of the twentieth century – shut on Saturday afternoon and Sunday.

It was not a particularly hot day by Bourke standards; mean December temperature was thirty-five degrees centigrade. December generally records fewer than four days on which temperatures are above forty.

A combination of failure to find a repairer and a large thirst drove Grant to abandon his attempt to have the electrical components repaired.

The Oxford Hotel was an ugly single-storey building in Anson Street. The Oxford was three blocks from the police station and a considerable distance from the Mitchell Caravan Park, where Grant lived. The caravan park was on Mitchell Street, which became the Kamilaroi Highway leading to Brewarrina. Grant arrived at the Oxford around 2.30 p.m. He stayed there until 4.30 p.m. and drank six middies of beer.[4] At 4.30 p.m. he left the Oxford and made his way to the Central Hotel, where he drank a further middy.

The Central, whose full name was the Central Australian Hotel, was a two-storey art deco building overlooking the site of the former railway station. Grant rarely drank at the Central, preferring instead the less salubrious Oxford or the Royal. Grant went to the Central to try to find someone to fix the parts. More than five hours had elapsed since the breakdown, yet his motivation to have them repaired seemed undiminished by time or drink.

Unable to locate the person he was looking for, he left the Central and drove to the BP garage to see if he could get the battery recharged or replaced. The BP servo was across town on the North Bourke Road. There were other servos in town but it is not clear why Grant chose to drive from the Central to BP. He was, however, unsuccessful in his attempt to replace or recharge the battery so he went to a third hotel, The Royal, or Old Royal as it was known, where he had a further single middy. Grant appeared to have entered both the Central and the Royal looking for company or looking for someone who could assist him with his problem. Finding neither, he then left the Royal and returned to the Oxford, where he drank eight more beers and where he stayed until around 8.30 p.m.

Meanwhile, as Grant was immersing himself in alcohol, having eaten nothing since early that morning, Mona and Cindy Smith, along with their other cousin Lisa Edwards, decided after dinner on Saturday evening to wander down to the park. Convent Park, as it was known, was on Meek Street and gained its name from its proximity to the Convent of Mercy and St Ignatius' school. Shortly after they entered the park, Cindy and Mona changed their minds and went into town to buy cigarettes. Given the cultural context, there was nothing unusual in that. Large numbers of teenagers in outback and coastal towns across Australia spend aimless hours looking for entertainment. In 1987, cigarettes, alcohol, marijuana and sex provided the outlet. Today the addition of methamphetamines has exacerbated the problem.

On any summer night in Bourke, the sun sets well after 8.30 p.m. At 7.30 p.m. it's still full daylight, so walking around town posed no threat to the two teenaged girls. In fact, the boundaries of their world were defined by the distances they could walk. Car ownership was not widespread.

The neighbourhood was the neighbourhood. There was sufficient light to enable identification of individuals, known or unknown. In this, at around the same time that Cindy and Mona left the park to buy cigarettes, Cindy's brother Lloyd left his aunty's house in Anson Street, preparing to walk home to Meadows Road. It was a reasonably direct route along flat ground.

Meadows Road ran off Anson Street at the eastern end of Bourke township. Lloyd had been at the western end of Anson Street, near Yanda Street, where his aunty lived. For whatever reason, Lloyd's route was not straightforward. He detoured up Yanda Street to the corner of Adelaide Street, where he saw Cindy and Mona at around 8.30 p.m. Half an hour earlier, at around 8 p.m., Mona Smith had knocked on the door of a house at number 20 Adelaide Street. The door was opened by Daniel Booth, an eighteen-year-old, who knew Cindy and Mona. Mona asked him for a cigarette. The house was close to the corner of Yanda Street, so it was less of a hardship to try to persuade Daniel to give them cigarettes than to go into town to buy them. Sometime between 8 p.m. and 8.30 p.m., Lisa Edwards' sister, Betty-Anne, had left the Reserve to walk into town. The Reserve is located along Parkdale Road at the western edge of Bourke township. Parkdale Road is an extension of Adelaide Street so Cindy and Mona, hanging at the corner of Yanda and Adelaide Streets, were on the direct path being taken by Betty-Anne as she walked towards town.

At around 8.15 p.m., as she walked towards Adelaide Street, Betty-Anne was stopped by the driver of a white Hilux going towards town away from the Reserve. Betty-Anne was walking with a friend, Karen Johnson. Betty-Anne and Karen had a conversation with the driver of the vehicle, whom they later identified as Alex Grant. Grant then drove away. As Betty-Anne and Karen arrived at the corner of Yanda and Adelaide Streets, they saw Grant talking to Cindy and Mona. They overheard the girls asking Grant if he would turn round and drive them to the levee. The levee was an embankment that had its history in the 1890 flood that engulfed the town partly because of the construction of a railway embankment.[5]

It is unclear why Grant did not agree to give Mona and Cindy a ride to the levee. What he did instead was to drive away from the girls. He turned right into Yanda Street, crossed Mertin and Hope, then turned left into Anson. It was not difficult to watch the ute driving away; there were few houses in Yanda Street and a lot of open, flat ground. In fact, the corner of Yanda and Adelaide today remains open; there is a house on the north-west corner but all three remaining corners are vacant land as they were in 1987.

Grant continued east along Anson Street until he arrived at the Oxford Hotel, where he bought a six-pack of Fosters beer. He then drove north into town, where he stopped at the post office.

In 1987, the ubiquity of the mobile telephone was a long way off. Grant went to the post office to use the public telephones to attempt to contact his business in Wee Waa to report his unsuccessful attempts to fix the excavator. His lack of success continued as he was unable at that late time of night to reach the number in Wee Waa. Grant then left the post office and returned to the Mitchell Caravan Park with the intention of having something to eat.

For whatever reason, he was also unsuccessful in locating any sustenance at the caravan park. He got back in his ute and drove to the Carrier's Arms Hotel in Mitchell Street, where he stayed for at least an hour, consuming six glasses of bourbon and Coke and a further four full-strength beers. It is unclear why Grant chose the Carrier rather than returning to the Oxford, the Central or the Royal. What is important is that by 10 p.m. that night he had consumed thirty drinks in eight and a half hours. It may have been that the Carrier presented a straight-line drive down Mitchell Street which, by that stage of Grant's alcohol consumption, may have been all the encouragement he needed.

While Grant was in the Carrier, Mona and Cindy were still at the corner of Anson and Adelaide Streets hanging out, smoking, talking, chiacking each other and their mates. Lloyd Smith had already seen them sitting on the corner at 8.30 p.m. that evening. By 9 p.m., Daniel Booth, the boy they had persuaded to give them cigarettes, also saw them but by now they were walking in the direction of the Reserve, west of town.

Between 9 p.m. and 10 p.m. that night, Mona and Cindy were again approached by a white Hilux somewhere on Parkdale Road. The arrival of the ute and the decision made by the girls to go for a ride with the driver was most likely made at around 9.30 p.m. A number of elements of the chronology of what happened next were unclear. What was clear was that Grant was next seen and identified at the Riverview Hotel in North Bourke at 10 p.m., when he bought a half bottle of rum, two bottles of Coke and a further six-pack of stubbies. Grant entered the Riverview alone but the barman, Lawrence Charles

Barnett, claimed later in a statement of evidence that he saw a woman lingering in the doorway, ostensibly waiting for Grant to make his purchases.

The Riverview Hotel, now known as the Riverside Hotel or the Northey, was originally built around 135 years ago at the same time as the original bridge was built across the Darling. It was known then as the Telegraph Hotel. It was called the Riverview between 1940 and 2010, when it was razed by fire. It was located immediately adjacent to the old bridge. Today, the Riverside is some distance from the road. The old centre-lift bridge was built in 1883 and decommissioned in 1998.

In 1987, however, the ancient bridge and the highway crossed the Darling right beside the hotel. The relevance of the detail of the location of the bridge and the hotel relates to the time that Grant was last seen in Bourke and when he was seen in North Bourke. The seven-kilometre stretch of road between Bourke and North Bourke is today wide, well-maintained with long-sight curves and banking. In 1987 it was less well maintained and took slightly longer to travel, given that the newer stretch of road cuts out the old sharp turns and hairpin bends leading to the old bridge.

Nonetheless, the driving time at night with no traffic would not have been different. It may have taken an extra few minutes to traverse the road and the old bridge, but it would not have been much more than the ten minutes it now takes to drive from the centre of Bourke township to North Bourke at the junction of the Mitchell Highway leading north to Enngonia and the Bourke Hungerford Road. The Mitchell Highway takes a sharp right-hand turn at North Bourke before winding some way along the Darling then veering off straight north towards the Queensland border.

It was in the red dirt drain beside that stretch of long dark bitumen sixty-three kilometres from Bourke and thirty-three kilometres south of Enngonia that the lives of Mona Smith and Cindy Smith ended four or more hours after they drove away from the Riverview Hotel with Alex Grant in his white Toyota Hilux.

# 4

# The unremarkable lives

The lives of the three people involved in the accident on the Enngonia Road were unremarkable. Mona Smith and Cindy Smith were Aboriginal teenagers born in Bourke in far western New South Wales. Alex Grant was a middle-aged white man born in New Zealand. He had arrived in Australia ten years before. He was forty years old and lived in a caravan park. To piece together the events in the lives of all three is to construct images of individuals on the margins of society.

The elder of the girls, Mona Smith, was sixteen. She lived at 12 Yanda Street, Bourke. Cindy Smith was fifteen years old and lived at 143 Meadows Road, Bourke. Yanda Street consisted of a smattering of houses built of asbestos cement and corrugated iron. Most had high corrugated-iron fences on their boundaries. Yanda Street had a mix of residential and commercial blocks, many of which were vacant. Meadows Road was at the opposite end of town to the east and was the last residential street to the south of town leading in to vast tracts of flat scrub and grazing land. Meadows Road and Yanda Street were at the furthest ends of the town; Yanda Street ran north–south while Meadows Road ran east–west.

The Mitchell Caravan Park was located on the Kamilaroi Highway, which led out of town east towards Brewarrina. It was four blocks or roughly two kilometres from the town centre and two blocks from the junction of the Mitchell Highway and the Kamilaroi Highway. The caravan park was opposite the playing fields of the Bourke High School. The entrance to the park was on Becker Street. When Alex Grant lived at the park, it had eight cabins, eight powered sites, twenty-eight unpowered sites and twenty-five unpowered tent sites.

It is unclear where Grant lived at the park. The park reserved some cabins for workmen. He may well have lived in one of those. The whereabouts of possessions he may have acquired, those he either had with him in Bourke or had stored elsewhere, are unknown. We do know that there was a variety of tools and equipment in the tray of the utility at the time of the accident and they most likely comprised the sum of his working possessions.

What little is known about the life of Mona Smith is relatively simple. For sixteen years before her death, she lived in Bourke. There is a legend that poet Henry Lawson remarked that to know Bourke is to know Australia. Mona was part of that legend. She had lived in Bourke all her life, venturing no further afield than Enngonia to the north. The rail line from Nyngan had been abandoned by the New South Wales government before Mona was born. If there was a chance to travel to the nearest large regional centre of Dubbo, it would have been by bus or private car. Mona's mother had no need to travel to Dubbo, so neither did Mona.

Mona Lisa Smith was born on 29 November 1971, delivered at Bourke Hospital and taken home after a few days by her mother June. Like the lives of many women born in the middle of the twentieth century, June described her work as 'domestic duties'. It is unknown how long Mona's father remained with her mother after her birth. June was twenty-three when Mona was born and thirty-nine when she died.

Mona had brothers; one she was close to was two years older. Mona had attended the local primary school and high school until sometime around the middle to end of 1987. At some point, she made the decision to not return and spent her days in the company of friends, one of whom was Cindy. Mona and Cindy were cousins but the closeness of their ages also drew them together to become best friends. Mona had turned sixteen in November 1987 but she did not have a boyfriend. She was what was described at the time as a larger girl, which meant that she was overweight for her age and size; what might now be referred to as an inappropriate body-mass index, or BMI. She was described as being of short to medium height and of plump build.

Mona's mother June did not know when Mona decided to leave school and not to return nor did she know how much time Mona spent engaged in inappropriate activities such as drinking alcohol or having sex. Mona's mother did not approve of the girl's drinking habits but she consoled herself in the belief that Mona drank mostly beer. Beer was relatively acceptable. It was 'the hot stuff' – spirits and the like – that June was concerned with. She had never known Mona to drink the hot stuff but that did not mean she had not done so. Mona's mother, and her boyfriend Robert Nixon, spent considerable time drinking.

Mona lived with her mother, her mother's boyfriend and her brothers at the Reserve, a few blocks west of the main township of Bourke. The Reserve was within walking distance of the town, although access was easier and quicker by motor vehicle. Mona's mother did not own a motor vehicle but her boyfriend Robert Nixon did – a blue Ford automatic sedan. Like most cars owned by tenants on the Reserve, it was never without its keys in the ignition and at various times the vehicles could be seen being driven by teenagers keen to test their skills behind the wheel.

The day Mona died, she had dressed in black tracksuit pants, a navy blue hoody with a white band, red-topped football socks (also striped white and blue) and running shoes. She wore a silver earring in her left ear. She wore no other jewellery nor did she display any evidence of other body piercings or tattoos. While it may have been midsummer and therefore very hot weather, the wearing of such clothing was not confined to the cooler months. The white band on her hoody had printed on it the words 'Perisher Valley', referring to a popular ski resort in the Snowy Mountains of New South Wales. The irony of the statement emblazoned on the article of clothing would not have been lost in the town of Bourke, fewer than a thousand kilometres from the snowfields but, in the imagination, a world away.

Mona's slightly younger cousin Cindy led a parallel life. Cindy too had left school at an early age, spending her time wandering the streets, hanging out with her friends at the weir or the levee and generally being bored. Jacinta Rose Smith was born in Bourke on 23 October 1972. She was known as Cindy to her relatives and friends. Her mother, Iona, known by her middle name Dawn, called her Jacinta, as mothers frequently do when they have gone to the trouble of naming their babies. Cindy lived with her mother, three brothers and sister.

Her brother Lloyd, who was twenty-two at the time, played the role of protector, looking out for Cindy's well-being when he could. Despite his protector status, Cindy managed to spend a considerable amount of time wandering the streets of Bourke during the day, hanging with her friends at the weir or the levee and generally occupying her time in the pursuit of nothing. Like Mona, Cindy did not have a boyfriend but she spent most of her waking hours with groups of equally disadvantaged teenagers. Her short life was spent in and around Bourke. There were few opportunities to travel further and had they existed at all it is uncertain if they would have been grasped.

Cindy's mother Dawn lived with her children at Meadows Road. Dawn was thirty years old when Cindy was born. She had four children before Cindy and they all lived at the time of Cindy's death in the house in Meadows Road with their mother. Cindy was described as being short and of slight build.

On the day she died, Cindy was wearing a blue, yellow and white striped T-shirt, black tracksuit pants and blue and white running shoes. She was wearing white underpants with pink flowers.

Alexander Ian Grant was born in Hamilton New Zealand in September 1947. By his own account, he attended Fairfield College in Hamilton at the age of five. If so, his recollection would have had him attending the college in 1952. Fairfield College, however, according to its own records, was not established until 1957. Grant was not a person who had much respect for truth.

Grant's working life before being in Bourke in 1987 was haphazard and sporadic. When he was fifteen, he began work on his uncle's sheep farm in New Zealand. He claimed he milked cows, which is bizarre. Three years later in 1965, he claimed to have taken himself out of farm labouring and into truck, bus and taxi driving. It was unclear whether an eighteen-year-old was legally able to obtain a taxi driver's licence in New Zealand in 1965. Grant claimed to have got married in 1965 but by 1970 he was divorced. Around that time, he moved from Hamilton to Auckland, where he took up work in earthmoving and construction. Grant may have spent six or more years living in Auckland but his employment and relationships are not recorded.

What is known is that in 1977 he relocated to Australia sometime around his thirtieth birthday when he went to work at Groote Eyland. At the time, the far north of Australia, and particularly Groote Eyland in the Gulf of Carpentaria, was alive to the discovery and production of bauxite. Earthmoving contractors and drivers were in huge demand.

In 1979, after two years in the north, Grant relocated to Moree, New South Wales. Cotton was the new flavour of the month with international investors and there was huge demand on the massive broadacre farms for skilled excavators to dig the vast irrigation channels that were being constructed and maintained. Between 1980 and his arrival in Bourke in mid-1987, little is known about Grant's movements and whereabouts.

By his own account, he claimed to have become a partner in a business in Wee Waa in 1984. The business, known as Major Metals Excavations, was listed as a steel fabricator and steel merchant. It has since relocated to Moree, a much larger town than Wee Waa but less than a hundred kilometres distant. In November the same year, Grant obtained a Class 5B motor vehicle driver's licence (1883XA). He listed his address as care of the business, which was the address printed on his motor vehicle driver's licence. Grant had renewed his licence at a cost of $20. One might assume he lived in Wee Waa and such an assumption is validated, for a year later, on 29 November 1985, he renewed his 5B licence with the altered address of Mainway Caravan Park, Rose Street, Wee Waa.

While it is speculative, it is also interesting that Grant continued to present his address as a caravan park, when he had for most of the previous year claimed to be a partner in a business in the town. There is nothing unusual for one to live in a caravan park for a short period of time while working in a district. If one has a financial interest in a business, it seems unlikely that a caravan park would be an appropriate residence in the longer term.

Grant arrived in Moree in 1979. It was not long before he was breaking the law. In late October 1980, he was charged with driving under the influence and in Moree court of petty sessions disqualified from driving for three months. He was fined $250, which he accepted rather than the alternative ten days' hard labour. A month later in Lithgow, he was charged with exceeding prescribed content alcohol (PCA) and driving while disqualified. He registered a blood alcohol content of 0.20. The limit then was 0.08 (it is now 0.05). He was fined $500 for being a disqualified driver and received a further disqualification from driving for an additional six months. On the charge of PCA, Grant had a custodial sentence deferred on entering a 'recognisance of self' and being placed on a good behaviour bond for three years with a fine of $1,000. Grant received a suspended sentence under s.558 of the then Road Transport Act.[6]

It may be assumed that Grant was already uninterested in the consequences of his actions as, in Moree in early February 1981, he was booked for exceeding the speed limit. The speeding charge was dismissed in the Moree court of petty sessions as no evidence was offered. Why the charge was dismissed when Grant was clearly still disqualified from driving is unknown. What is known is that he did nothing in the face of all the court-imposed penalties to modify his behaviour.

A little over two years later, in May 1983, Grant was arrested again for driving while disqualified. He appeared in Walgett court of petty sessions on 3 May, was fined $800 and disqualified until a specific date: 22 November 1984. What is most intriguing about Grant's behaviour in relation to his driving record is that eight days after the expiry of his driving disqualification, 30 November, he was issued with a Class

5 driving licence. After the accident and in the two years leading up to his trial in Bourke, Grant continued to exhibit a pattern of behaviour similar to that in which he had previously engaged.[7]

Almost two years after the fatal accident, Grant's charges had not been tested in court. In October 1989, he was living in the southern Sydney suburb of Sans Souci. It is unknown how he had supported himself financially since leaving Bourke nor what his continued involvement may have been in the business in Wee Waa. Payment of his substantial legal costs were also shrouded in mystery. Who paid his massive legal bills? Who paid his rent? What is known is that in October 1989, four months before his trial date, Grant must have had a brain snap. He applied for a Sydney taxi driver's licence. Sanity prevailed. It was refused 'on the grounds of the conviction recorded and charges pending'.

On 12 February 1990, four days after his trial in Bourke, Grant appeared in Sydney's Waverley court on a charge of assault occasioning actual bodily harm. He had left Bourke a free man, gone back to Sydney and beaten someone up. There is no record to show who he attacked or why. It would be speculation but the stress and anxiety associated with the trial may have provoked him. Or it may have been, as his record showed, that he was downright antisocial.

According to a woman who claimed de facto relationship status with Grant, Linda Jane Windsor, she and Grant got together in mid-1988. Windsor, in a handwritten letter addressed to whom it may concern and dated 22 January 1990, stated that during that eighteen months Grant had 'never once driven a car after drinking alchol [sic]. We both always travel on Public transport. We have discussed his accident on several occassions [sic] and my honest opinion is that I find it very hard to believe that he was driving when this accident occurred. Even when he drank alchol [sic] in New Zealand I never seen him drive a vehicle after.'[8]

While he worked contract on the irrigation channels, Alex Grant had been living at the Mitchell Caravan Park. Aside from information supplied in a witness statement, Grant's time in Bourke leading up to the day of the accident was undocumented. When not employed excavating, Grant had little interest in anything about the town other than occupying a seat at the bar of one or other of the six hotels. He was a heavy drinker. There is no firm evidence that he maintained a permanent relationship while living in Bourke, so his leisure time was spent drinking or cruising the wide dusty streets in his Hilux. Like most itinerant workers, he kept his tools and other paraphernalia in the utility tray.

On the day of the accident, it is likely that the utility also contained parts of the excavation machine. The reason for his presence in town that Saturday afternoon was due to the breakdown of its electrical components. When he was questioned by police the day after the accident, Grant said he had removed some components and brought them in to town for repair. There is no evidence to show the parts were left somewhere in town during the afternoon, or that they were in the back of the ute when the accident happened, or that they were collected from the scene and taken to Enngonia with the ute. Like the steering wheel, there is a lot of mystery surrounding the excavator parts and whether they did, in fact, ever exist.

# 5

## The death scene

It was a little after 5 a.m. on Sunday when police Constable Kevin David Harper was awoken from a sound sleep by a loud knocking on his front door. He was not keen to answer the knock. Harper had been on sick leave, which meant he was not on duty at Enngonia police station when Shane Baty arrived at the front door.

The police station and the adjoining police residences were low, iron-roofed, single-storey buildings joined by a roofed walkway. A large coolibah grew at the front, south corner of the station, otherwise the surrounding vegetation was sparse. In marked contrast to the surrounding scrub country, a shock of green grass sprouted between the buildings and the highway. There was a wire fence separating the residences and a steel fence along the front boundary.

Constable Harper dragged himself out of bed and answered the door. He took a few moments to grasp the situation but, having done so, went out to the side fence and shouted out at the house next door. When there was no response, he picked up some small stones and began chucking them on the roof. A short while later, a person emerged from the house half asleep, dressed in boxer shorts and a T-shirt. He went over to the fence and spoke with Constable Harper.

At the conclusion of their brief conversation, Constable Kenneth John McKenzie went back inside the second police residence, changed out of his sleeping gear and pulled on a pair of blue police-issue overalls. He put on his boots. He grabbed his notebook and left the house. McKenzie had been a police officer for five years. Before joining the police force, he had worked in Sydney for five years as an ambulance officer.

Constable Harper, despite being on sick leave, dressed and went outside to where the police vehicle was standing. He and Constable McKenzie got into the vehicle, turned onto the Mitchell Highway and headed south towards the accident site. They had no need of the police siren as there was no traffic on the highway other than 'Kingy', a roo shooter travelling south. About halfway between the accident site and Enngonia, Kingy waved as he passed Tex Johnson in the second ute heading towards Enngonia.

Tex, his wife Adele and Joe Baty arrived at the police station not long after. Although they were not far into their drive to Quilpie, Tex, Adele and Joe accepted the hospitality of the policemen's wives, who had dressed and made coffee. As they sat recovering from the event, sipping their coffee and talking about what they had witnessed, only one other vehicle passed through town, a road transport heading north towards Cunamulla across the Queensland border.

When McKenzie and Harper arrived at the scene, McKenzie stopped the police vehicle on the road shoulder, turned across the highway, and pulled up facing north, on the same side as the smashed utility. Both police constables sat for a few moments looking at the scene.

Police observation skills allowed McKenzie to grasp the situation quickly. As he later recalled,

> I arrived at the scene about 5.45 a.m. and saw a white Toyota Hilux four-wheel drive utility resting on its wheels, facing in a south-easterly direction at a forty-five degree angle to the south, in the western table drain. I saw the vehicle had sustained extensive damage to the roof portion of the vehicle and there was a male person standing near the passenger side door.
>
> I stopped the police vehicle on the western side of the highway, got out and walked toward the male person. As I approached this person I saw what appeared to be the body of a person which was lying on the western gravel shoulder, between the road and the front of the vehicle. I then saw another body, that of a female person, which was lying on top of a canvas tarpaulin on the northern side of the

vehicle, further toward the line of the scrub, behind where the male person was standing.

In what appeared to be a minor contradiction, Constable Harper claimed to have 'alighted from the vehicle on the near side and walked across the roadway'. It may be that Harper's sickness impaired his ability to recall minor details, such as where the police vehicle may or may not have been parked. As McKenzie mentions later, Grant was very intoxicated and needed to lean on the police vehicle to stay upright. He would have been unable to do so if the vehicle had been parked across the highway, as Harper indicates.

Nevertheless, both police proceeded towards Grant, who was by then standing near the passenger side of the smashed utility.

McKenzie asked Grant directly if he had been involved in the accident.

'Yeah, mate,' Grant replied.

'Are you all right?' McKenzie asked.

'Yeah, I'm all right.'

'Who was driving the ute?' McKenzie continued.

'I was.'

'Who owns it?'

'I do, or the business does.'

As McKenzie sought some initial answers to his questions, Harper cast his eyes about the scene.

I saw a deceased female Aboriginal person lying on the shoulder of the roadway. I then saw another female Aboriginal person lying on a tarpaulin on the nearside of the white Toyota utility. This person was partly undressed, being naked from the shoulders to the ankles. All items of clothing had been pulled up or down.

As Harper took in the scene, McKenzie did something really stupid. When he finished his initial conversation with Grant, he walked over to where the body lay on the tarpaulin. He squatted to get a better perspective and saw there the body of a 'young deceased Aboriginal female, which was naked from the shoulders to the ankles, laying on its back'. McKenzie then stood and, as he did so, he took unusual and inappropriate action. He grabbed hold of the edge of the tarp and pulled it from one side to cover Cindy's body. McKenzie covered Cindy completely with the tarp and as he did so, Grant, who had been leaning against the side of the ute, remarked, 'They're only asleep, aren't they?'

In disbelief, McKenzie responded angrily and aggressively, 'No. They're both dead.'

Grant appeared to be confused. He became evasive. 'No. They're all right. They're only sleeping.'

'I assure you,' McKenzie responded assertively in a louder tone, 'they are dead.' McKenzie stepped closer to Grant and asked him if he could explain what happened.

'I don't know,' Grant replied.

'Which way were you travelling?'

'I was going that way,' he replied, pointing south towards Bourke.

'Where did you come from?'

'Bourke.'

'Where were you going?'

'North Bourke.'

'Do you know where you are now?'

'Oh, not far from Bourke, aren't I?'

McKenzie shook his head. 'No. You're nearly at Enngonia.'

As McKenzie later recalled, Grant appeared to be talking in riddles and to be badly affected by alcohol, slurring his words and finding difficulty in remaining awake.

McKenzie pursued a different line of questioning. 'Were there any other vehicles involved?'

'I didn't see any other cars,' Grant replied. Then he changed tack. 'Are you sure they're both dead?' he asked McKenzie.

'Yes,' the constable replied, beginning to grasp the enormity of the situation.

Grant then pointed directly at Mona lying face down dead in the dirt. His statement surprised McKenzie and Harper. 'Ah, she was driving,' he said.

The police officers looked at each other. McKenzie then asked the man to produce his driver's licence. As he did so, McKenzie was close enough to him to determine his deep state of intoxication.

I noticed that his breath smelt strongly of intoxicating liquor, his eyes were very bloodshot and when he spoke, at times he was incoherent and slurred in his speech, having to be asked to repeat himself on a number of occasions. I saw that [he] was unsteady on his feet and on occasions he had to support himself against the police vehicle. [He] was dressed in a khaki shirt and trousers, wearing work boots. I saw that his clothing was disheveled [sic] and he was dirty and untidy in appearance. I formed the opinion that [he] was well affected by alcohol.

Having determined the man's state of intoxication, McKenzie then asked where he had been drinking.

'At the Post Office Hotel and some other places,' he replied.

McKenzie then turned the conversation back to Mona and Cindy. 'Who are the two girls?'

'I don't know their names. They just asked me for a ride out to the North Bourke Hotel.'

By now, McKenzie and Harper had been at the scene for around three quarters of an hour. According to McKenzie, at a little after 6.30 a.m., two ambulances arrived from Bourke. McKenzie continued to examine the scene, taking particular note of the vehicle.

I made an examination of the white 1985 Toyota Hilux four-wheel drive utility number OGQ921. I saw the vehicle had extensive damage to the roof, the offside toward the front and the forward nearside panels. The rear nearside wheel rim was buckled, however, all the tyres fitted were inflated and appeared in roadworthy condition. I was unable to open either of the vehicles [sic] doors as they were both jammed closed and it was necessary for me to reach through the drivers [sic] window to check the steering. On reaching through the window I found the keys were missing from the ignition and the steering was locked. I inspected under the front of the vehicle and saw all the steering linkages were intact and undamaged. There was a large quantity of tools and equipment scattered over the side of the road.

McKenzie noted that the key to the vehicle was not in the ignition. It was never found.

# 6

## The ambos and the detectives arrive

Kelvin John Brennan was the first on-call station officer at Bourke ambulance station on Sunday morning 6 December. At 5.18 a.m., Brennan received a call from Bourke Hospital. A patient needed to be moved from the hospital to the airport. At the same time, Brennan received notification of an accident on the Mitchell Highway south of Enngonia. Bourke ambulance station provided services across a wide area as it was the central station for the district. Brennan knew he needed to transport his patient to the airport before proceeding to the crash site, so he radioed his second on-call officer Ronald Francis Willoughby. Willoughby was at home in Bourke. His ambulance was parked in the driveway. Willoughby got the call from Brennan at 5.18 a.m. Willoughby dressed in his ambulance officer's uniform, closed his front door behind him and drove north along the Mitchell Highway.

Willoughby said he arrived at the scene 'just after 6 a.m.' in car 131. Police Constable McKenzie noted, however, that the 'ambulance' arrived at 6.35 a.m. It may have been that the second ambulance driven by Brennan, car 123, arrived at 6.35 a.m. as it was delayed by the patient hospital airport transfer. Whatever, unsatisfactory protocols and procedures were beginning to be put in place.

Thirty-four-year-old Ron Willoughby arrived at the scene, parked his ambulance as close as possible and immediately spoke with Ken McKenzie. McKenzie told him the details, or at least the information he had himself gathered by that stage.

'You've got two female patients there that are both deceased and that fellow over there is the driver and he appears to be okay,' McKenzie said.

Grant was by then leaning on the police car and within earshot of the conversation between McKenzie and Willoughby. 'No, she was the driver,' he called out, pointing in the direction of Mona lying face down in the dirt.

McKenzie gave him a death stare. 'Oh, she's the driver now, is she?'

While he was speaking with McKenzie, Willoughby looked over towards the ute and determined immediately that it had rolled.

Meanwhile, twenty-nine-year-old Kel Brennan had arrived in the second ambulance. Brennan directed Willoughby to check on Grant, who was by now, as Willoughby observed, 'standing around smoking a cigarette'.

Willoughby took Grant's pulse and checked his blood pressure, which appeared normal. When he had made his initial observations, he went to check Mona and Cindy, who he said were 'two young Aboriginal females which had both been covered'. 'One of the deceased was located near the roadside in a prone position covered by a tarp or something similar,' Willoughby noted. 'The other deceased female was found adjacent to the vehicle covered by a sheet of plastic or something similar.' He removed the covering and 'found that the deceased was partially naked'. Willoughby then checked for 'their vital signs', which were found to be absent.

It is unclear whether officer Willoughby re-covered either or both of the bodies. It is also not known if they remained in the position in which he found them.

What he did next was under further instruction from Brennan and McKenzie. Willoughby went over to Grant standing near the police vehicle. He assisted him into the front passenger seat of the ambulance. He then had another brief conversation with Constable McKenzie. Willoughby said later that McKenzie had instructed him to 'do certain things when I got to the hospital'.

Willoughby left the scene at 6.25 a.m. in car 123, the ambulance

Brennan had driven to the scene. Willoughby recalled some years later that the switch had been made because car 123 'had more room to convey the two deceased'.

On the drive to Bourke, Willoughby had a conversation with Grant. He asked a few questions. 'Who was driving the car?' Willoughby asked.

Grant was in a less than sober state, so any conversation was limited. 'I wasn't driving. One of the girls was,' Grant replied.

Willoughby thought it unusual that Grant had not said specifically which girl was driving. A little later he asked, 'Have you been drinking?'

Grant replied, 'I had a couple of stubbies since the accident.'

They drove on in silence for a while. When they were on the outskirts of Bourke, Willoughby was shocked when Grant asked him if he could drive him to the caravan park before going to the hospital.

'Can you take me to the Mitchell Caravan Park so I can tell my wife what happened?' Grant pleaded.

'No,' Willoughby said firmly, 'I have to go straight to the hospital.'

The ambulance station and hospital to the east of Bourke in Tarcoon Street were one block from the caravan park, north-east on Mitchell Street. The ambulance would have left the Mitchell Highway, turned into Tarcoon Street and travelled south for five blocks before arriving at the hospital.

As Willoughby conveyed Grant back to Bourke, Officer Brennan waited with the second ambulance at the crash site until detectives could arrive from Bourke. In gathering evidence, Constable McKenzie had determined that detectives from Bourke would need to be involved. Enngonia was not a big police station and did not have a detective on duty.

While waiting at the site, Kel Brennan contacted the ambulance coordination centre in Dubbo to ask that the male patient, Alex Grant, be held at Bourke Hospital until police could speak to him. Aside from the direct communication technology in the ambulance, which allowed Brennan to convey his message to Dubbo, there were no mobile telephones and the police radio was unable to make contact in that vast featureless landscape.

Kev Harper, Ken McKenzie and Kel Brennan decided that it would be best if Kev, as he was unwell, was taken back to Enngonia by Kel in the ambulance as it was uncertain how long Ken would be needed at the site and it was from Enngonia that the detectives could be alerted. With that, Brennan drove Harper back to Enngonia, arriving at 6.45 a.m. Brennan and Harper spoke little on the drive to Enngonia, then Brennan turned round and headed back to the crash site. He waited there with Constable McKenzie for the arrival of the detectives.

McKenzie wrote up his notebook. Officer Brennan recalled that the detectives arrived at the crash site at about 7.50 a.m. but this does not coincide with the time the detectives themselves say they arrived. It was the second time in a matter of hours that the first responders got it wrong.

Peter John Ehsman was the detective on duty at Bourke police station on the morning of 6 December 1987. He had logged on at 6.30 a.m. His log records that shortly after he entered on duty he drove out from Bourke along the Mitchell Highway thirty-four kilometres from Enngonia 're double fatal accident involving vehicle OGQ921, examine scene, 2 deceased females, photo scene confer with const Mckenzie [sic] from Engonia [sic] (females unidentified) then return to Bourke police station, speak to then R.O.I. with Alexander Ian Grant'. As far as his actions between leaving Bourke and entering the accident site were concerned, Ehsman said some time later that he recalled leaving Bourke around 6.30 a.m. on Sunday 6 December. On arrival at the scene, he said he saw a white Toyota Hilux four-wheel drive utility bearing registration plate OGQ921. The vehicle was in the western table drain resting on its wheels facing at an angle of forty-five degrees to the south. It had extensive damage on the offside and roof section; the roof on the driver's side was crushed onto the top of the driver's seat.

Ehsman was based in Bourke and McKenzie in Enngonia but they

42

knew each other reasonably well. Ehsman spent some time conversing with McKenzie while ambulance officer Brennan looked on. While McKenzie drew a pretty good sketch map, Ehsman made a close visual inspection of the scene. While waiting for Ehsman to arrive, McKenzie had taken extensive measurements of the roadway, the vehicle and the gear scattered all over the place. He had made precise measurements of the relationship of the vehicle to the bodies and to the tarpaulin, the windscreen of the ute, which had been popped from the vehicle as it rolled, the auxiliary fuel tank and a large toolbox. On returning to the police station, McKenzie had converted the sketch map in his notebook to a larger-scale drawing of the scene. It included wheel marks and the measurement of gouge marks in the bitumen surface of the road.

Ehsman recalled seeing the body of a 'female Aboriginal' lying face down on the western table drain between the front of the vehicle and the roadway. He saw that she had a large graze over the entire side of the left of her face, the left ear was missing and there was a large gaping wound from the left eye back to the base of her skull. He saw that she was dressed in dark tracksuit pants, tracksuit top and joggers.

Ehsman then went to the rear of the truck and on the northern side he saw a green canvas tarpaulin spread out on the ground. He saw the body of a 'female Aboriginal' lying on her back; her legs were spread apart and she had a pair of dark tracksuit pants pulled down to her ankles, a bra had been pulled down below her breasts and her top was pulled up under her chin. He saw that she was deceased and had a large cut under her left nostril and an amount of blood on her face. He saw a number of lacerations on her right side and upper arm and a large gash and lacerations to the area of her right pelvis and hip.

When he had completed his examination of Mona and Cindy, Ehsman turned his attention to the utility. He saw that the vehicle had extensive damage to the roof, offside panels towards the front, the front of the vehicle and the front nearside panels. He saw that the tyres were in a roadworthy condition but he was unable to open the doors.

The driver's door and the passenger's door were both jammed shut. Ehsman saw a large quantity of tools, toolboxes and a spare tyre, and a large metal fuel tank all scattered over the side of the road. He saw that the roadway was approximately six metres wide, constructed of sealed bitumen and in good condition. He saw a wide table drain on both sides of the road extending about six metres. He saw a skid mark on the roadway about two hundred metres south of the utility going from the eastern side of the centreline to the western side onto the dirt shoulder. He saw heavy skid marks in the dirt for a short distance then deep gouge marks facing east where there was broken glass.

Ehsman went to his police car and took a camera from the passenger seat. He snapped a number of photographs of the bodies, the ute, the skid marks and the scene more generally. He put the camera back in the car then went to the ambulance to, in his words, 'assist with the removal of the bodies who were then taken to Bourke Hospital'.

Ambulance Officer Brennan, however, provided a very different version of events. Brennan recalled later that 'detectives' arrived, implying there was more than one. To this he added, 'after the detectives left I assisted the other police officer at the scene to load the deceased into the rear of the ambulance'. The 'other' police officer Brennan referred to was Ken McKenzie, who had remained throughout. It is of little consequence whether or not Ehsman assisted in moving Mona and Cindy to the ambulance, nor of whether Officer Brennan made an error by saying 'detectives' rather than the singular. What is crucial is that before the scene had been cleared of its actors and props, the police and ambulance officers were at variance with the facts.

Brennan closed the rear door of the ambulance, walked to the driver's side door, climbed into the ambulance and at precisely 8.32 a.m. on that clear Sunday morning in midsummer, drove the sixty-three kilometres to Bourke. Brennan arrived at the hospital with the bodies of Mona and Cindy at 9.06 a.m., a little less than twelve hours after they had set out from the North Bourke Hotel with Alexander Ian Grant to go for a drunken Saturday-night joyride.

# 7

# The interview at the hospital

After a fatal motor vehicle accident, a variety of governmental and civil actors are mobilised and deployed. The most immediate are police and ambulance officers. There are two distinct frames and one less distinct frame.

Actors can be described as primary: the victims, the perpetrators and witnesses to the crime. Secondary actors include police officers, ambulance officers, hospital staff such as medical examiners, and family members of the victims and perpetrators. Tertiary actors include the prosecutor, the defendant's barrister, the trial jury, and character witnesses for both the victims and the defendants.

Many primary and secondary actors were active that Sunday morning in Bourke. The victims arrived at the hospital in Officer Brennan's ambulance, car 123. They were removed from the ambulance and taken into the hospital morgue. The owner of the ute, Alex Grant, also arrived by ambulance at the hospital. Grant was not at the hospital for long. On his arrival, he was assisted from the ambulance by Officer Brennan and taken inside. According to Officer Brennan, he arrived at the hospital at 9.06 a.m. Immediately after his arrival, Grant was asked for a blood sample which, according to hospital records, was taken at 9.10 a.m. Here there is another variance in the time scale of events.

There is no question that at the accident site Alex Grant was questioned by Constable Ken McKenzie. It is also not in question that Grant was conveyed from the site by ambulance before the arrival of Detective Peter Ehsman. Thus when Grant arrived at the Bourke Hospital, McKenzie was the only police officer to have interviewed him, however informally. Constable Harper was present at the site but did not take part in the conversation with Grant.

On his arrival at the hospital, Grant was met by Constable Peter Christopher Clarke of Bourke police. Constable Clarke, twenty-nine years of age, was at the hospital much earlier than Grant's arrival, for reasons unknown. At a later date, he claimed to have been engaged in conversation with 'other police' at precisely 7.10 a.m. Clarke made no clear distinction between the time of his conversation with other police and the time he met Grant and recorded an interview with him. At a much later date he stated, 'Whilst present at the Hospital, and awaiting medical personnel I had a conversation with the person Grant where I recorded the following version of a motor vehicle collision which had occurred on the Mitchell Highway, Enngonia.'

Clarke recorded that Grant then said of his actions the previous day,

> I was ringing up from the Post Office here in Bourke, I was ringing a partner in Wee Waa. These two Murrays [sic] asked me to give them a ride home. I said I'm going this way. I thought they lived in North Bourke or something. The two girls and myself got in the Toyota and headed towards North Bourke. One of the girls said 'give us a drive'. I said 'No. Nope.' I thought from a moment, there was no traffic about so I thought 'OK. Why not'. I don't know which one it was, I don't know their names. Got in and headed towards Enngonia, just past North Bourke pub. She started driving and away she went. Got out on the road there, I thought a bit too far there and I said 'Come on, lets [sic] go back.' The girl turned around and I didn't come very far down the road and bang that was it. After the accident I got out and one of the girls got out and took off her clothes and said 'Ya, want me?' I said 'No, we've got a problem here.' I then looked around and there was no traffic and that and I said to myself 'What the hell, we've got a rolled Toyota here'. She layed [sic] down on the ground and I didn't touch her. A car came along and asked if we were all right. They left and then the Police came.

Clarke recorded further details. In the meantime, Detective Ehsman had returned to Bourke police station. Constable McKenzie had waited at the accident site until a tow truck arrived to take the smashed ute back to Enngonia. It is unknown what McKenzie did following the departure of the tow truck. It is possible he followed it to Enngonia then sometime late drove to Bourke, where he wrote up his occurrence pad and prepared other information about the event. More likely, he went straight to Bourke to make sure he got all his ducks lined up.

If the ambulance officer was correct about his arrival at the hospital, placing the time at 9.06 a.m., and if blood was taken from Grant at 9.10 a.m., then Clarke began his interview with Grant sometime immediately after that. The length of the transcript of the recorded interview indicates it would have taken around thirty minutes to complete. Clarke said later he 'attended the Bourke District Hospital Morgue where I inspected the bodies of two deceased females'. The timeline for this appears reasonable, given that Clarke claimed to have spent some time after the interview going over each word with Grant for the purposes of precision. The language is interesting. Clarke refers to him as 'Grant' or 'the person Grant'. But there is no pattern in his use of either.

Clarke recorded the following.

'You mentioned to me, prior to me taking your version of the collision, that at one stage you grabbed the wheel. Is that correct?'

Grant[9] replied, 'I grabbed the wheel, that's correct I grabbed the wheel and said "slow down". She was going all right then, Well, then after that, she was going all right, then was going a bit quicker obviously, then she went off the road and that was that.'

I said to the person Grant, 'Where [sic] you sitting in the vehicle?'
Grant replied, 'Left hand side.'

I said to Grant, 'Where abouts in the vehicle were you seated?'
Grant replied, 'On the outside left.'

I said to the person Grant, 'Where were the other girls [sic] positioned in the vehicle?'

Grant replied, 'Both on the right, the same bench seat.'

I said to the person Grant, 'The girl who was naked, where was she seated?'

The person Grant replied, 'In the middle, the other one was driving, that's it.'

I said to the person Grant, 'What time did you leave Bourke?'

Grant replied, 'I don't know what time it was, about 11 or 12.'

I said to the person Grant, 'How long after you left Bourke was it that the accident occurred?'

Grant replied, 'I don't honestly know, I can't honestly say, I don't know, say about 2 o'clock, 3 o'clock, I don't know I can't confirm it. It was around, let me think, I'd be telling lies if I said, it could have been 1 o'clock 2 o'clock. I don't know, it could have been later.'

I said to the person Grant, 'What was the speed of the vehicle prior to the accident?'

Grant replied, 'About 70-80 kilometres per hour, it wasn't real quick, not once, or maybe once she got to 100 kilometres per hour then I jumped on her.'

I said to the person Grant, 'Have you consumed alcohol between the time of the accident and prior to being spoken to by the Police?'

Grant replied, 'No.'

I said to Grant, 'How much alohchol [sic] have you had to drink recently, prior to the accident?'

Grant replied, 'I was down the Carriers for a while before the accident, 6 to 8 or 10 middies. I don't keep count of 'em.'

I said to the person Grant, 'What time did you have your first drink?'

Grant replied, 'About 5 last night, about 5.30–6 last night.'

I said to the person Grant, 'What time did you have your last drink?'

Grant replied, 'Had a couple of stubbies on the way out along the road. I don't know, say maybe about 11 or 12 last night.'

I said to the person Grant, 'Are you injured in any way?'

Grant replied, 'No.'

I said to the person Grant, 'Did you see the woman, you allege was driving, drinking at any stage?'

Grant replied, 'She had one stubbie I don't know what she was drinking before that. I'd say she hadn't had a lot. But on the cards she could have had a lot.'

I said to Grant, 'When did you see her consume the 'Stubbie'?'

Grant replied, 'When she got into the Toyota cause it was one of mine.'

I said to the person Grant, 'Which way were you travelling at the time of the accident?'

Grant replied, 'I don't know, I think we were heading back towards Bourke, I'm not real sure.'

# 8

# The interview at the station

At the conclusion of the interview, Grant was asked to sign what Clarke described as 'a record of conversation', which he did. This was the first formal interview between Alex Grant and the police. While he was waiting at the hospital, Constable Clarke left Grant alone while he went to speak to medical staff. He then returned to speak to Grant. In a statement at a later date, it is unclear where Clarke may have been at the time. He states, 'I later again spoke to Grant, recovered my notebook and left the Police station.' It may be that Clarke meant he left the hospital. There is no evidence of Grant's movement from the hospital to the police station, a distance of five blocks or a kilometre that would have required the services of a car.

There is evidence that Grant was at the police station before 10.30 a.m. because he was interviewed by Detective Ehsman at that time. The interview was long and detailed. It did not conclude until 12.20 p.m. The interview between Grant and Ehsman was in the presence of another police officer, whose signature appears at the bottom of the last page of the interview transcript. The signature is illegible but the notation Sgt appears beside it with the time noted as 12.38 p.m., which was the conclusion of the interview.

The transcript of interview bears no notation on the first page that a witness other than Detective Ehsman was present. There is an illegible sign-off on the bottom left-hand corner of each page. Grant and Ehsman also signed the bottom of each page. At a later date, Ehsman explained that on his return from the accident site he observed Grant sitting at the inquiry counter at the police station. This was the first time Ehsman had come into contact with Grant. Ehsman had seen the bodies of Mona and Cindy at the scene but when he arrived, Grant had already left to be transported by ambulance to Bourke Hospital.

Ehsman walked over to Grant sitting at the inquiry counter. 'I am Detective Ehsman. I am going to interview you about the fatal motor vehicle accident you were involved in earlier this morning. Before I do I am going to make further inquiries. I will speak to you shortly.'

Grant remained seated. He said that he understood.

Soon after, Ehsman returned and took Grant into the detectives' room, where he conducted and recorded his interview.

Ehsman sat Grant down and looked him over. 'I intend to record these questions and any answers you may care to give on a typewriter, do you understand that?'

Grant said that he understood. It is important to keep in mind that while it was early Sunday morning, Grant was still severely intoxicated. And he had been wearing the same work gear for more than twenty-four hours.

Ehsman began.

'I am Detective Ehsman, I am going to ask you some questions concerning a motor vehicle accident which occurred earlier this morning about thirty-four kilometres south of Enngonia on the Mitchell Highway in which two females were killed. I want you to understand that you are not obliged to say anything unless you wish as anything you do say will be taken down and may later be used in evidence. Do you understand that?'

Grant replied yes, he understood.

'At the conclusion of the record of interview you will be given a copy of this interview and you will be given the opportunity of signing it if you wish. Do you understand that?'

'Yes.'

'For the purpose of this record of interview, what is your full name, date of birth and address?'

'Alexander Ian Grant, 22/9/47, Mitchell caravan park.'

'Are you married or single?'

'The woman I'm living with is a partner in the company.'

'Where are you employed?'

'Self-employed, excavator.'

'What is the name of your business?'

'Major Metals excations [sic].'

'How long have you been employed here at Bourke?'

'I started in July, the 20th. I work for Westbeef, Tancred, Jack Buster. I've had the company going for about three years.'

'Earlier this morning there was an accident involving a vehicle registered number OGQ921 on the Mitchell Highway, thirty-four kilometres south of Enngonia. What can you tell me about this?'

'I was down the post office here ringing up, I was trying to ring Ron over Wee Waa, my partner, I never got on to him. That's when they asked me if I could give them a lift. I said where you going, they said, over north Bourke, I said I'm going the other way, they said it wouldn't take you long to get over there. I said all right, they got in and we drove to North Bourke. The bigger one of the two asked me if she could drive. I said if you're real steady you can have a drive. I let the bigger one drive. She drove a fair way along the road, I would have thought it was thirty or forty kilometres. I said, pull up, we're going back. We stopped and had one stubbie. I said, right we're turnin' around and going home.'

'What happened when you pulled up and had a stubbie?'

'Nothing happened much at all. I went out to the toilet had a smoke, we had a yarn.'

'What were you talking about?'

'I told her I was working at Bourke, excavations, you know nothing of any substance really.'

'Did you make any advances to either of these two girls?'

'I had my arm around her, she was cuddling up to me, I didn't touch her or no sexual advances, all she wanted to do was drive my Toyota.'

'Did you ask the bigger of these girls if they had a licence?'

'No, I didn't, I should have, I suppose, but I didn't.'

'You say that the girl was driving along at about seventy to eighty. Do you know what caused the vehicle to slide?'

'She was only going steady. I was sitting back, not taking a lot of notice. Being a four-wheel drive and a fair bit of weight in the back, she might have over corrected, I don't know, it may have been a roo, it could easily happen. I just don't know why it happened.'

'Can you explain to me what you did after the vehicle came to a halt after the accident?'

'I got out the passenger door, the one that was in the middle, the smaller one was out, the other one I do not know if she was thrown out or what. The smaller one, I don't know if she was stunned or not, that's when she came on to me, do you want me now, that sort of thing. The [sic] was lying back there on the cover pulling her clothes up and I just wanted a beer.'

'Did you go and have a look at the other girl?'

'She was lying up near the road. I went to her and asked her if she was all right. She just groaned and I thought she was all right so I left her. Perhaps it was just air coming out of her, I don't know. I just was looking at my gear lying around all over the place, not realising that anyone was dead or not.'

'You say that you went and had a beer with this other girl. Did you make any advances to her then?'

'I just sat down with her and I didn't even finish my beer she just layed [sic] down and maybe she passed out then, I don't know.'

'How much beer did you consume last night?'

'1 went down the Oxford for a while, then I went and saw Dusty at the Carriers. I had about four middies there. I was at the Oxford for about three hours. After the Carriers I went to the Royal for a while, had about three beers, then I headed off home and I thought I'd better ring up so I went back to the post office.'

'What time did you pick the girls up at the post office?'

'I reckon it would have to be about eleven to half past eleven last night.'

'What time did the accident happen?'

'I don't know. I suppose it was about 1 or 2 o'clock, I don't know. I don't know.'

'Were you drunk last night?'

'A little bit.'

'What speed was the vehicle travelling prior to the accident?'

'I'd say about 70 to 80 kilometres per hour.'

'What position in the cabin were you sitting?'

'Passenger side on the left-hand side, the larger girl was driving and the smaller one in the middle.'

'Have you seen either of these girls before last night?'

'No.'

'Is there anything further you wish to say about this matter?'

'I don't think I can add anything to it really.'

'Will you now read this four-page record of interview?'

'Yes.'

The interview was handed to Grant.

'Do you agree that you have just read this four-page record of interview?'

'Yes.'

'Is it a correct record of our conversation?'

'Yes.'

'Have the answers that you have given been made of your own free will?'

'Yes.'

'Was any threat promise or inducement held out to you to give the answers as recorded?'

'No.'

'Will you now read the additional questions and answers?'

'Yes.'

'Will you sign this record of interview?'

'Yes.'

At the conclusion of the interview, Ehsman said he witnessed

Grant signing each page of the transcript. He then left the detectives' office and spoke with a Sergeant Stace. Ehsman said he returned to the detective's office with Sergeant Stace and told Grant that Stace would speak with him about the interview. Ehsman then left Stace and Grant alone in the room while he went off in search of a cup of coffee. A short time later, Stace came out of the detectives' room and handed Ehsman the copy of the record of interview.

Ehsman said he then returned to the room and looked more closely at Grant. 'I saw that Grant was in a dirty appearance. He was dressed in khaki pants and shirt, he was wearing work boots, he smelt strongly of intoxicating liquor, his eyes were very bloodshot and I formed the opinion that he was well affected by alcohol.'

Ehsman did not further caution Grant nor did he charge him at that time with any offences. What he did do was bizarre. He advised Grant to leave town. According to Ehsman's logbook, it was not a direct piece of advice, more a thought that he planted in Grant's head. Ehsman said, 'I am going to make further inquiries about this matter and I will talk to you again at a later date. If you leave town, let me know where I can contact you.' A more likely unrecorded directive was 'Fuck off out of town before this thing gets out of hand.'

Ehsman's log shows Grant replied, 'Yeah, it might be a good idea to get away for a while. I'll let you know where I'll be.'

Ehsman said he then took Grant out of the detectives' room and through the station to the front desk. What Ehsman said he saw next is most interesting. 'I took him to the front desk, where I saw a blond [sic] woman waiting for him. They both walked out of the police station.'

Ehsman must have been pretty keen for Grant to vanish. He took no mugshot of him, no fingerprints, no photographs of Grant's proclaimed head injury. In fact, it was as if Ehsman wanted the whole thing to just go away. Why did he not ask Grant for details of where he would be? Why did he not explain to the blonde woman what had happened? How did the blonde woman know to come to the station to collect Grant? Who contacted her? Who was she? We can assume that

Grant gave her contact details to the desk office at the station while he was waiting for Ehsman and that someone contacted her by telephone. There was no recorded evidence of her existence.

# 9

# The unanswered questions

Part of the problem for the prosecution concerned the question of who was at the wheel of the vehicle at the time of the accident. The utility sustained critical damage to the driver's-side roof, windscreen and door. While he was charged with two counts of negligent driving causing death, Grant's defence counsel argued that the damage to the driver's side and the injuries sustained by Mona Smith were clear evidence that Alex Grant had not been in control of the vehicle at the time of the accident. It was not in question that Mona and Cindy were killed as a result of the accident on a long, straight stretch of the well-maintained Mitchell Highway.

What was known was that Grant had that Saturday afternoon and evening consumed thirty standard alcoholic drinks. In 1987, there were six hotels and two clubs in Bourke. Today there is one hotel and one club, and the bottle shop has restrictions on the type of containers in which it may legally sell alcohol. It doesn't sell long-necks. Other questions, however, remained unanswered. What had really played out between 10 p.m., when Grant was last seen buying alcohol at a North Bourke hotel, and 4.30 a.m., when the five people driving through to Queensland stopped to investigate? When had the accident happened? How did it happen? Before the crash, what did Mona, Cindy and Grant do? What went on between the three people in the utility between 10 p.m. on Saturday and 4.30 a.m. Sunday? What motivation did Mona and Cindy have for getting into the utility in the first place? Why did Grant allow Mona to drive north towards Enngonia when both girls lived in Bourke, as did Grant himself? Why did the police case against Grant alter in substance some time after the event? Why did the attorney-general no-bill the charge of offer indignity? Why did the media, specifically the local newspaper *The Western Herald*, report the accident but not report nor analyse anything about the committal hearing or the trial? Why did ABC regional radio not pick up at all on the case? Why did the local radio station report nothing? Why was Grant free to leave Bourke immediately after being questioned by the police? Where were the bodies of the girls taken after autopsies were performed at Bourke hospital?

Other more technical questions remain about the Hilux. It was towed from the accident site to Enngonia police station. Vehicles that have been involved in accidents are frequently left to rot on the grass in front of the police station. Not the Hilux.

Later that same day, it was towed again, this time back to North Bourke's Darling Farm, the massive cotton-growing spread where Grant had been working. The vehicle itself was owned by a small business based in Wee Waa, 370 kilometres east of Bourke. At three o'clock that afternoon, a police officer from the crime scene unit at Dubbo made the four-hour drive to Bourke and photographed the vehicle at Darling Farm. Sometime in the six weeks between Sunday 6 December and Thursday 21 January, the ute was transported to Wee Waa.

On 21 January, it was sold to Wee Waa Electrics. Five months later, on Saturday 14 May at 3.20 p.m., a detective sergeant visited Wee Waa Electrics to inspect the wreck. One day before the detective arrived, the owner of Wee Waa Electrics removed the steering wheel from the vehicle and shipped it to Alex Grant in Sydney or other parts unknown. In what appears to be bizarre behaviour, he unbolted the steering wheel from the ute and sent it to the defendant. There are too many questions surrounding the shipping of the steering wheel. All of them unanswered. Why was it shipped one day before the planned police inspection? Who arranged the shipment? How was it shipped? What was the motivation for removing the steering wheel from the vehicle? Why did Grant want the steering wheel? From where did Grant collect the wheel? Why did the police not ask for its immediate return? Was the wheel ever recovered by the police?

# 10

## The defendant leaves Bourke

Alex Grant left the police station. Whether he then made his way with the blonde woman the 1.2 kilometres from the police station to the Mitchell Caravan Park is unknown. What is known is that it was now well into the afternoon and some time before nightfall Grant left Bourke for Nyngan, two hundred kilometres away.

Grant's blood alcohol reading, taken at the hospital at 9.10 a.m., was 0.159 grams in 100 millilitres of blood. There is no evidence to support the consumption of fluids to counteract the blood alcohol level from that time until the time he left the police station at 12.45 p.m. It is therefore unlikely that he got behind the wheel of a vehicle and drove. As there was no longer a train service between Bourke and Nyngan nor a bus service on Sunday afternoons, the most likely scenario is that an individual known to Grant at the time drove him from Bourke to Nyngan sometime during the afternoon or evening, or sometime the following day, Monday 7 December.

A plausible explanation of both the presence of the blonde woman at the police station and Grant's delivery to Nyngan is bound up in the location of his excavation work. It is possible that someone from Darling Farms, the wife of one of the managers perhaps, was directed to collect Grant from the police station and to transport him out of town so that there was no possibility of trouble, given the circumstances he had found himself in. The farm owner probably knew only too well that Grant had a taste for sex with Aboriginal women – that he was a 'gin jockey'.

When asked by Ehsman whether he was married or single, Grant was evasive. In his interview with Ehsman, Grant had recorded that he lived with a woman who was a partner in the company he worked for. No such woman came forward nor was one sought at a later date to corroborate any of Grant's statement. In fact, it was difficult to place any real credence on Grant's statement that he lived with a woman, was married to one, or had ever been since his alleged short-term marriage in New Zealand.

When interviewed by Ehsman and Detective Sergeant Vaughan Reid in Nyngan a few days later, Grant said, 'I'm a nervous wreck. My wife has kicked me out for being with those darkies.' It is doubtful that Grant was either married or living with a woman at the time of the accident. It is more likely that he lived alone at the caravan park and that he was assisted in some way to leave Bourke either on Sunday afternoon 6 December or sometime on Monday 7 December. The most plausible, given that in Nyngan on Monday night he was still dressed in his stinking work gear, was that he left Bourke immediately after the conclusion of his interview with Ehsman.

Nonetheless, while Grant was either at the caravan park or preparing to leave for Nyngan, Ehsman was making inquiries about the identities of Mona and Cindy.

Bourke is a town in which everyone knows everything that goes on. When news of the accident spread quickly, it did not take long for June Smith, Mona's mother, to make the three-kilometre journey from the Reserve to the hospital. June Smith arrived at the hospital at around the same time that Dawn Smith, Cindy's mother, arrived at Bourke police station. Ehsman had gone to the hospital to be there when Mona's mother identified her daughter. He then returned to the police station, collected Dawn Smith and her friend Yvonne Howarth, who had gone with her in support, and returned with them to the hospital so Dawn could identify Cindy.

For the mothers, it was a harrowing process – a thing that no parent should ever have to confront. Both girls had sustained injuries that were difficult to mask. The hospital morgue was a basic room in which the relatives of the deceased were expected to be in close quarters with their dead daughters.

The mothers identified the dead girls as their daughters Mona Smith and Cindy Smith. Not long after, Ehsman drove Dawn and Yvonne to Anson Street to the home of some relatives who were there in support. For Ehsman, it was just routine. He dropped them off and drove away.

Ehsman then returned to the station, where he busied himself with 'inside duties' and record keeping until he knocked off at 5.30 p.m. He had been on duty for eleven hours and had claimed neither a meal allowance nor overtime. It is not recorded where Ehsman went after he knocked off nor with whom he may have spoken.

# 11

## The witness interviews

On Monday morning, Ehsman reported for duty at Bourke police station at 8 a.m. He began his day by making 'further inquiries' into the fatal accident that had taken the lives of the two teenaged girls. He began making arrangements for post-mortems to be undertaken. Later in the day, after lunch, he arranged for Dr Clive Pringle, a well-respected pathologist from Dubbo, to travel to Bourke to conduct the examinations. Dubbo was the closest regional centre and even then it was more than four hours' drive from Bourke. It would be necessary for Dr Pringle to come to Bourke the following day, Tuesday 8 December. And it would be necessary for him to stay overnight before returning to Dubbo.

While Ehsman was continuing his inquiries, Mona and Cindy's families were mourning the deaths of their loved ones and preparing for their funerals. It was a sombre mood that descended upon the Aboriginal community in Bourke that day. It was made more sombre and to an extent aggravated by the discovery that Alex Grant had been allowed to leave town without being charged while the bodies of the girls lay in the morgue awaiting forensic examination.

Nobody knew precisely what had transpired out on the Mitchell Highway but they all had their suspicions. Two of those with suspicions beyond doubt were friends of Mona and Cindy – Betty Edwards and Karen Johnson. Both girls had seen Mona and Cindy that fateful evening. The following Monday morning they gave statements to the police. Their statements were taken by Detective Sergeant Vaughan George Reid.[10]

Bourke police station was a relatively large, single-storey brick building situated at 46 Oxley Street, across the road from the courthouse. The station was built on a square in the colonial Georgian design. It had low-slung eaves along its two street-front faces and sported three brick chimneys with two chimney pots each. Unlike the courthouse across the road, the police station was not an imposing building. But it was there and it was there for a purpose. It had a flagpole on the Richard Street corner flying the Australian flag.[11]

For a number of years before 1987, across the district the relationship between the police and Aborigines was not good. It had deteriorated significantly as police had a very different view of how public space should be used. From 1987, there was a large increase in assaults against police by local indigenous community members due in part to the changes the police had made to how they confronted people using public spaces. The control of Aboriginal behaviour in public places extended in late 1987 to the issuing of riot gear to Bourke police patrols and to the provision of tactical response training.[12] Increased violence against police occurred most often when police gave directions or attempted to change behaviour in public spaces.

Betty Edwards and Karen Johnson had intimate knowledge of the Bourke police station. While there is no evidence that in their short lives they had been charged with any offence, the percentage of juvenile offenders within the indigenous population was so high that it was inevitable that they would have had friends or relatives who had. Between 1980 and 1992 police laid 1,916 charges against 387 juveniles and made 1,107 arrests.

Betty-Anne Edwards and Karen Anne Johnson were both fifteen at the time of their friends' deaths. Karen Johnson was in Year 8 at Bourke High School. Both girls had been among the last people in town to see Mona and Cindy alive. On Monday they recalled to Detective Sergeant Reid what they had seen earlier on Saturday night.

According to Karen Johnson, she was walking along Adelaide Street with Betty-Anne at 8.15 p.m. When they got to the intersection of Adelaide and Yanda Streets, they saw Mona and Cindy sitting in the street outside Booth's place (a cousin).

A man in a white coloured Toyota utility pulled up along side of us. He was driving in the same direction as us along Adelaide Street. When he pulled up he leaned over and opened the passenger side door, then he sort of pulled himself back behind the wheel. I saw that he had what looked to me to be a half carton of stubby beer on the seat beside him. He also had a beer bottle, a stubby size beer bottle in his left hand, and he had hold of the steering wheel with his right hand. He called out to us through the open door, 'Do you want a lift home?' Betty-Anne said something to me and said back to him, 'No. We're going home now.' He called out, 'Do you want to come for a drive with me?' I said, 'No, we have to go home.' Then I saw Mona and Cindy come over to the car. I could tell that they had been drinking, and they were carrying on the same way. Cindy said to Mona, 'Go on, ask him.' Mona said to the man, 'Would you run us over to the levee to see if any boys are coming?' He said, 'Yeah, jump in.' Cindy asked us to jump in the back of the truck but we said no. Mona got into the truck first, and then Cindy got in and closed the door. I then saw the vehicle turn to its right, into Yanda Street. It drove all the way down Yanda Street and turned left into Anson Street. That was the last time I saw the vehicle. I have seen a lot of people who have been drinking alcohol. I have seen what people look like when they have been drinking small amounts of alcohol and what they look like when they drink a lot of alcohol. I have seen people who are a little charged, up to when they are drunk and really drunk. When the man in the utility stopped and spoke to Betty-Anne and me, from the way he acted, spoke and sat in the vehicle, I thought he was almost drunk.

Karen's statement was composed on a typewriter in the police station by Detective Sergeant Reid. It was dated 8 December but the time of the interview was not recorded. It was signed by Detective Sergeant Reid as a witness. There was no additional witness signature as there had been for Alex Grant.

Betty-Anne Edwards was also interviewed that day by Detective Sergeant Reid but it is unknown if the girls attended the station together or separately. Betty-Anne's statement read,

Last Saturday night about 8.15 p.m. I was walking towards my home on the Reserve along Adelaide Street with Karen Johnson. When we got to the corner of Adelaide and Yanda Streets outside Gladys Edwards place, a man driving a white Toyota utility stopped beside us. He had driven along Adelaide Street going in the same direction that we were walking. When he stopped, he leaned over and opened the passenger side door. He said, 'Do you want a lift home?' I turned to Karen and told her to say no and Karen called to him, 'No, we're going home now.' He said, 'Do you want to come for a drive with me?' Karen said, 'No, we have to go home.' Then Mona and Cindy run [sic] over to the car. They had been sitting on the corner of Adelaide and Yanda Street outside Booth's place. I asked Cindy for a smoke. When she spoke back to me, I could smell alcohol on her breath. The two of them were acting sort of silly. They said they had been drinking that night and I thought that they were charged. Mona was also carrying a bottle of rum but I didn't see the bottle, that was what Cindy said. Cindy told Mona to ask the man driving the utility, 'Go on, ask him, Mona.' Mona said to the man, 'Would you run us over the levee to see if any boys are coming?' He said, 'Yeah, jump in.' Cindy asked us to jump on the back of the truck but we said no. Then Mona and Cindy got into the truck. Mona got in first and Cindy was next to the door. The utility moved off and he turned to his left a bit as if he was going to make a U and then he turned up Yanda Street. He drove all the way down Yanda Street to Anson Street, where he turned left. When the man first pulled up and opened the passenger door of the utility, I saw that he had had to lay [sic] across the front seat of the utility to open the door, and he was very slow getting up again. When he did get up, I saw what appeared to be a half carton of stubbie-sized beer on the seat alongside of him. He also was holding what appeared to be a stubbie of beer which he was drinking from as he spoke to us. I have seen a lot of people who have been drinking alcohol and I have seen what alcohol does to them as they drink more and more. I have seen people who have had a little bit of alcohol, and what they look like when they are drunk, that is stubling [sic] around, not knowing what they are doing. I would say, from the way the man was speaking, slowly and dopey like, and the way he was so slow in getting up after opening the door, that he was almost drunk.

A number of similarities existed in the statements so it appears probable that the girls were in the room together during the interview process. It also appears probable that when the first had made her statement the second repeated much of what was said with a few minor word and phrase changes. It was unclear who was interviewed first and who second and it remains speculative as to why these girls where interviewed on Monday 7 December but no other family members or friends of the deceased were called to make statements. The police case continued to be mismanaged and random in its evidence gathering.

Ehsman, Reid and other detectives on duty at Bourke that day bundied off at 5.50 p.m. Before heading home they called in for a few beers at the golf club.[13] The off-duty police talk that afternoon may have been typical of the times. It may have centred on the idea that the only good Abo was a dead one, a white bloke who liked a bit of black velvet and how little needed to be done to make the case go away.

# 12

# The autopsies

On Tuesday morning, Clive Pringle left Dubbo by car to make the long boring drive to Bourke. He had an overnight bag packed with clothes and he threw his battered straw Akubra hat into the back seat. As one who have lived all his adult life in the west of New South Wales, Pringle knew the ravages of too much sun on the body. He was never without his hat.

Pringle had established a rural pathology service in Dubbo in 1962. While he was based in Dubbo, he spent a lot of time in outlying districts and in the late 1980s, given his wide-ranging work, he was invited to provide expert advice to the Aboriginal Deaths in Custody Royal Commission. Pringle retired from active practice in 1984. Yet in December 1987 he agreed to perform autopsies on Mona and Cindy. It is unknown why he would have accepted the assignment. Pringle had been contacted directly by Ehsman the day before. As Ehsman was in charge of the accident investigation on the ground in Bourke, it was his responsibility to arrange such matters.

The day was to be a long and eventful one for Ehsman. He was on duty at Bourke at 8 a.m. and did not clock off until 10.30 p.m. Ehsman worked in the detectives' office for most of the morning making further inquiries about the accident and undertaking administrative matters of record and other occurrences before heading out to the hospital to meet Pringle. Ehsman and Pringle were well acquainted. Ehsman had seen many autopsies in his police career as a detective.

Two days had passed since the accident. Pringle began his examination of Cindy Smith at 12 p.m. His report opened by identifying her as 'Jacinta Smith, 15 years, DOA, Bourke District Hospital 8.12.87. 12.00 midday'. It indicated she was identified by 'Det. P. Ehsman, Bourke Police'.

Pringle performed external and internal examinations. Of the external appearance he noted,

> the deceased was a short adolescent female Aborigine of slight build dressed in a blue yellow and white striped T-shirt and black tracksuit trousers. The T-shirt was drawn up across the top of her chest exposing her breasts and the tracksuit trousers where gathered about her legs just above the ankles. She was thus naked from her breasts to her ankles. She had also been wearing bikini-type panties and blue and white running shoes, but no socks. [Pringle makes no mention of the deceased wearing a bra.] A conspicuous area of lividity like discolouration was present across the lower part of her abdomen, in both inguinal areas and on the top of the front and inner aspects of both thighs. The pelvis was noted to be excessively mobile when traction was applied through the anterior superior iliac spines to pull them apart – this indicated that the pelvis was fractured.[14]

Dr Pringle's internal examination followed.[15] He commented that the injuries sustained by Cindy would have prevented her walking or arranging her clothes so that she was rendered naked. The comments are interesting in that they relate directly to Grant's statements when interviewed by the police that Cindy was up and walking around after the accident.

Pringle stated that death may not have been immediate but it would have induced semi-consciousness in the girl immediately after the accident. Pringle's comments raise questions about his conversations with Ehsman before, and during, the autopsies. Did any part of the conversations shift the frame of the autopsies so that Pringle was looking to obtain information on the basis of the building of police evidence rather than straightforward and face-value observations? Was it usual for a pathologist to look for, or assist in the building of, a police case of evidence against an individual?

Pringle was exhaustive in his examination and his final comment reflected his knowledge that he was in the presence of a police witness and that information had been passed to him by way of conversation and professionally.

He stated,

> she would not have been able to arrange her clothing in the fashion observed at the post mortem examination which according to the information provided to me by the police was the same as at the scene of the accident.

Pringle's penultimate statement in the report of the death of Cindy Smith is revealing and yet it too raises other questions. Both girls died at the scene of the accident sometime between midnight on Saturday 5 December and 4.30 a.m. Sunday 6 December. Yet it was Tuesday after midday that the autopsies were being carried out, possibly as much as sixty hours after their deaths but at the least fifty-four hours.

The families of the dead girls identified them forty-eight hours earlier around lunchtime on Sunday. It is not in question that a place as remote as Bourke did not have a resident pathologist. Nor is it that one was unavailable until Tuesday. What comes into view is the question of whether the bodies of the two girls remained alone in the hospital morgue for at least forty-eight hours after they were identified by family and before Pringle was available to examine them.

In New South Wales, a death is referred to the coroner if the death was the result of an accident, even if the cause appears clear. The coroner then decides, within forty-eight hours of the death, if it is necessary to perform an autopsy. At the conclusion of an autopsy, it is usual to engage a funeral director to effect the transfer of the deceased to a funeral home. At the same time, a medical certificate is issued by the coroner or the medical examiner so that interment or cremation can take place.

It is an indictment of Australian society that much is written about death and funerary practices in white society but very little information is available about Aboriginal deaths. Certainly there is a sensitivity and deep respect associated with death and funerary rights in Aboriginal society but the same requirements attach to secular and non-secular rights and rituals among whites. Contextualising and extrapolating events involving death in white society, even if much is initially unknown, is not a difficult task. History, chronology and volumes of information make it relatively easy. Not so Aboriginal deaths and funerary practices. Of course, many Aboriginals belong to white faiths and churches, or they are practising Muslims or Buddhists, so their deaths and funerals are undertaken in accordance with those rituals and beliefs.

What we are interested in here lies at the intersection of Aboriginal society and white society in a remote location. Aside from the initial identification of the bodies of the dead girls by their mothers, every encounter they had from late Saturday night until they were released from the hospital morgue into the embraces of their families sometime on Tuesday evening or Wednesday morning was with non-Aboriginals. The first witnesses, the police, the ambulance officers, the hospital staff, the medical examiner and, one would assume, the funeral director, were white. There is no evidence to suggest that either Mona or Cindy were religious in the traditional white sense. Nor that they had been initiated into Aboriginal cultural practices. It remains unknown whether or not 'sorry business' – the mourning of a family member – was enacted; whether the families followed traditional Aboriginal death ceremonies; or whether they followed the traditional practice when someone dies of moving out of their houses, swapping houses with other family members.

Clive Pringle began work on the body of Mona Smith at precisely 4.20 p.m. on Tuesday 8 December. He had spent some time examining her cousin Cindy and for unknown reasons had arranged to examine the older girl second. He began by stating the girl's name, her age, the time and the name of the witness to the procedure, Detective P. Ehsman. It is most likely that Ehsman wanted Cindy examined first to discount the possibility that Grant had sexually assaulted her. Throughout the two years of the case, the dried matter taken from Cindy's leg and sent for examination never again surfaced.

Pringle's external examination of Mona noted the deceased was an adolescent female Aborigine of short to medium height and plump build. It can be assumed that he and Ehsman discussed various aspects of the accident, the possibility that Mona was the driver, given her injuries and the smashed driver's side of the utility, and that neither of the girls had been wearing seatbelts at the time of the crash. It would be speculative to say that Grant was or was not wearing a seatbelt but it may have been that his reaction to the ute rolling over was to grasp tightly the handle near the front of the passenger-side window and to therefore avoid being thrown through the front window opening. The jammed doors, though, would have made it hard for him to get out of the ute.

Pringle recorded his findings.[16] While the external injuries to Mona Smith appeared to have been caused by accident and to have occasioned death, Pringle was required to undertake an internal examination. What was most important to the internal examination was that the incisions to open the body cavities and the transection of major blood vessels 'were accompanied by the escape of very little, and often no blood. The major veins which normally are swollen and filled with blood were collapsed and almost empty.' As Pringle stated, his observations were consistent with 'massive haemorrhage from the wound seen on the left side of the scalp'.[17]

At the conclusion of his report, Pringle signed his name C.T. Pringle as he had done with Cindy's autopsy. No indication is provided of the length of time taken for the autopsy, other than a notation made by Ehsman in his log back at the police station. Ehsman wrote, 'see Dr Pringle of Dubbo re same, also see S/C of Dubbo Scientific so engaged to 3 p.m. to 6.p.m. then return to office inside records and occurrences'. It is reasonable to assume that the autopsy on Mona Smith thus took until 6 p.m. to complete. Ehsman's log, however, states that he had a

71

meal break between 3 p.m. and 3.30 p.m., which would be consistent with his being present for the second autopsy at 4.20 p.m.

It seems reasonable to assume that by now, with the autopsies completed and sundry other tasks concluded, such as statements made by the people who came upon the scene of the accident, statements by the police and ambulance officers, there remained no barrier to charges being pressed against Grant. But, with the agreement of the police, he had left Bourke sometime within the previous two days and was two hundred kilometres away in Nyngan, where he had holed up at the Alamo Motel.

The Alamo is one of two motels operating today but in late 1987 it was one of five in the town on the Bogan River. Nyngan was also on the rail line with branches from there making their way to Cobar and Bourke. It has a population of around 2,000. It is located at the junction of the Barrier Highway, which leads west to Cobar, and the Mitchell Highway leading north-west to Bourke.

Grant was right in that his presence at his place of residence at the Mitchell Caravan Park might have caused anxiety and distress to the families and friends of the dead girls. The question remains, though, why he had been allowed to leave town without being charged. It is at this point that difficulties begin to surface for the police in the question of the charges. As we will see, Alex Grant was initially charged the next day with two counts of 'wilful neglect or misconduct causing grievous bodily harm' and 'owner permit unlicensed driver'. The charge of 'indecently interfere with a dead body' was made later. The police were beginning to look as if they wanted the case to go away quickly.

When he had completed his observation of the autopsies at Bourke hospital, Detective Ehsman thanked Clive Pringle, shook hands and returned to the police station. It is unknown whether or not officer Ludewig stayed around after taking photographs of the corpses.

At 6.30 p.m. Ehsman logged off for half an hour and went out to get something to eat. There was a takeaway around the corner that was still open. Sometime shortly after 7 p.m. he and Detective Sergeant

Reid left Bourke by car to travel to Nyngan. It seemed unusual that, during the initial conversation between Grant and Ehsman, Ehsman did not have the foresight to order Grant to stay in Bourke until such time as the police were ready to charge him, if charges were to be laid. It seemed beyond reasonable doubt that some charges must be laid, so the resources required to find him in Nyngan would have been conserved.

The level of resources required was not outstanding; it required Ehsman and Reid to travel to Nyngan and return, to secure accommodation for themselves for the night in Nyngan and for the police department to invest at least ten hours of overtime in the pursuit of charges against Grant. Ehsman's log for Tuesday 8 December noted five hours overtime, including an evening meal. This log was submitted on Tuesday 9 December on his return to Bourke. It is reasonable to assume Reid logged the same amount of overtime and meals. The local area command of Darling River included the towns of Nyngan and Cobar so it may have been that had Grant not existed Ehsman might have been required in Nyngan and Cobar for a few days on other matters which he subsequently pursued after dealing with Grant.

It was also in question why neither Ehsman, having interviewed Grant in Bourke on the morning after the accident, nor Reid, having interviewed two friends of the deceased who made statements on their whereabouts on the Saturday evening, did not photograph Grant for the record. One would assume a picture of the man involved in the deaths of the two girls would have 'assisted police with their inquiries'. No picture of Grant ever made its way into the files.

# 13

# The police culture in the 'Aboriginal' towns

In Bourke in 1987, the population of 3,400 sustained a police force of twenty-six. Three years later, there were thirty police officers stationed in the town, a ratio of police to population of 1:113.[18] Nearby Brewarrina, with a population of 1,600, had seven and eleven respectively, with a ratio of 1:145, while Walgett further to the east had seventeen and twenty-six, with a ratio of 1:96. Wilcannia, the fourth of the so-called Aboriginal towns in New South Wales, had six police in 1987 but increased to eleven in 1990 for a population of 800 or a ratio of 1:73.

Chris Cunneen, a university academic, questions the motives for such large police numbers given the public policy of community policing which was designed such that practical police work was a community endeavour – in other words, it had a focus on preventive policing; the presence of the police and their relationship-building with townspeople would be sufficient to deter crime and misbehaviour. This was meant to counteract the alternative policy of proactive policing. This policy allowed discretionary measures to be taken to aim resources at groups or categories that the police thought required special attention.

More recently, the focus for New South Wales police was on motorcycle clubs and their involvement in organised crime and drug trafficking. But as Cunneen notes, proactive policing had the potential to amplify conflict which in turn was self-fulfilling and justified additional police intervention and resources. Cunneen makes an important contribution to the police/community narrative suggesting that the idea of community was in fact presented as an uncritical solution to a variety of problems without an understanding of what community actually meant. He noted that the rhetoric employed in towns or districts with large Aboriginal populations amplified the idea that everyone was part of the same community. Those who framed the ideal of community, however, had the most social and economic power and used such rhetoric to admonish any Aboriginal dissent.[19]

The same could be said for governments, both state and federal in Australia in the twenty-first century, where the use of the word community has increased and become diffuse to the extent it is now a word with little true meaning. Every organisation, every suburb, every town, every interest group is a community.

The website of the police force in New South Wales has a tag titled 'community issues' under which there are thirty subheadings ranging from Aboriginal issues through alcohol, community safety precinct committees, drugs, firearms, mental health, rural crime and youth. For one wishing more information on the topics, the site invites selection from the 'community issues menu'.

Under the Aboriginal heading, it provides a 36-page document entitled 'Aboriginal Strategic Direction 2012–2017'. Part 1 of the document includes a section entitled 'Current challenges facing Aboriginal communities'. It remarked that twenty years had passed (the strategy was published in 2011) since the report of the Royal Commission Into Aboriginal Deaths In Custody yet the percentages of Aboriginals in the criminal justice system continued to grow.

In 1987, it remarked Aboriginal representation in the criminal justice system (that is, behind bars) was fourteen per cent. By 2011 it had increased to twenty-six per cent of the total prison population, with twenty-nine per cent of women being what it described as 'considerably higher'. The document added that after the 2008 Council of Australian Governments conference, various ideas were put forward to resolve some of the issues. They included the idea of safe communities, better practice community policing for indigenous communities and the identification of 'key drivers' that impact on policing in indigenous communities including building better relationships between police and indigenous communities. The term Aboriginal or indigenous communities was used five times in seven paragraphs yet there was little evidence that it was understood.

As mentioned above, there were twenty-seven police stationed at Bourke in 1987. By 2015, five years after the Aboriginal Strategic Direction paper was published, there were forty. In late 2014, as reported in *The Western Herald*, a fourteen-year-old Aboriginal boy was arrested at 1 a.m. after attempting to kick in the door of the Bourke police station and assaulting an officer.

Bourke, Brewarrina, Wilcannia and Walgett are towns in which an Aboriginal community liaison officer operates as part of the local area command (LAC). The community liaison officer is a member of the LAC crime management team with responsibility for providing advice and support to police and the management of Aboriginal issues. The community liaison officer is meant to work closely with Aboriginal communities and to encourage positive working relationships and partnerships between the police and Aboriginals.

In 1987, at the time of the accident, any liaison between Aboriginals and the police in Bourke was a matter for the individual officers. As we will see in a later chapter, one of the officers who was deployed to Nyngan to charge Alex Grant, Detective Sergeant Vaughan Reid, had been directly involved in the Brewarrina riot earlier in August. While it is speculative, one must look to Reid's involvement in the Brewarrina riot and his injuries sustained there as a marker for any future feelings or attitudes towards Aboriginals in Bourke from where he was operational.

It is not suggested that Reid influenced or attempted to influence the course of justice as it related to Alex Grant and the charges laid against him. There is, however, a causal link requiring substantiation around the question of the initial charges laid against Grant and later charges that appeared to be more substantial.

# 14

## The detectives mount up

On Tuesday evening, having taken a meal break from 6.30 p.m. to 7 p.m., Ehsman and Reid left Bourke to travel to Nyngan to find Alex Grant who, as previously mentioned, was holed up at the Alamo Motel. Nyngan is a good stopping point between Sydney and Broken Hill but it has little else to recommend it. Like Bourke, it has deteriorated substantially since the late 1980s, when there were several more motels and hotels.

Ehsman and Reid found Grant at the motel in pretty much the same state he had been in when he was interviewed in Bourke two days earlier. As Ehsman remarked later, Grant appeared to be wearing the same clothes he had worn on the Sunday and he was in what Ehsman described as an 'unkept' [sic] state. Ehsman and Reid went into the motel room, where Grant was seated on the edge of the bed. There was little furniture in the room, a bed, a small bench, two chairs. A television. Ehsman and Reid stood while they spoke with Grant.

After a few moments, it became clear that Grant was in no fit state to accompany them to the police station. It was unknown whether or not he had continued drinking.

Nonetheless, Ehsman said, 'I want to interview you further about the fatal motor vehicle accident you were involved in last Sunday up at Bourke. Will you come down to the police station with us?' Ehsman said he could see that Grant was still in a dirty and 'unkept' state.

Grant replied, 'Sure I'll come down but I'm dead tired and I'm a nervous wreck. My wife has kicked me out for being with those darkies. Can it wait until the morning? I'll come down to the station first thing.'

Ehsman nodded. 'Right, I'll talk to you then.'

He and Reid then left the motel, went to the Nyngan police station and, as Ehsman recounted later, made a number of further inquiries.

The inquiries were not related to the accident but to stolen sheep at Cobar, with which Ehsman dealt the following day. The sheep stealing matter goes some way towards providing an understanding of the depth and breadth of activities that a detective in the western part of the state was required to pursue. It also assists in an understanding of the relative importance or otherwise of the cases under investigation by the detectives. To have been present at the autopsies of two dead teenage girls then to be making inquiries about stolen sheep in the space of a fourteen and a half hour working day might be considered unusual. But there is little doubt that both events were on an equal footing in the eyes of the police.

It is unclear where Ehsman and Reid spent the rest of the night in Nyngan, most likely, though, not at the Alamo. Did they go to the local for a couple of schooners? Did they go to the club to eat? Did they talk about the case or was it as interesting to them as stolen sheep?

The following morning they arrived on duty at the Nyngan police station at 7.30 a.m. Shortly after that, they returned to the motel, where they collected Grant and took him to the police station. It is unknown whether or not Grant had made an attempt to clean himself up or whether he had eaten or slept during the previous twenty-four hours or more. What is known is that he was about to be interviewed again and then charged in relation to the accident. It is also clear that he had had time to consider his position and he made several attempts to distance himself from the action and the deaths of the girls.

At 8 a.m., Grant was taken to an interview room at Nyngan police station.

Ehsman said, 'I intend to conduct another record of interview with you. Sergeant Reid will type out the questions and answers as I ask them, do you understand that?'

Mr Grant replied that he understood and the interview began at 8.37 a.m.

'As you know, I am Detective Ehsman and this is Detective Sergeant Reid. I am going to ask you some further questions in relation to a motor vehicle accident which occurred on the Mitchell Highway, thirty-four kilometres south of Enngonia on the 6 December 1987. I want you to understand that you are not obliged to say anything unless you wish as anything that you do say will be taken down and may later be used in evidence. Do you understand that?'

Grant answered yes.

'Do you agree that on the morning of the 6th of December, I conducted a record of interview with you?'

'Yes,' Grant replied.

'I will now show you that document. Do you agree that it is a true and correct record of our conversation that morning?'

'Yes.'

'I now propose to ask you some further questions about this matter. At the conclusion of this interview you will be given the opportunity of reading the document and signing it, if you wish. Do you understand that?'

'Yes.'

'On the afternoon of the 5th of December 1987, that is, Saturday afternoon last, will you tell me where you were that afternoon from 12 midday?'

'Well, after my machine broke down, I come into town to try an auto electrician to fix it, to repair it. Being a Saturday, I went down to the Oxford for a while, and I had a few beers there. Then, I was probably a couple of hours there. Then I just went from one pub to another trying to find a bloke there. I went home at one stage, then went back out again.'

'Will you tell me, what time you went to the Oxford Hotel?'

'Well, I said the other day, I'm not sure of the exact time. It was later in the afternoon. I think I was there about half past two, I think it was.'

'How many beers did you drink at the Oxford Hotel?'

'I went there first and had three or four middies. Then I went around to the Central, had about five beers there. Then went around to the Royal, and I think I had two beers there. Then I went to the Carriers and had a few beers with Dusty Harvey and a few other blokes down there.'

'What happened then?'

'I must have gone back to the Oxford. I tried to make the Oxford my regular pub to get to know a few people.'

'How long did you stay at the Oxford that time?'

'I don't know. It must have been about closing.'

'What were you drinking?'

'Beer and bourbon.'

'How may bourbons did you consume?'

'Two or three.'

'What did you do after the Oxford closed?'

'That's when I went to ring up and I thought I met the girls.'

'When you left the Oxford Hotel, how would you state your condition of sobriety?'

'I was obviously pretty drunk.'

'When you left the hotel, that is, the Oxford, did you buy any bottles of beer to take with you?'

'I think I got a small bottle of rum and a six-pack.'

'What sort of beer was it that you bought in the six-pack?'

'Forsets [sic], I think.'

'Did you buy any Tooheys beer?'

'I can't remember.'

'When I examined the scene of the collision of your vehicle, OGQ921, I saw a half bottle of rum that had been almost totally consumed. Can you tell me who drank that?'

'I wouldn't have had much of that.'

'Also at the scene of the accident, I saw two bottles of Tooheys stubbies. One was totally consumed, the other half full. Can you tell me who drank those?'

'I think the young one in the middle that's come out the same side as me, she was on her feet and she must have had part of that and I had the other one.'

'You say the younger one came out the same side as you. Can you explain that to me?'

'I'm not sure if I just fell out the door and I think she must have got out a similar way, but I don't know.'

'What happened then?'

'She, well, she sort of da[ ]ed around. She was standing there, and she said, "Have you got a beer or not?" I said, "Yeah, there's a beer there," and I must have opened it and gave it to her. Then I opened a bottle of beer. Then she said, "Do you want me?"'

'Did you lay the green canvas cover on the ground?'

'No, it fell that way.'

'How did the smaller girl get on to the canvas?'

'She was wandering around there, and she walked there herself.'

'When she asked you for a beer, where did you get the beer from?'

'I don't know if I saw it on the road or in the vehicle or what.'

'When did the smaller girl pull her pants down?'

'I think it was just after she had a mouthful of beer.'

'What did the smaller girl do after she had the mouthful of beer?'

'She was wandering around. That must have been when she wandered over to the canvas and she must have put it down there.'

'What happened then?'

'That's when I thought she was having a wee or something. I just tried to check the other girl, tried to pick her up a bit, and asked her if she was all right, and that's when she kind of groaned, and I thought she was saying "yeah". Then I went back to the other girl and the other one was just lying there, right back, I didn't know whether she was dead or not.'[20]

'What did you do then?'

'I don't know if I blacked out or what, there's just too long a blank spot.'

'What do you remember happening next?'

'I don't know what time, but sometime, a vehicle pulled up and said, "Are you all right?" I said, "I think so." And then I can't remember what happened until the police pulled up. He was talking to me, but I don't think I was making much sense. Then he said, "She's dead." And then he said, "The other one too" and then he put a cover over it.'

'What did you do then?'

'I was going to pick up some gear, and the policeman said, "Just leave it there."'

'Who [sic] did you get to Bourke?'

'The ambulance.'

'Did you go into Enngonia?'

'No. The ambulance took me to Bourke.'

'Did you have sexual intercourse with either of those two girls that night?'

'No.'

'Did you pull the smaller girl's pants down after the accident?'

'No.'

'Did you pull her top up?'

'No.'

'Did she have her pants down, or her breasts exposed in the vehicle before the collision?'

'No.'

'Can you tell me how her clothes came to be in that state after she lay on the canvas?'

'She pulled her pants down herself and then she pulled her top up and she she [sic] lay back and said, "Do you want me?" I thought she must have been thinking of someone else, and I said, "No. That would be bloody right. Help me pick this gear up."'

'When you say that you picked these girls up from outside the post office, where did you drive to?'

'Started to drive out on the North Bourke Road.'

'Why did you drive out towards North Bourke?'

'That's where they wanted to go. They wanted a lift home. When they asked to go there, I thought they must live there. I didn't know where they lived.'

'Did they ask you to drive them to North Bourke before or after they first entered your vehicle? '

'Well, they first of all said, "Can you give us a lift home?" And I said, "Oh well, where you going?" They said, "North Bourke."'

'Were the girls inside or outside of the vehicle when you had that conversation with them? '

'They were out. Just close to the vehicle.'

'Are you saying, then, that you agreed to drive them to North Bourke before they actually entered your vehicle?'

'Yeah. They said it wouldn't take long to get over there, so that's when I said I'd do it.'

'Where did you drive to when you first drove away from the post office?'

'Just drove towards North Bourke.'

'Did they direct you to any particular location in the North Bourke area?'

'No. When it happened, when we got over that way, the bigger one asked if she could have a drive.'

'What did you say to her then?'

'My first remarks was not really. I don't really let anyone drive it. After a couple of minutes, we turned onto the Enngonia Road, and she asked me again. I said, "All right, if you take it steady."'

'Why did you refuse her first request to drive the vehicle?'

'Well, I just don't usually let anyone under those circumstances drive it.'

'What circumstances are they?'

'Well, normally if you don't know somebody, you don't normally do it.'

'Did you have a load in the rear of the ute?'

'There was a fair load in there. I don't know how much it weighed. Probably a ton, or something like that. There were tools and things.'

'Is that utility an easy vehicle to drive, for someone who's not experienced with it?'

'Well, it's not really difficult to drive.'

'Did you ask the girl if she was a holder of a current licence to drive a motor vehicle?'

'No. That was one mistake I made. I didn't ask her.'

'You were saying earlier that you had stopped at the side of the road and had a stubby of beer. Was that the point at which she commeced [sic] to drive the vehicle?'

'No. She had already been driving along the road. I said, "You'd better pull up here. You've had your drive now. We'll go home."'

'After you said that to her, did she commece [sic] to drive again?'

'Yes, she kept driving.'

'While you were stopped at that time, and before she drove off again, did the girl who was driving have a stubby of beer to drink?"

'Yeah. She had a stubby, and that was all.'

'And did she drink the entire contents of that stubby bottle of beer?'

'I don't honestly know, but I presume so.'

'You also said earlier that when she was driving, when she got to speeds approaching 100ks, you told her to slow down. As 100 kilometres is the speed limit in the area in which she was driving, why did you insist she drive slower?'

'Honestly, it was late at nigjt [sic], just the safety factor, really.'

'Is the reason that you insisted that she drive slower because you did not feel she was competent enough to drive the vehicle at that speed?'

'Yeah. When people first drive it, I prefer that they get to know how to drive it.'

'When you first picked the two girls up, did they, or either of them, have the appearance of having already consumed alcohol that night?'

'I wouldn't know.'

'Is there anything further that you wish to say about this matter?'

'I don't think so.'

'Will you now read this five-page record of interview?'

Grant answered, 'Yeah.'

The interview was suspended at 10.33 a.m. The typescript was removed from the typewriter and handed to Grant. The interview resumed at 10.45 a.m. Grant was asked a few more questions by Ehsman.'

'Do you agree that you have just read this five-page record of interview?'

'Yeah.'

'Is it a correct record of our conversation?'

'Yeah.'

'Have the answers been made of your own free will?'

'Yeah.'

'Has any threat promise or inducement been held out to you to give the answers as recorded herein?'

'No.'

'Will you now read the additional questions and answers?'

'Yes.'

'Will you sign this record of interview?'

'Yeah, right,' replied Grant, and the interview concluded at 10.50 a.m.

The notation at the end of the interview transcript read 'received from detective Ehsman one copy of this five record [sic] of interview', which is then signed by Detective Senior Constable P.J. Ehsman and by Alex Grant. At the conclusion of the interview, Ehsman watched as Grant signed each page. He then left Grant for a moment and spoke with a Nyngan police officer, Senior Constable Boland. Ehsman and Boland returned to the interview room, where Ehsman introduced Grant to Boland.

'This is Senior Constable Boland. He is going to ask you some questions about the interview we have just completed. Do you understand that?' Ehsman asked Grant.

Grant replied yes, he understood, and Ehsman and Reid left the room. A short time later, Boland left the room and handed Ehsman the record of interview. Boland had signed and dated each page of the transcript.

Ehsman returned to where Grant was sitting. He said to Grant, 'Shortly you will be charged with two counts of wilful neglect or misconduct causing grievous bodily harm and owner permit unlicenced [sic] driver, do you understand that?'

Grant must have been mightily relieved. 'Yes,' he replied.

Grant was then taken to the charge room, where he was charged with the three counts. He made no comment nor spoke while in the charge room. Under the *Crimes Act 1900*, which was in force at the time of charges being made against Alex Grant, Section 54, causing grievous bodily harm, carried a liability of imprisonment for two years. Wilful neglect under Section 53 carried a similar penalty. The charge of 'owner permit unlicensed driver' carried a penalty of $1,000 and a term of community service up to five hundred hours. It is almost incomprehensible that these were not the charges that Grant ultimately defended himself against. Incomprehensible until one grasps the significance of the influence that was brought to bear on the case by external, anonymous individuals.

# 15

## The Brewarrina riot

Vaughan Reid had arrived at Bourke police station on duty in July 1983. He had thus been active in and around Bourke as a detective for more than four years at the time of the accident. From 1977 until 1994, when technology known as computerised operational police systems (COPS) was invented, all police stations across New South Wales maintained typed records of events. These records were known as occurrence pads; they were a running log of arrests, serious offences and deaths. In the event of a report of an indecent assault, which was under the umbrella of the *Crimes Act 1900*, police would decide whether to investigate the matter or take some other step.

In 1983, shortly after his arrival in Bourke, Detective Reid was invited to investigate complaints in Brewarrina against the owners of Bethcar, a children's home. Until 1984, Bourke police station was head station in the division. Uniformed and plain-clothed police covered three shifts. A daily roster was maintained showing the date, officer name and attached duties. Several detectives worked out of Bourke. Brewarrina was a substation with no detective attached, as was Enngonia. Matters of a criminal nature from Enngonia and Brewarrina were attended to by Bourke detectives.

In the January 1995 Australia Day honours, Sergeant Reid was awarded the Australian Police Medal. The medal was awarded for '15 years ethical and diligent service on or after 14 February 1975'. It provided recognition for the 'unique contribution and significant commitment of those persons who have given ethical and diligent service as a sworn member of an Australian police service'.

Four months before the accident on the Enngonia Road, Detective Sergeant Reid had been directly involved in what became known as the Brewarrina riot, following the death in custody of Brewarrina man Lloyd James Boney.

Detective Reid was one of two officers injured during the riot. *The Sydney Morning Herald* headlined the event on 17 August 1987, 'Blood on the streets the night a town exploded'. The event became legend as a violent confrontation between Aboriginals and police. A similar event the year before in Bourke (the Bourke post office riot) had left extensive property damage but no human injury, while another, the Bourke Bowling Club riot of 1985, had done the same.

The Brewarrina event was ignited by the death of local man Lloyd Boney, who was at the time in police custody. Boney's death on 6 August and the consequent events inspired the Royal Commission Into Deaths In Custody but at the time the events a few days after his death were the main focus of attention from the media and the police. The Australian Broadcasting Corporation had sent a reporter and camera crew to cover Mr Boney's funeral and wake and it was the gathering for the wake in the park opposite the main hotel that became the news.

A group of people in the park were allegedly goaded by the owner of the hotel and others on the first-floor veranda of the hotel as they called out and brandished shotguns. The group in the park smashed the windows of the hotel bar and caused general disruption in the main street. Reid was one of two police officers injured that night in the line of duty. Two other officers, Senior Constable T.J. McGregor and Detective Constable G. Connelly received serious injuries. For his courage in shielding McGregor from further attack, Connolly was the first ever recipient of the Commissioner's Valour Award. Other police involved were awarded the Commissioner's Commendation.

In preparation for the potential for violence following Boney's burial, additional officers had been brought in from other places, including Bourke. By early evening, most reinforcements were sent away from Brewarrina, but Reid, for an unknown reason, was called back from Bourke at around 7.30 p.m.

At around 9.30 p.m., a few people in the park began throwing rocks at the hotel – action which brought forth eight police with riot shields and batons. The police arrived at the scene in two cars; Reid was in the second with two constables, Bordin and Fernandez, and another sergeant, Morgan. The cars were positioned at either end of the park. Reid was in charge of the second vehicle group and had ordered a 'baton and shield' line to disperse people from the park and then to pursue four or five people who had been throwing things at the hotel. They were confronted by thirty or more, who then also began throwing sticks and bottles, so they retreated to the vehicle parked in Bathurst Street.

Some time later, Reid described the situation as 'a very intense barrage of flagon bottles, beer bottles and pieces of wood. I could not believe how many bottles were coming through the air. The sky seemed to turn brown. It was absolutely incredible.'

From there, Reid's group joined with the other four police, including McGregor and Connolly. It was at this point that McGregor was confronted by a man wielding a star-picket fence post. The man raised the picket and fractured McGregor's leg with it. Connolly shielded McGregor from the continuing barrage of bottles and sticks. A diversion – the fire alarm bell at the fire station – allowed them to get McGregor into an ambulance but, as Connolly noted later, 'as I got into the back of the police truck, a beer keg was thrown at us, lighted fire buckets and burning logs were thrown and sticks and bottles were still being skimmed across the road at us as we left the scene'.

Reid observed a similar scene in the moments before the fire alarm sounded. 'We were unable to have any impact on them at all. In fact, the crowd just seemed to get bigger and bigger and they seemed to be coming towards us. We couldn't advance any further. We couldn't get to the police vehicle. We stood where we were.'

The police returned to the station and by 10.15 p.m. the riot was over. The hotel resumed trade.

It is unknown when Reid was treated for his injuries nor when he returned to duty at Bourke. Three of the men involved in the riot were charged with numerous offences. Initially, a charge of attempted murder of Constable McGregor was made but it was later dropped. Charges of assault causing actual bodily harm on Bordin and Reid were made and further charges of maliciously wounding with intent to do grievous bodily harm to McGregor and assault occasioning actual bodily harm to Reid were made. The three accused were also charged with riotous assembly.

It is not here relevant to provide additional information or narrative about the Brewarrina riot and those charged. What is relevant is to point out the fact that Vaughan Reid had spent some time before his involvement in the Grant case investigating and being part of crimes against, and perpetrated by, Aboriginals in the district. It is reasonable to assume that Reid had formed clear and unambiguous opinions about the 'community' in which he lived and about the various groups and individuals who also occupied that space. The award of the police medal in 1995 was testimony to Reid's diligence and ethical approach to this space despite the Brewarrina attack and, possibly, undocumented occurrences of a similar nature.

Reid's personal views of the conditions under which the dead girls lived their lives or of the manner of their deaths is unknown. His behaviour, however, along with that of detective Ehsman, indicates that his view may have been sympathetic to Grant's situation rather than to that of Mona and Cindy.

# 16

## The defendant vanishes

We know definitively that on Tuesday 8 December at 11a.m., Alexander Ian Grant was charged at Nyngan police station with numerous offences under the Crimes Act. The charges were laid by Peter John Ehsman, the Bourke detective assigned to the case two days earlier. But it was not until Wednesday 16 December that Grant was formally charged at Nyngan.

What did he do during that unaccounted-for week? How did he spend his time? Did he go anywhere before he appeared in Nyngan court? Did he go back to Bourke to collect his things from the caravan park? Did he go to Darling Farm?

It would be logical to assume he did. He must have made contact with his employer. There were no mobile phones, no Skype, no text messages to keep him in constant touch. Did he make a call to his employer from the motel? Did someone from Darling Farm bring his stuff to Nyngan? Did he go to Sydney by train then return the following week to be charged? Did he go to Wee Waa, where he claimed to be the owner of a business? If so how did he get there? By car? Did he make contact with his business partner who, as a matter of interest, was never asked to supply a character reference. The business partner, if in fact one existed, was never identified by anything other than his first name of 'Ron'.

Grant was formally charged at Nyngan local court and remanded to Bourke local court for 22 February 1988, two months thence. Grant may have travelled to Sydney and then returned to Nyngan for the remand, or he may have remained at the Alamo Motor Inn for the week. We know Ehsman did not return to Bourke until late on the evening of Wednesday 9; he made 'further inquiries' at Nyngan to deal with stolen sheep, then travelled to Cobar 130 kilometres west, where he examined a sheep property then charged the sheep rustler at Cobar police station. Ehsman later ate dinner, then drove back to Bourke. His most likely route was directly north from Cobar to Bourke rather than driving back east to Nyngan; the road was good dirt between Cobar and Bourke, about 160 kilometres or two hours' driving. It had not yet succumbed, with its neighbours through Louth and Tilpa, to New South Wales Tourism public relations' boosting of outback touring by naming it Kidman Way.

Ehsman left Cobar around 8 p.m., and clocked off at Bourke police station at 10.30 p.m. He submitted a claim for a further five hours overtime. Ehsman was again on duty at Bourke on Thursday 10 December and Friday 11 December, dealing with standard office procedures. He then had three days off before returning to duty on Tuesday 15 December.

While we know from official records that Ehsman came back on duty at 7 a.m. at Bourke and then drove back to Cobar to charge the sheep rustler before driving over to Nyngan and logging off at 6 p.m., we know nothing of Grant's whereabouts. There appeared to be no conditions attached to his bail. We may assume Grant appeared in Nyngan local court on Wednesday 12 December to hear the charges against him read out. Ehsman's log of the same day is silent on the matter.

We know Ehsman returned to Bourke at 12.30 p.m., where he remained until logging off at 5 p.m. Ehsman was then on sick leave for the following two days, on rest leave the next, then on annual leave until 3 January 1988. We might assume Grant remained absent from Bourke until such time as he was required to attend court there. But he may have returned. An important aspect of the case is undocumented – where was Grant and why was he allowed to roam free when he had been charged with crimes that carried gaol time?

# 17

## The Toyota Hilux

In the meantime, other events that had a strong bearing on the case were playing out. Sometime on the morning of the accident, the Toyota Hilux had been towed to Enngonia police station, where it was parked on the dirt and grass verge. In the following few days, it was again towed, this time back to Bourke to the cotton gin at Darling Farms. The ute remained at the cotton gin until early January the following year. The ute had been the subject of a serious inspection the day after the accident, when Senior Constable John William Ludewig of the Crime Scene Unit Physical Evidence Section travelled from Dubbo to Bourke on Monday 7 December.

Ludewig first drove to the site of the accident. He took eight photographs of the gouge marks on the road and the strewn debris. He then returned to North Bourke, where he inspected the ute. He stated, 'this vehicle was extensively damaged in the offside and roof area, it was apparent to me that this vehicle had been overturned. The roof on the driver's side was crushed onto the top of the drivers [sic] seat at the rear section and to the centre of the steering wheel at the windscreen.' Ludewig took three more photographs. He then went to the hospital, where he assisted in the autopsies and took more photographs. It is interesting that Ehsman gave no indication in his logbook that Ludewig had been at the autopsy. Nor was he mentioned by Dr Pringle.

The vehicle was registered to the business for which Alex Grant worked: Major Metals Excavations, based then, in 1988, at Wee Waa, some 370 kilometres or five hours' drive or more from Bourke. In

1988, the Kamilaroi Highway was unpaved for a considerable distance so the drive was not nearly as easy as it is today. It would have taken six hours or more to transport the smashed utility that far. It was, however, transported to Wee Waa early in January 1988, where it stood outside in the yard of Major Metals until Thursday 21 January.

On that day, it was sold, in its written-off state, to Peter Hurle, owner and operator of Wee Waa Electrics. The negotiated price is unknown. Nor is it known why Peter Hurle wished to purchase the smashed vehicle. Wee Waa is a small town in which everyone knows everyone. A week later, on Wednesday 27 January, Hurle collected the vehicle from Doug Innes of Major Metals and took it to his factory. Spasmodically and over a period of a few months, Hurle made some attempts to correct the damage to the ute.

He said later that when he first saw the ute it was 'extensively damaged, with the driver's side of the cabin crushed down to within eighteen inches of the bench seat. The driver's door was sprung and the top of the window frame was bent. I straightened the driver's door. The passenger's side door was open and the lock area was damaged, consistent with some person having forced the lock with a crow bar or similar.'

Hurle's statement about the condition of the passenger-side door accorded with the observations made by Constable Ken McKenzie at the accident scene but not with the defendant's statement about it. Grant claimed that he had got Cindy out of the smashed ute through the passenger door, yet, if what Hurle said was correct, the door required some type of violent action against it to get it open. Hurle concluded that when he took delivery of the vehicle from Major Metals it was in a locked yard covered by a tarpaulin and 'it did not appear that any person had tampered with the vehicle in any way, except for the forced door'. To add a complication to the evidence of the passenger-side door, the damage, according to Doug Innes, had been caused while the vehicle was at the yard owned by Major Metals. Innes, in a statement, recollected that the passenger door was 'in good order at the time it was left', meaning presumably the time it was left after being transported to Wee Waa from North Bourke. Innes claimed, 'an accident involving a forklift which was moving in the yard caused damage to the left hand side of the vehicle'. This seems highly improbable, yet Innes went on to state that he 'was asked to search the interior of the vehicle for ignition keys to it and other vehicles that had gone missing, at this point I found I was unable to gain entry so I levered the doors open with a crow bar'.

It is not known who Innes is referring to when he says he was asked to search for ignition keys. At the site of the accident, Constable McKenzie said he was unable to locate them and it remains unknown whether or not the ignition key and any associated keys that may have been attached to it, such as a key to Grant's room at the caravan park or others, were ever located. Grant, being relatively itinerant, may not have carried many or any keys other than one for the ignition of the utility. Nonetheless, Innes's statement seemed unusual. It was highly improbable that, having transported the ute from Bourke to Wee Waa, he or anyone else would have let further damage be caused to it, given that it may have been necessary for further police examinations to be made.

A further examination of the vehicle was indeed made but not until 15 May, four months after the vehicle had been sold to Peter Hurle. By then, the police case against Grant was being rethought and looking very much like a dog's breakfast. The initial charges may have been considered unsustainable, given that the condition of the utility now played a prominent role in determining whether or not Grant had been driving. The condition of it was such that the driver of the utility would have sustained grievous injuries when the roof was crushed down hard against the steering wheel. As had sixteen-year-old Mona Smith.

There was an alternative scenario. Grant had in fact been driving. Mona, on the passenger side, was thrown through the windscreen as he braked, before the vehicle spun out of control. Cindy, in the middle, was also pitched out through the windscreen but slightly later. Grant, wearing a seatbelt, was tossed sideways before the roof was crushed. When the ute came to rest on its wheels, he was unhurt and able to climb through the gap where the windscreen had been. This scenario accounts for both doors being jammed shut and for the fatal injuries to both girls.

# 18

# The defendant's lawyers

After he had been charged in mid-December, Alex Grant left Nyngan for Sydney. He may have returned to Bourke to collect his possessions; he may have travelled to Wee Waa. It was from Sydney, however, that he or someone acting for him engaged a firm of solicitors.

In 1988, Picone & Howes was a suburban practice located in Kogarah. Its principals were Lawrence L. Picone B Juris LLB, and William V. Howes B Juris LLB. Bill Howes was the solicitor who took the case. He in turn engaged the services of a Sydney criminal barrister, Anthony Quinlivan. At the time, Tony Quinlivan worked from University Chambers, in Phillip Street, Sydney. In correspondence from Howes to Quinlivan dated 1 February 1988, Howes outlined the case.

We are the Solicitors for Alexander Ian Grant of 54 Caledonian Street, Bexley. Our client was charged in relation to three offences which occurred at Enngonia on 6 December, 1987.

Counsel is briefed with the following:

1. Charge in relation to permitting Mona Smith, 16 years old, an unlicenced [sic] and unexperienced [sic] driver to take control of his motor vehicle which resulted in the bodily harm to Jacinta Smith.

2. Charge in relation to permitting Mona Smith, 16 years old, an unlicenced [sic] and unexperienced [sic] driver to take control and drive his motor vehicle and did cause to be done bodily harm to Mona Smith.

3. Charge in relation to permitting Mona Smith to drive a motor vehicle whilst not being licenced [sic].

We confirm that this matter is listed for mention at Bourke Local Court on the 15 February, 1988.

Mr Quinlivan also received from Mr Howes copies of the original charge sheets from Nyngan local court, a copy of the record of interview between Detective Ehsman and Alex Grant conducted at Bourke, a copy of the second interview between Ehsman and Grant conducted at Nyngan, and an undated, unsigned statement purporting to be made by Mr Grant sometime after he engaged Picone & Howes.

Grant's statement informed the barrister's early understanding of the case. On taking delivery of the written matter and before arranging to meet with Bill Howes and Grant, Tony Quinlivan sat at his desk in chambers and read Grant's statement. He highlighted in yellow certain parts of the interviews and parts of Grant's statement. A number of things were puzzling. Grant had on a previous occasion told Ehsman and Reid his 'wife' had kicked him out. He told McKenzie and others that he was a 'partner' in a business.

Grant's statement read,

> I am a single man aged 40 years of age. I am employed by Major Metals Excavations of 33 Boocarol Road, Wee Waa, New South Wales. The following is a Statement in relation to events which occurred on 6th December, 1987 at Enngonia, New South Wales. At the time of the offences I was living at The Mitchell Caravan Park at Bourke. I recall leaving the Pub at Bourke on *6th December, 1987* at around *10 p.m.* I can't recall whether I was at the Oxford Hotel or The Royal Hotel. I had been drinking since 2.30 p.m. that day. I think I was drunk. *Two Aboriginal girls approached me outside of the Hotel as I was about to get into my car. The girls asked me for a lift.* First of all, I refused but when the girls asked me to take them to *North Bourke* I said, 'I will do so.' I thought both girls were about 18 years old. I did not ask them their age. I now know from what the Police have told me, that the girls were aged 15 and 16 respectively. I did not know the girls [sic] names at the time. I had not seen these girls around before. As the girls only wanted a lift home, I agreed. I don't normally agree to give people lifts home that I don't know. On this occasion I don't know why I agreed

to. It could only have been because I was too drunk and too silly at the time. When about two or three kilometres from North Bourke, the bigger girl asked me if she could drive my car. I said, 'Oh, no, I just don't let anyone drive it.' As we had just turned into the *Enngonia Road, I pulled over North Bourke Hotel at the request of the girls.* One of the girls said, 'Can you get us a six pack of Tooheys, a small bottle of rum, and a bottle of a Coke.'

I said, 'I suppose so.'

I did so and paid for it thinking they lived in *North Bourke Village*. We then *drove off to Enngonia.*

The *bigger girl said, 'Give me a drive, I can handle it.'*

I *said, 'OK, If you take it steady.' What is then contained in the Statement concerning the driving of the vehicle is true as best as I can recall, when the big girl pulled up off the road to turn around,* I realised that the girls had just wanted a joy ride and some alcohol.

I said, 'We're off the road, I'm just going to have a leak, then we're going home.'

They said, 'We'll have a drink.'

I said, 'OK.' I then drank a stubby and a mouthful of rum straight. The girls mixed the rum into the Coke bottles. The girls drank their rum and the Coke. I think we stayed there for about ten to fifteen minutes. We were *20 kilometres out of North Bourke on the Enngonia Road.* The big girl sat in the driver's seat the whole time. The bigger girl kept driving and didn't turn around. I didn't realise that at the time as it was very dark, around 11 p.m. at night. We were driving along steady, the vehicle then left the road, it may have been a kangaroo which the girl tried to avoid hitting. *The vehicle rolled, I don't know how many times,* and ended on its wheels. *The bigger girl had been thrown through the windscreen. The smaller girl got out.* I think I helped her, and *walked her away from the vehicle.* I don't recall what is in the *Statement* as now being factually true. I don't remember her pulling her pants down etc. I did check the bigger girl, I put my arm around her, and lifted her up and thought she groaned. I put her down. I went over to the other girl, I don't remember what happened. Next thing I remember, is a *four-wheel drive vehicle pulled up.* The man said, *'Are you all right?'*

I said, 'I think so.' The next I recall is the Police arriving. I must have blacked out as I don't remember, the girls being dead until the Police told me. *What I told the Police about the scene of the accident must not have been true.*

Quinlivan's highlights appeared in italics. He also bracketed the sentence 'I don't recall what is in the *Statement* as now being factually true'. Quinlivan read the observations to counsel again, made some notes, and prepared to take the case. He would wait until Bill Howes arranged a conference with him and the defendant.

Meanwhile, the police case was still struggling to take shape. On 3 February, as part of the inquest into the deaths of Mona and Cindy Smith, Senior Constable John Ludewig made a statement at Dubbo police station. Ludewig described how he had gone to Bourke police station on Monday 7 December, where he had spoken at length with Detectives Reid and Ehsman. He described driving to the scene of the accident but did not indicate whether or not he was accompanied. He described taking eight colour photographs of the scene (which he tabled as part of the inquest). He described how he then went to the cotton gin and took three colour photographs of the utility, which he also tabled. He then described how he attended the autopsies conducted by Dr Pringle, of which he took nine colour photographs. He then 'collected specimens from each body and subsequently caused them to be forwarded to the Analytical Laboratories at Lidcombe and Glebe for examination'. Ludewig indicated that results of the examinations from the Department of Health were attached.

# 19

# The vital evidence of Shane Baty

A short time after Ludewig gave evidence to the inquest, the police attempted to fill in some of the blanks by interviewing one of the first people to view the accident scene: Shane Baty. Mr Baty was interviewed at Dareton police station on Tuesday 8 March 1988 by Constable K.J. McKenzie of Enngonia police. It is unclear why Baty was interviewed at Dareton other than its proximity to Mulurulu Station, where Baty's parents lived.[21] How did McKenzie get from Enngonia to Dareton? Did he hitch a ride on a plane? The drive from Enngonia to Dareton would have been somewhere between ten and thirteen hours, one way.

It may be unusual to interview a witness so long after the event. A likely explanation is that Mr Baty, who described himself as a 'seasonal worker' and gave his address as his parents' farm near Mildura, could not be located before that time. Mr Baty declared that he was born on 9 September, 1962. At the time of the accident he was twenty-five years of age and claimed to have been 'following full-time employment for the past nine years'. Mr Baty had therefore been working since he was sixteen. He owned a 1984 Toyota Hilux utility. The Toyota Hilux was and remains the number one selling utility in Australia but it is interesting that throughout the investigation and in statements made by various people, the make and model of Grant's ute were cited but the year of manufacture was not mentioned other than by Constable McKenzie in a statement made on 6 May 1988, five months after the accident.

Baty identified the smashed vehicle as a Toyota Hilux but did not name the year of manufacture (1985) even though he and his brother were driving the same kind of vehicle.[22] Mr Baty's statement did, however, include other information that was to prove highly valuable. It was so important that it presented a platform for an additional charge to be made against Grant, namely that at some time between when he was seen by Baty lying on the ground beside Cindy Smith, and when McKenzie arrived some time later from Enngonia, Grant had interfered with the corpse of the fifteen-year-old girl. Mr Baty said he arrived at the scene after his brother Michael (known as Joe) and that he and Texter Johnson were the individuals who went to render possible assistance to the occupants of the smashed vehicle. It was he who first declared Mona Smith dead. He also declared Cindy Smith to be dead but in Cindy's case he also took note of the state of her clothing.

It must have come as a shock to Baty, despite his isolation on a sheep farm and all that that entailed, to come across two dead Aboriginal girls on the side of the road. What must have been more shocking, and is most likely why he took note of the state of Cindy's state of undress, was to find a man lying next to her; lying with his arm draped across the near-naked body of the young Aboriginal girl.

Baty said he was unable to find Cindy's pulse in her neck or under her armpit, the two most likely places even if it were faint. Baty said he 'noticed that her panties were on her left ankle and that she was naked from her ankle to her waste [sic], but her blouse was buttoned up and she was clothed from her neck to her waste [sic]'. This was to become a crucial part of his statement. But it did not fit precisely with the occurrence pad entry made by Constable McKenzie on Sunday 6 December, in which McKenzie wrote that Cindy was 'Dressed in light T-shirt top white blue and yellow stripped [sic], short sleeve. Black track suit pants and black and white joggers with the Edna Smith 1987 written on the soles'. More importantly, as it may have been difficult to distinguish in the semi-dark whether the girl was wearing a buttoned blouse or a coloured striped T-shirt, McKenzie wrote in his occurrence pad that 'The deceased person 1 was located at the side of the vehicle, laying [sic] on a green plastic sheet and her track suit pants and underpants were around her ankles and her tee shirt top was pulled up above her breast [sic] to her neck. This rendered her naked from the ankle to her neck.' This was the apparent state in which McKenzie found Cindy but it was not the state in which Shane Baty first saw her. Further statements and photographs of the position of Cindy's body added weight.

But there was also uncertainty about other aspects. When one of the ambulance officers, Kelvin Brennan, arrived at the scene from Bourke he noted that 'There was one occupant, female, prone on her back, covered with a tonneau cover. She was about 2 metres off the road. The second patient was female, she was adjacent to the vehicle on the northern side covered with a plastic sheet. Upon examination she was found to be practically naked.'

At some point, both girls had been covered by Constable McKenzie or someone else. When Ehsman arrived on the scene, both girls had been uncovered by Ambulance Officer Ronald Willoughby. Ehsman photographed the bodies. The photograph of Cindy indicates that she was indeed naked from neck to ankle and that her legs were not straight. Her left leg was bent outwards so that the lower half of her leg formed nearly a right angle to the top half.

Until now, the police case against Grant had its basis in wilful neglect or misconduct, causing grievous bodily harm and permitting an unlicensed driver to drive. Mr Baty's statement about the position of Cindy's clothing added a layer of information that may have previously been in the minds of some of the actors or it may not; either way, such thoughts had remained unformed.

It may have been in Ehsman's mind. When he interviewed Grant on Sunday 6 December, he asked, 'Did you make any advances to either of these two girls?' The question had its basis in the time before Grant and the girls drove out of Bourke. Secondly he asked if Grant had 'made any advances' to Cindy after the accident.

In Nyngan three days later, Ehsman was more direct. 'Did you have sexual intercourse with either of those two girls that night?' he asked in the record of interview with Grant. In this he was not asking Grant if he had had sexual intercourse after or before the accident. He was not specific in his questioning, so it is unclear whether or not Ehsman was thinking that Grant had had sex with Cindy after she had died. Such a complicated thought would be difficult to ask as a direct question in the expectation that one would receive anything other than an answer in the negative.

Throughout the process of being interviewed and examined in the few days after the crash, Grant told a story about Cindy 'coming on to him' soon after the utility rolled. He provided a few variations of the story, first to Constable McKenzie, then to Ambulance Officer Brennan, then to Constable Clarke, then to Ehsman.

Grant himself provided a handwritten statement on Sunday 6 December refuting a claim made by McKenzie that he had had sexual intercourse with Cindy.

> I remember dragging the younger away from the Vechilce [sic] and must have put her on the tarp don't remember anything until a mans [sic] voice you all right I said yeah I think so the next thing its [sic] almost daylight and the Police were there one constable from Enngonia he woke me up and said you all right I said yeah I think so, he went to the one that [sic] was driving and said she's dead then went to the other one and said the same then said you been screwing her, I said like hell, that was the first time I realised they had been killed, I think I must have blacked out in shock I don't really now [sic] but there seemed to be along [sic] time after the accident that I can't account for.

Early on Sunday morning, while still under the influence of alcohol, Grant had told Constable Clarke that 'After the accident I got out and one of the girls got out and took off her clothes and said, "Ya want me?" I said, "No, we've got a problem here." I then looked around and there was no traffic and that and I said to myself, "What the hell, we've got a rolled Toyota here." She layed [sic] down on the ground and I didn't touch her. A car came along and asked if we were all right. They left and then the Police came.'

There was no compelling reason at all for Grant, at this stage, or any stage in the future, to offer information regarding the possibility that sexual play had or had not taken place with one or either of the girls. McKenzie may have remarked to Grant at the accident site that he had 'been screwing' one of the girls. It may have been reasonable for Ehsman to ask Grant the question of sexual intercourse given the state of undress of Cindy Smith. What is unclear is why Grant would first make any comment at all about what Cindy may or may not have done before death, and second, why he would embellish the story a number of times before coming to rest sometime later, denying that anything had occurred. It seems that Grant may have inadvertently given the police something to think about beyond the culpable driving charges.

# 20

# The investigation squad pokes around

For a few weeks following Shane Baty's sworn testimony at Dareton police station, the police quietly gathered further evidence while Grant's lawyers framed his defence against the initial charges. Grant had been remanded to appear at Bourke local court on 15 February 1988.

As Bill Howes stated in his first communication with Tony Quinlivan, the matter had been 'listed for mention'. A mention is part of the procedural business of a criminal charge. It means a magistrate in a local court will seek to ascertain from a defendant whether they wish to plead guilty or not guilty. It is usually incumbent upon the defendant to attend the court and wait until such time as their matter is mentioned; it might be the last case on the list and a defendant must wait the whole day in or near the courtroom. It is possible that a case may be assigned a particular time for mention on a day. At what time on Monday 15 February Grant's case was listed is unknown. It is also unknown but inferred that certain actors attended the court for the mention. We might assume that lead actors such as Grant himself attended and others such as Ehsman and Reid. We might assume too that under normative conditions, the parents and other relatives of the deceased would also attend. Bourke, however, does not present a normative socio-legal environment, so the possibility of Mona's and Cindy's families being informed of the court date remains unclear. The Aboriginal liaison officer attached to Bourke police station may have informed them and they may in fact have attended the mention. A more likely scenario is that the first they knew of the hearing date was in early May when they were invited to make statements about Mona's driving ability.

For Grant, the financial cost associated with attendance at Bourke local court must be contextualised. If he attended with his solicitor and his barrister, he would have accumulated the direct cost of representation and the associated costs of travel, accommodation and meals. Grant's financial support for his case, which we know took another two years to come to trial, came from anonymous sources. He may have secured employment or he may have had a benefactor. His financial support may have come from the business for which he had worked at the time of the accident. The vehicle was registered in the name of the business so there may have been some legal or moral obligation attached, although that is doubtful. Another assumption we might make is how Grant and his legal entourage travelled from Sydney to Bourke, a not inconsiderable distance by car. There is evidence that Quinlivan spent a few nights during the following two years at a motel in Dubbo, which is roughly the halfway point between Sydney and Bourke. We may assume that Grant, his solicitor and his barrister travelled in one car, booked three separate rooms and returned the same way.

We know that Grant appeared in front of a magistrate at Bourke local court on Monday 15 February and that he pleaded not guilty to the charges made in Nyngan local court on 16 December 1987 relating to permitting unlicensed driver resulting in bodily harm to Mona Smith and Jacinta Smith and in relation to permitting Mona Smith to drive while unlicensed. Grant had stated from the time of the accident that he had not been the driver. The only time he had admitted guilt was in his first encounter with Constable McKenzie when McKenzie said to him, 'Who was driving the ute?' According to McKenzie's testimony, Grant replied, 'I was.' McKenzie then asked, 'Who owns it?' to which Grant replied, 'I do, or the business does.' Given the damage to the driver's side of the utility, it was clear that Grant was not the driver, so the charges appeared to be reasonable at the time. As Grant was not the driver, then charges relating to high-range alcohol content did not apply.

Somewhere in between the time of the mention on Monday 15 February and the committal hearing on Tuesday 8 November – for that was the time set down at mention – the police case altered dramatically in shape and content. In the cold light of the courtroom, when the case was listed for mention, police prosecutors and lead police actors looking closely at the original charges made almost two months earlier may have considered they had been made in haste. The police conversations after the court mention may have been framed around the probability that Grant may walk away from the charges. The conversations may have conflated and made transparent the various statements and the evidence, especially that of the location of the tarpaulin, the location of Grant relative to the body of Cindy Smith and the savage way in which both girls had died.

Whatever the reasons, by early April the case had come to the attention of the commander of the North-west Accident Investigation Squad at Parramatta, Sergeant Raymond George Godkin. In 1988, Ray Godkin was not only a distinguished policeman he was also deeply involved in cycling; he was at the time the manager of a team of cyclists from the St George Cycling Club in Sydney's southern suburbs. In that capacity, he travelled to the Seoul Olympics with six fellow cyclists, the largest representation by St George at a summer Olympics. Godkin was in Seoul in September and October 1988.

But six months before that he was the senior officer in charge of the investigation in relation to the indictable matters then before the court. Godkin had examined closely the charges against Grant as they related to him being a passenger in the utility. During the process of considering the charges and the evidence against Grant, Godkin had conversations with numerous lead actors, including Ehsman, Reid and McKenzie. It was his conversation with McKenzie that provided the catalyst for Godkin to conduct further interviews with Grant and also for him to become convinced that the initial charges did not reflect the actual events as they had occurred.

McKenzie's conversation with Godkin was underpinned by the remark Grant made to McKenzie early in the morning at the scene of the accident that he (Grant) was the driver of the vehicle. As mentioned above, Grant's first response when asked who was driving was to say that he had been. The remark was sufficient for Sergeant Godkin to seek to investigate further, which he did. Godkin asked for statements from a number of people, including lead actor Ken McKenzie, Mona Smith's mother June, Cindy Smith's mother Dawn (Iona), Douglas Smith, Sharon Smith, Lisa Smith and Lloyd Smith. It had been a long time coming. The police case now began to look like it might go somewhere significant.

On Friday 6 May, Constable McKenzie was interviewed at Enngonia police station by Richard Le Merton, a twenty-nine-year-old constable with the North-west Accident Investigation Squad, Parramatta. Le Merton had been sent to Enngonia and Bourke by Sergeant Godkin to tie up a few loose ends.[23] It had now been exactly five months since Constable McKenzie had attended the scene of the accident. But he was able to recall for the investigating officer considerable detail of the event.

About 5.15 a.m. on Sunday the 6 of December, 1987, a male person came to the police residence at Enngonia Police station and as a result of certain information I left and attended the scene of a fatal motor vehicle collision on The Mitchell Highway about 34 kilometres south of Enngonia. I arrived at the scene about 5.45 a.m. and saw a white Toyota Hilux four wheel drive utility resting on its wheels, facing in a south easterly direction at a 45 degree angle to the south, in the western table drain. I saw the vehicle had sustained extensive damage to the roof portion of the vehicle and there was a male person standing near the passenger side door. I stopped the police vehicle on the western side of the highway, got out and walked toward the male person. As I approached this person I saw what appeared to be the body of a person which was lying on the western gravel shoulder, between the road and the front of the vehicle. I then saw another body, that of a female person, which was lying on top of a canvas tarpaulin on the northern side of the vehicle, further toward the line of the scrub, behind where the male person was standing. I walked up to the male person the defendant, Alexander Ian Grant, and said to him, 'Were you involved in the accident'? He said, 'Yeah, mate.' I said, 'Are you all right'? He said, 'Yeah, I'm all right.' I said, 'Who was driving the ute'? He said, 'I was.' I said, 'Who owns it'? He said, 'I do, or the business does.' I then walked over and stood next to the body ~~of Mona Smith~~ that lay in front of the vehicle next to the road and saw it was ~~the body of~~ a young deceased Aboriginal female. I then walked to the body that lay on the tarpaulin and saw it was also a young deceased Aboriginal female, ~~which was naked from the shoulders to the ankles,~~ laying [sic] on its back. I stood up and pulled the tarpaulin over that body to cover it. The defendant said to me, 'They're only asleep aren't they'? I said, 'No, they're both dead.' He said, 'No. They're all right. They're only sleeping'. I said , 'I assure you they are dead'. I then said to him, 'Can you tell me what happened'? He said, 'I don't know.' I said, 'Which way were you travelling'? He then pointed in a southerly direction toward Bourke and said, 'I was going that way'. I said, 'Where did you come from'? He said, 'Bourke.' I said, 'Where were you going'? He said, 'North Bourke.' I said, 'Do you know where you are now'? He said, 'Oh, not far from Bourke, aren't I'? I said, 'No. Nearly at Enngonia.' I then said to the defendant, 'Were there any other vehicles involved?" He said, 'I didn't see any other cars.' He then said, 'Are you sure they're both dead'? I said, 'Yes.' He then pointed at the deceased female Mona Smith at the front of the vehicle and said, 'Ah, she was driving.' I then said, 'Could you give me your licence'? The defendant then produced his licence and I obtained his particulars. Whilst I was speaking to the defendant, I noticed that his breath smelt strongly of intoxicating liquor, his eyes were very bloodshot and when he spoke, at times he was incoherrent [sic] and slurred in his speech, having to be asked to repeat himself on a number of occasions. I saw that the defendant was unsteady on his feet and on occasions he had to support himself against the police vehicle. The defendant was dressed in a khaki shirt and trousers, wearing work boots. I saw that his clothing was disheveled [sic] and he was dirty and untidy in appearance. I formed the opinion that the defendant was well affected by alcohol. I then said to the defendant, 'Where had you been drinking'? He said,

'At the Post Office Hotel and some other places.' I said, 'Who are the two girls'? He said, 'I don't know the names. They just asked me for a ride out to the North Bourke Hotel.' I then made an examination of the white 1985 Toyota Hilux four wheel drive utility number OGQ921. I saw the vehicle had extensive damage to the roof, the offside toward the front and the forward nearside panels. The rear nearside wheel rim was buckled, however, all the tyres fitted were inflated and appeared in roadworthy condition. I was unable to open either of the vehicles [sic] doors as they were both jammed closed and it was necessary for me to reach through the drivers [sic] window to check the steering. On reaching through the window I found the keys were missing from the ignition and the steering was locked. I inspected under the front of the vehicle and saw all the steering linkages were intact and undamaged. There was a large quantity of tools and equipment scattered over the side of the road. The vehicle was later towed to Enngonia police station. The ambulances arrived about 6.35 a.m. and conveyed the bodies of the two deceased girls and the defendant to the Bourke Hospital. Prior to the bodies being removed, Detective Senior Constable Esheman [sic] of Bourke Police attended the scene and I was present whilst he took a number of photographs. I also obtained a number of measurements at the scene and have prepared a plan of the collision scene. The Mitchell Highway where the collision occurred is a public street in the State of New South Wales, being of all weather bitumen construction about 6.5 metres wide, with a broken white centreline and white edgelines. The roadway is level and straight for about 2 kilometres to the north of the collision scene and for about one kilometre to the south. The carriageway is in good condition, being a rural area with a 100 kilometre per hour speed limit applying. At the time of the collision the weather was fine. [On a photocopy, Grant's lawyers have scored through some of the words and sentences as indicated above.]

Some of McKenzie's statement accorded with his occurrence pad entry from the date of the accident. He left out his estimation of the time of the accident and the direction the vehicle was travelling. His occurrence pad noted that it would appear that the deceased person number 2 was the driver and the other deceased female and the owner were passengers in the ute. As the vehicle travelled along a straight portion of roadway about 260 metres south of the Bourke 63 kilometres [sic] marker peg the driver has lost control of the vehicle and the vehicle has left the left side of the roadway and travelled with the near side wheels in the gravel for a distance of approximately 32 metres. The vehicle has then veered [sic] to the centre of the roadway in a curve for a distance of about 36 metres before veering [sic] to the near side of the roadway again. The vehicle has again left the roadway on the western side and travelled a distance of 35 metres in a left hand broadside and then rolled over. The vehicle rolled once and came to rest on its wheels again near the side of the bitumen [sic] and then rolled back down the slight embankment of the roadway shoulder and stopped on the edge of the light scrub. The vehicle is expected to be a total right [sic] off as a result of the accident. A large quantity of tools and other equipment that was stored in the rear of the ute was scattered over an area of xx about 100 square metres. It would appear that from the damage to the vehicle and the injuries to the suspected driver, the [sic] she was thrown out of the vehicle through the drivers [sic] door window as the vehicle rolled and the vehicle has rolled onto her body on the ground causing massive head injuries. The other deceased person had no obvious injuries that may have caused her death. Both deceased person 1 and the other uninjured passenger were not thrown out of the vehicle during the accident.

McKenzie appears to have made some unfortunate inferences during his initial observations of the scene. Aside from the word of the defendant, which was proving to be highly unreliable, there was no evidence to suggest that the passengers had not been thrown from the vehicle. His log contradicted his statement; the log stated Mona Smith was driving, the statement that Alex Grant was driving.

By the following Wednesday, 11 May, Le Merton was back in Sydney but returned to Bourke a week later in the company of Sergeant Godkin. While in Sydney, Le Merton accompanied Godkin to Hurstville police station, where Godkin interviewed Grant. It is unclear why the interview occurred at Hurstville, other than that it may have been the closest station to where Grant lived at the time. Why was Grant not instructed to make his own way to the accident squad at Parramatta? It was beginning to seem that Grant had more than nine lives.

Sergeant Godkin introduced himself and Constable Le Merton and explained where they were from and that they were making further inquiries into the accident in which he had been involved. Godkin referred to it as a 'motor vehicle collision'. There was no collision. The vehicle had collided with nothing and no one.

In reply, Grant said, 'Yes, I am still trying to sort that out myself.'

Godkin said it was his intention to conduct a record of interview and asked if Grant was prepared to participate.

It is unclear why Grant did participate given that he had by now engaged the services of his solicitor, Bill Howes, and had been represented in court by his barrister, Tony Quinlivan. It would seem logical that Grant was advised by his solicitor to have him present at all subsequent police engagements. It was not to be, though Grant hesitated: 'Well, I have been talking to my solicitor. I'd be happy to talk to you about it but I would not like to have a record of interview unless my solicitor or barrister is [sic] present.'

This did not deter Godkin, who countered by asking if there was anything Grant wanted to tell him about the matter. It was as if Godkin were acting as a confessor to whom Grant appeared to succumb.

Grant replied, 'Well, I've thought about it and a lot of the stuff I told the detectives is not right and some of the things I said is really bullshit.'

Godkin pursued his line of inquiry: 'It is my intention to ask you a number of questions about the matter. I want you to understand that you do not have to answer or say anything. However, anything you do say may be later used in evidence, do you understand that?'

Grant replied, 'Yes, of course.'

Godkin then took a line of questioning that was similar to previous interviews Grant had done, but there was enough difference for Godkin to be convinced that further charges could be laid. Questions remain, however, as to why Godkin persisted when Grant had said he wanted his lawyer present. Why did Grant change his mind and answer Godkin's questions?

Godkin: 'Can you tell me when you first picked the girls up that were involved in the incident?'

Grant: 'I was really rotten that night and a lot worse than I told the detectives. I remember talking to the girls, I don't know where, it's just still not there.'

'Are you able to tell me whether you asked them to get into the vehicle or whether they approached you?'

'I think they came to me asking for a lift to North Bourke.'

'What happened after that?'

'Well, it's a bit hazy but we went across to North Bourke and I bought them a bottle of rum, they asked me to get it. I think it was the older one. After we left the North Bourke, the older one said to me, "Can I have a drive?" After a while I said, "All right," and she got into the driver's seat and I sat on the left-hand side. I could see that she drove pretty good and handled it real well, really good on the gears. I had to speak to her a couple of times as she was getting up over 100ks. While we were driving along I could see out the front, the lights were working okay and she was going straight up the road no problem.'

'How do you know what speed she was travelling?'

'I can just tell.'

'Can you remember how far this other person was driving the vehicle?'

'She drove for a while, about 10 to 15 ks. I said, "That's it, pull up and turn around now," but instead of turning around she just pulled off the road and stopped. One of the girls then poured the rum into the bottle of Coke. They drank the rum and Coke and I had a stubbie. I didn't drink the rum. Then she started driving again and the next thing we flipped.'

'What happened then?'

'The bigger one, that's the one who was driving, she was the older one who went through the windscreen.'

'What happened to you?'

'I'm not sure if I was knocked out or not. I know I had a good hit on the top of the head, there was a big lump there and I was still sitting in the seat next to the left hand door. The smaller girl she was still in the ute with me.'

'What happened then?'

'I opened the passenger door, got out, then I pulled the other girl out of the vehicle.'

'Can you tell me if anyone in the vehicle was wearing a seat belt?'

'I'm not sure.'

'Do you recall telling the detectives from Bourke that the girl you dragged out of the vehicle was walking around in a dazed state after getting out of the ute?'

'From what I have heard since about her injuries, that can't be right. Like I said, a lot of the things I have said isn't right.'

'Did you have a look at either girl after you got out in regard to their condition?'

'I know what I said before but fair dinkum I was that rotten I really don't know if I did or not.'

'Can you recall how the tarpaulin got to the position it was in beside the utility?'

'That's where it fell out the back of the ute.'

'Do you recall lying on the tarpaulin with the girl?'

'Like I said, I was right out of it. I remember opening the door and dragging her out, that's how her clothes got pulled down. I thought she asked me for a drink, I'm not sure now.'

'Do you recall being spoken to by a person in the vicinity of 4.30 a.m. whilst you were lying on the tarpaulin with the girl?'

'I can vaguely remember hearing a diesel engine but not seeing any person.'

'Prior to the vehicle leaving the roadway and rolling over, did either of the girls have any of their clothing removed or partly removed?'

'Definitely not.'

'I have a statement from a person who has stated that the young girl was naked from the waist down and that you had your arm over the top portion of her body. Would you care to comment on that?'

'No. I was too out of it.'

'Can you now recall if you at any time interfered with or removed any clothing from the young girl after the accident.'

'I don't think so. I have to say no.'

'Was there any other person other than you and the two girls involved in the vehicle prior to rolling over?'

'No. Only us.'

'Are you able to tell me the state of sobriety of the girls when you picked them up at Bourke?'

'I honestly wouldn't have a clue. Like I said, I was drunk. I honestly don't know. The older one must have been all right because she could drive so well.'

'What injuries did you have in the incident?'

'A good hit on the top of the head and a bit of a scrape on the elbows.'

'You mentioned earlier that you got out of the passenger door after the accident. Do you recall if you had any trouble opening the door?'

'No, I just pushed it open with my elbow and got out.'

'Do you recall when the police first arrived at the scene of the collision?'

'Only vaguely. I was still a bit out of it at the time.'

'Do you recall the constable asking you who was driving the utility when it rolled over?'

'I remember talking to him about things. Like I said before, I was pretty rotten drunk that night but I am very clear that I wasn't driving.'

'Have you ever let other young people drive your vehicle prior to this occasion?'

'That's what I don't understand. I never do. It must have been because she kept asking and I was so drunk.'

'Are you able to tell me how the top part of the young girl's clothing was pulled up below her chin?'

'Only like I said before, when I pulled her out of the truck, it must have happened.'

'I have information that the girls [sic] clothing was interfered with sometime after you were told that she was dead. Do you care to comment on that?'

'No. I can't understand it.'

'After the vehicle rolled over, did you have anything to drink prior to the police arriving?'

'Well, the best I can do is say I think I had one stubbie of Fosters.'

'I have a copy of a blood test certificate no 76588 which indicates that you had a blood alcohol level of 0.159 when a sample was taken from you at the Bourke hospital on the morning of the accident. Can you tell me where the vehicle is at the present time?'

'It was sold as a wreck to Peter Hurle of Wee Waa.'

'It is my view that you were the driver of the vehicle OGQ921 when it left the highway and rolled over in the collision we have been discussing. It is my intention to charge you with two counts of culpable driving and also with driving with the prescribed concentration of alcohol. Is there anything else you would like to tell me about this matter?'

'I can't think of anything other than to say that no way was I driving. I know I did the wrong thing letting her drive without a licence.'

Godkin charged Grant at Hurstville police station at 7.45 p.m. on Wednesday 11 May. Three extra charges were added to Mr Grant's sheet:

1. Charge in relation to culpable driving causing the death of Mona Lisa Smith.
2. Charge in relation to culpable driving causing the death of Jacinta Rose Smith.
3. High-range PCA.

The following day at Parramatta, Sergeant Godkin made a statement of his action which was witnessed by Constable Le Merton. What is most interesting about the change of direction of the charges added by Godkin is that they appear to be at odds with the earlier charges: Grant was either in charge of the vehicle or he was not. He could not be charged with permitting an unlicensed driver if he himself was driving. But Godkin had not yet finished with Grant. There was a further charge to be added.

# 21

# The steering wheel

Before being present at the interview at which Sergeant Godkin added charges against Alex Grant, Constable Richard Le Merton had travelled to Bourke, as indicated above, where he gathered statements from various actors including Constable Ken McKenzie. Le Merton was in Bourke from Friday 6 May when he interviewed McKenzie until at least Sunday 8 May, when four other actors were interviewed. It may not have been unusual for the Bourke police to take statements on any day of the week. As it happened, Mona and Cindy's mothers, along with brother Doug Smith, were interviewed on Sunday 8 May. The information that Le Merton returned with from Bourke increased substantially the opportunity for Godkin to apply additional charges. Le Merton was to return to Bourke again before the end of the month, where he continued to gather statements from important actors.

We will return to the statements, but for now it is important to imagine two events that transpired immediately after Grant was interviewed by Godkin at Hurstville. Keeping in mind that he was interviewed by Godkin on Wednesday 11 May at 6.30 p.m., the following day, Thursday 12 May, Godkin made a statement at Parramatta at the Accident Investigation headquarters.

At 9 a.m. the next day, Friday 13 May, Godkin telephoned Inverell police station and had a conversation with thirty-four-year-old Detective Sergeant Patrick Bernard Moss. Detective Moss was stationed at Inverell and engaged in physical evidence collection. His duties were to examine items of physical evidence, make a photographic record of those examinations and submit items for forensic testing. He had been engaged in these activities for nine years so it could be inferred that Moss was an expert investigator. Inverell is a pleasant wheat and sheep town almost 600 kilometres east of Bourke or more than seven hours' drive. It was however, only a smidgen over three hours' drive from Wee Waa, along the Newell and Gwydir Highways, where the smashed ute had come to rest at the business premises of Peter Hurle. Closer centres to Wee Waa included Walgett and Coonamble but at the time neither town supported an investigation unit within the police station.

The nature of the telephone conversation between Godkin and Moss was to arrange for Moss to set up a time to drive to Wee Waa and have a look at the smashed ute. Keeping in mind that the ute had already been examined by Senior Constable Ludewig shortly after the accident, it had now become necessary to take another look at it given that extra charges had been laid. What happened next was a bizarre event that remains unexplained to this day.

When Moss had finished with the call from Sergeant Godkin, he made a call to Peter Hurle at Wee Waa Electrics to arrange a suitable time to examine the utility, or what might have remained of it. Hurle, as we recall, had bought the ute in January. Hurle said it was okay to come over the following day, Saturday 15 May. At the time, Peter Warren Hurle, who was born on 23 February 1936, referred to himself as a company director.

Moss arrived at Wee Waa at 3 pm, called in to the police station to use the toilet and get a drink of water (no bottled spring water back then), then drove to Hurle's place where, at 3.20 p.m., he began his examination. He examined the ute, took photographs and, by his own account, 'made a presumptive test for the presence of blood on the roof liner, the sun visor, a mat and the dashboard panels'. A positive result was made from the roof liner, nearside front and the nearside sun visor. Moss secured these items and later on sent the roof liner and sun visor to the Division of Forensic Medicine at Glebe, New South Wales, for further examination. He was unable, though, to examine the steering wheel from the ute because it was not there. We might assume he questioned Mr Hurle as to the whereabouts of the steering wheel. Hurle, we might also assume, was forthright in his response, given what Moss later recalled in a statement of record. Hurle said that the steering wheel had the day before been sent to Alex Grant. If it occurred to Moss to question the logic of such unusual action, knowing that it had been sent from the scene the day before he was to examine vital evidence, he did not record it in his later statement.

Some months later, Hurle made a statement about Moss's visit. In it he said,

> included in the items stored inside the shed were the roof liner and both sun visors from inside the vehicle. Prior to the attendance of Detective Moss I had sent the steering wheel to Alex Grant, at Alex's request. I sent the steering wheel to Alex the day before Detective Moss attended my workshop. On 14 May [sic], 1988 I gave Detective Moss a number of items, including the roof liner and the two sun visors. I have since received the steering wheel from Alex Grant.

Bizarre as the act of shipping the wheel to Grant seems, it is even more nonsensical that at some time between May and September, when Hurle made a statement of the events, Grant returned the wheel to him. There are many questions about these actions. It is not so much a question of why Hurle sent the wheel in the first place. It is a question of how Grant knew that Moss was making an inspection of the ute. Given the familiar tone Hurle uses in his statement – 'at Alex's request' and 'I sent the steering wheel to Alex' rather than Grant or Mr Grant – we can infer that Grant and Hurle were well-known to each other. Secondly, service providers in small towns are not known for their enduring friendships with the police. Even though Moss himself, as a policeman, could be viewed as a service provider, small towns such as Wee Waa have strict vertical social hierarchies; and Moss was from Inverell, so Hurle would have had no commonality of purpose. If, as we suspect, Hurle knew Grant because Grant was based in Wee Waa and had lived there for some time before relocating to Bourke, Hurle may have been quick to contact Grant to tell him of the impending inspection. Grant too had used similar familiar terms when interviewed by Sergeant Godkin a few days earlier. He may have feigned amnesia when it came to knowing what happened at the time of the accident but he was quick to respond that '[the ute] was sold as a wreck to Peter Hurle at Wee Waa'. Grant had left Bourke quickly after the accident so unless he was back in Wee Waa, or knew Peter Hurle personally, there is no reason he would have had information about where the ute had gone or to whom it had been sold.

Grant had had three extra charges laid against him four days earlier. Wherever he was, in Sydney or Wee Waa, by Saturday when Moss visited Wee Waa Electrics, the steering wheel had gone walkabout. The items Moss was able to secure he took to Wee Waa police station later in the day. As to the question of whether the steering wheel was ever actually shipped to Grant, the balance of probability was that Hurle telephoned Grant in Sydney or found him in Wee Waa and told him of Moss's impending examination. Grant, in what would by then have been a furious state of mind given the extra charges, told Hurle to hide the steering wheel until such time as Moss went back to Inverell. Hurle had made contact with Grant, so it seemed logical to follow through on his instructions and to hide the item from the police.

Hurle's and Grant's actions raise other questions. What was it about the steering wheel that required it to be removed before the police could examine it? If reason is applied to the question, the only possible answer is that Grant thought it might reveal in some way that he had been the driver at the time of the accident. If he believed that, then it follows that he truly believed he had been the driver, despite his statements to various police officers that he had not.

When Peter Hurle gave his statement to police at Wee Waa police station on 8 September 1988, he signed it in the knowledge that 'I am aware that if I sign this statement and any part of this statement is untrue to my knowledge I may be liable to punishment'. While it is irrelevant that Hurle said he spoke with Detective Moss on 14 May, rather than the actual day, 15 May, it is important that his statement contained vital information as to the whereabouts of the steering wheel, but the information lay dormant and did not surface until September.

# 22

# The charges mount up

By the middle of the following week, Constable Le Merton was back in Bourke and this time he was accompanied by Sergeant Godkin. Le Merton invested some time in finding and talking with witnesses who had seen Mona and Cindy the night before they were killed. He interviewed Sharon Smith, Lisa Smith and Lloyd Smith on Friday 20 May and Daniel Booth on Saturday 21 May.

Booth provided a statement about the driving ability of the two girls. Ironically, when Grant finally came to trial, Dan Booth was also on the court list for escaping from lawful custody and assaulting two police.

Le Merton also interviewed the barman from the hotel where Grant had last been seen buying grog. Lawrence Charles Barnett was the barman at the Riverview Hotel in North Bourke. He recalled selling beer and rum to Grant and seeing someone waiting at the door for him as he left the hotel.

While Le Merton interviewed witnesses, Godkin was busy deep in conversation with Constable McKenzie. McKenzie had come down from Enngonia to talk about what exactly Grant had said the morning of the accident. Godkin needed to be certain, absolutely certain, if he was going to continue with the additional charges against Grant. At issue was the question of Grant being the driver, but additionally there was the question of whether Cindy Smith had been dead when Grant interfered with her clothing and her body. At this stage of the investigation, Grant had not been charged with anything in relation to Cindy other than causing grievous bodily harm, as he had with

Mona. Godkin spoke at length with McKenzie. It is unarguable that he would also have spoken at length with Ehsman and Reid and with the ambulance officers Brennan and Willoughby. Godkin was getting close to adding an additional charge unrelated to the driving offences; a charge that would make it almost impossible for Grant not to go to trial in the event that he defended himself against the driving charges.

On Sunday 22 May, Godkin and Le Merton returned to Sydney with enough evidence to add the additional charge. On Tuesday 24 May, accompanied by his solicitor Bill Howes, Alexander Ian Grant attended Kogarah local court at Hurstville, where he was charged with culpable driving causing the deaths of Mona Smith and Cindy. Smith under the *Crimes Act 1900*, No 40 Sec 52A(1)(b); high range PCA under the *Motor Traffic Act 1909* No 5 Sec 4E (1G)(a); and, under the *Crimes Act 1900*, Number 40 Section 81C(A), he was charged with misconduct with regard to corpses. The charge read

> That Alexander Ian Gratn [sic] on the 6th day of December in the year 1987 at Enngonia in the State of New South Wales, did indecently interfere with a dead human body. The dead human body being that of Jacinta Rose Smith.

On the first three, Grant was charged by Sergeant Godkin and Constable Le Merton. On the fourth, Grant was charged by Constable Le Merton. The first three charge sheets were dated 11/5/88, the day they were laid. The charge of interfere had the notation 'charged at court' rather than where the other three had been made, at Kogarah police station. Godkin and Le Merton had visited Bourke after laying the first three charges and had found enough information to be beyond reasonable doubt that he had interfered with Cindy after she had died.

All four charges were adjourned for mention at Bourke local court on 4 July.

# 23

# The Hilux again – who was really driving?

As Bill Howes was in Sydney drafting a letter to Tony Quinlivan with information about the charges made against his client, Godkin and Le Merton were arriving again in Bourke to further their investigations. Quinlivan retrieved Howes's letter from his document exchange. The Sydney document exchange was a central facility from where law firms, courts and other associated businesses could deposit and retrieve documents. Picone & Howes used DX430 in Sydney and DX11136 in Kogarah. Quinlivan used DX509. Correspondence sent to Quinlivan needed only to be addressed A.P. Quinlivan, Barrister at Law, DX509 Sydney and it would find him. It was also a way for law practitioners to maintain a semi-private function; unless they were suburban street-front practitioners. Howes wrote to Quinlivan to say that his client had been charged with two further offences in relation to culpable driving causing death (two counts) and in relation to high-range PCA. He included a copy of the blood certificate that Grant had received from the police and a copy of the bail undertaking into which Grant had entered. The *Bail Act 1978* allowed a defendant to remain at large with no financial burden if the court so chose. In Grant's case, he agreed to appear in Kogarah court of petty sessions at 10 a.m. on 24 May. There was no other undertaking imposed upon him. Given the charges, it is beyond belief that Grant was let off so lightly.

Howes suggested to Quinlivan that

> this matter is returnable in the first instance at Kogarah Local Court
> on 24th May, 1988. The writer will represent Mr Grant on that

occasion as we understand the matter will thereafter be transferred to Bourke local court. It would be appreciated if you kindly telephone the writer with a view to making an appointment next week to discuss this matter with our client and the writer prior to the mention at Court on 24th May, 1988.

The meeting with Howes, Quinlivan and Grant did not take place until 14 June.

In the meantime, Godkin and Le Merton were busy gathering more evidence that would underpin the driving charges against Grant and create the interference charge. A week earlier, the mothers of the dead girls had been interviewed, as had Douglas Smith, Mona's twenty-one-year-old brother. Doug gave his address as Cottage 17, the Reserve, and his occupation as unemployed. Unemployment rates in Bourke were highest then among young Aborigines, very much as they are now. It was nothing for unemployment to be passed down through generations.

Mona's mother June, who was thirty-nine years old at the time, gave her occupation as domestic duties. This was a standard for women throughout most of the twentieth century if they were what are now called stay-at-home mums. June provided a one-page statement at Bourke police station on Sunday 8 May. She had walked from the Reserve to the police station.

When told that Mona might have been the driver, June said, 'I was later told that it had been suggested that Mona was driving the four-wheel drive that was involved in the accident. I know that this is not possible as she could not drive any manual type of cars. The only car that I have ever known her try to drive was a blue Ford automatic and she reversed that for a short distance and ran into a steel peg. I then told Mona to get out of the car and to my knowledge, that is the only time she ever tried to drive a car.'[24]

Dawn Smith also walked to the police station but from the other end of town, where she lived at 143 Meadows Road. Dawn was about to turn forty-four and gave her occupation as pensioner. While Dawn had not provided a telephone number, June had a telephone at her house. Dawn was Cindy's mother and Mona's aunt. In her statement, Dawn raised an issue that was later bracketed in red ink on the copy held by the defence team and may have gone some way towards confirming Sergeant Godkin's decision. Dawn said, 'We are a very close community and if Mona was driving at any time then I would hear about it.'

We will return to the image of community in more detail; what is important here is that such a usage portrayed significantly the divisions within the triangulation of groups within the town, namely Aborigines, service providers and landowners.

Dawn confirmed that Mona had driven the blue automatic Falcon. 'One of the Police told us that it was suggested that Mona was driving the vehicle involved in the accident. We are a close family and I see the girls all the time. There is no way that Mona could have been driving a car as she could not drive, other than mucking around on the Reserve, which I found out later on, and that was only an automatic car. We are a very close community and if Mona was driving at any time, then I would hear about it. Anybody who said that Mona was driving the four-wheel drive that was involved in the accident, would be lying, because she just couldn't drive it.' Dawn was very specific in her statement. She then added some important information about Cindy, information that would have compelled Sergeant Godkin to add the interference charge. Dawn said, 'It was also said that my daughter was sixteen but in fact she was only fifteen, having been born on the 23rd of October, 1972.'

Ray Godkin was a man deeply involved in his own community, the cycling community of Kogarah and his own family. It would have been beyond his comprehension that a forty-year-old man could entertain the thought of being sexually involved with a fifteen or sixteen-year-old girl, let alone the possibility of doing what he now believed the defendant had done to Cindy after her death.

Doug Smith's statement confirmed that his sister Mona was not

127

a driver but it denied the fact that the car belonged to his mother's boyfriend, Robert. He described the car as being owned by a 'friend'. 'My sister had just turned sixteen years of age. I once saw Mona try to drive a blue Ford automatic sedan down at the Reserve. She drove the car for less than five minutes around a little dirt road within the Reserve and then she got out. The car belonged to a friend who was visiting us. That is the only car that she has ever driven as far as I know and I am sure that she has never driven any other car. If someone told me that Mona drove a manual car, I wouldn't believe them because she just doesn't know how to drive.'

Like June and Dawn before him, Doug Smith made his statement at Bourke police station at an unknown time on Sunday 8 May. To whom all three gave their statements is also unclear. While the statements were signed by June, Dawn and Doug, the witness signature was unknown. It did not belong to Godkin or le Merton and it did not belong to Ehsman, Reid or McKenzie, whose signatures appeared on other related documents.

The following week, the statements given by Sharon Smith, Lisa Smith, Lloyd Smith, Daniel Booth and Lawrence Barnett were all taken down on Friday 20 May by Richard Le Merton. Le Merton's signature appears below each one. While June and Dawn Smith had made one-page statements, those interviewed the following week provided more detail. The form of the statement was different to the interviews with the defendant and some of the police. The statements did not have associated questions; they were simply statements made by the individuals. They were very specific in their focus, so they must have been underpinned by information from the police for them to be relevant.

Sharon Smith provided information that was designed to show that the defendant might have been involved in similar actions prior to the night of the accident. Sharon was sixteen, a cousin of both Mona and Cindy, and lived at Cottage 13, the Reserve. She listed her occupation as unemployed. Like many young Aborigines of her age in and around

Bourke, she had quit school as she found no point in it. She had done so with the prospect of no other institutionalised activity taking its place. Sharon said she remembered being approached by a man a week or so before the accident.

It was just after darkness and I was walking along Mitchell Street near the park going up towards the Reserve, after being at the Carrier Hotel, we were coming back with my cousin Julie Smith. As we were walking a set of headlights came up behind me then a white four wheel drive, I think it was a Toyota, pulled up beside me on the right hand side. A man spoke to me through the window and said, 'Can you tell me where the rodeo is?' I said, 'I'll show you.' Julie and I got into the four wheel drive and took him to the rodeo. I sat on the passenger side and Julie was in the middle and Julie said, 'Will you shout us a beer?' The man stopped at the Oxford Hotel and went in then came out with a half dozen pack of Tooheys beer. We then directed the fellow to the showground and when we got there we started drinking with this man. When we were having a drink I saw Jacinta and Vivienne and they called out to us. Julie, the man and I then went for a drive out along the North Bourke Road towards the levy and he was driving. When we first met the man he smelt strongly of beer and while he was with us he drank even more. We were just talking in the truck and having a drink and he offered me a drive of his car. I said, 'I can't drive.' There was more talk and then the man pulled over to the side of the road as you go over the levy and he jumped out of the driver's side. I slid over on the seat behind the wheel and the man got into the passenger seat. Julie said, 'Let's go back and get Cindy', so I turned around and drove back to the showground to get my cousin Jacinta. When we got to the rodeo Jacinta was waiting behind the tents and she got into the four wheel drive between me and Julie. As we drove out I stopped at the Oxley Club and the man got out and came back with another half a dozen pack of beer. Julie and Jacinta got out and he jumped back into the middle and put the beer on the floor. Julie brung [sic] the subject up about going to Enngonia and the man never said nothing. Julie wanted to go out to Enngonia so I drove and on the way out the man was rubbing his hand up and down my leg and when Cindy seen [sic] him doing that she put her hand in and moved it away. The man was trying to do the same thing to Cindy and Julie but since I was driving I couldn't see exactly what he was doing. When we got to Enngonia I stopped at my cousin's place and after a while we got back in the car and went back to town. On the way back he was trying to rub our legs and we ran out of diesel. The man got out and filled the utility up with fuel again while us girls sat in the front seat. When it was full I drove back into town towards the showground. Some of my other cousins wanted a lift, Carl Smith, Dwayne Robinson, Alan Moore, Sally Edward [sic] and another girl. They got in the back of the utility and I drove them to Church Street I think it is. They got some parts out of the back of the ute from under the big black cover and then we were going home. I then drove the four wheel drive down to the Reserve. We stopped in front of Cottage No. 12 and Jacinta jumped out. While all this was happening the man was really drunk and he didn't seem to know what was happening. The man wanted to be friendly and he said, 'We'll go for a drive and I'll give you some money.' He wanted me and Julie for a girlfriend, to have sex with him. I drove the four wheel drive down to the drain near the weir and we stopped there. He kept saying, 'If you let me do sex with you I'll give you money.' Julie said, 'No, cause I'm a virgin.' He asked me and I said, 'No, cause I'm pregnant.' I started the car up and drove back to the Reserve then we jumped out and left him. The man then drove away.[25]

A statement was made by Lisa Patricia Smith, who was also known as Lisa Edwards. Lisa lived at Cottage 13, the Reserve. She was Mona and Cindy's aunt and she was born on 28 July 1962. Despite her being a few years older than Mona and Cindy, she too was unemployed and spent her days hanging around the Reserve and drinking. On the day before Mona and Cindy died, Lisa had been at Mona's house. While she was there, Mona and 'another fella from the Reserve', Gary Cook, went to get 'some grog'. Lisa's statement reflected that she and Mona and Cindy had been drinking in a 'little blue caravan' with another man named David Corn but when Lisa's mother arrived and 'belted us with a stick to make us stop drinking', they left the caravan and walked to the levy. While her statement may not have been accurate, given that others placed Mona and Cindy elsewhere before dark, it is relevant that she painted a picture of a community in which even a twenty-four-year-old was subject to control, or attempted control, by the parent.

Lloyd Smith was the last person to be interviewed by Richard Le Merton on Friday 20 May. Lloyd too walked to the police station, where he stated that he lived at 143 Meadows Road, was born on 18 December 1965, and was unemployed. He had lived with his mother, three brothers and sister Cindy. Another sister lived in Anson Street. He was the only one of Cindy's siblings to be interviewed because he was the last to see her alive. Lloyd had been at his auntie's at 15 Anson Street for most of the day on Saturday 5 December. He left there at 7.45 p.m. to walk home. At intervals on the way, he stopped and spoke with friends and relations. It was part of Aboriginal community life to spend time on the street among friends and relatives. At 8.15 p.m. he saw his sister Cindy and cousin Mona in Yanda Street. He spoke with them. They began walking towards the Reserve while Lloyd continued into town, stopping at the Post Office Hotel. He did not get home until around 10.30 p.m. Lloyd did not find out about Cindy's death until after midday on Sunday, when he went to his sister's house. Lloyd added to the information about Mona's driving ability in stating, 'To my knowledge, Mona didn't know how to drive and I have never seen her behind the wheel.'

It is clear from the statements made to Constable Le Merton that the frame around which they were developed was directly related to Mona's capabilities as a motor vehicle driver and thus to confirm the relevance of the charges against the defendant.

The following day, Constable Le Merton took a statement from Daniel Booth, the last of the 'aboriginal statements' as Mr Quinlivan was later to refer to them, and from Lawrence Charles Barnett, the barman at the Riverview Hotel in North Bourke. Mr Booth said he lived at a cottage on the Reserve, was born on 15 June 1969, and referred to his occupation as tech student. Mr Booth recalled seeing Mona and Jacinta between 8 o'clock and 9 o'clock on the Saturday night. He also said he did not think Mona could drive. 'To my knowledge my cousin Mona couldn't drive. No one had shown her how but one day I seen her trying to drive a old blue Falcon around. She drove the car around the dirt in the Reserve, but she was only going real slow and she didn't know what she was doing. That was the first time she had been trying to drive a car and even then it was an automatic. I never heard of her driving after that and it was awhile ago, about 6 or 7 months before the accident happened.'

The last statement taken by Constable Le Merton was from the barman at the Riverview Hotel, Lawrence Charles Barnett. Mr Barnett provided a piece of information that was important in constructing a time scale for the whereabouts of the three people in the utility late on Saturday night. There was plenty of guesswork as to the timing of the accident; and there was some expert testimony as to the possible times of death of Mona and Cindy. Nonetheless, the space of time between 10 p.m., when Mr Barnett spoke with Mr Grant at the Riverview Hotel and 4.30 a.m., when Shane Baty and his party came upon the accident site, is unaccounted for. Grant was the only person alive who could have shed light on those missing hours. But he chose not to or, in his defence as his counsel was later to argue, he was unable to because of his state of inebriation.

Laurie Barnett gave his address as 20 Mertin Street, in the heart of town. Mr Barnett was forty-eight years old and gave his occupation as barman. He had begun his shift at the hotel at 1.30 p.m. on Saturday 5 December. Barnett, by his own account, stated that he would not normally remember specifically who came into the bar or for how long or at what time, but in this instance he had met Grant the day before over a potential business transaction.

On Saturday night the 5th of December, 1987, I was working at the hotel from 1.30pm to 10.30pm. About 10:00pm that night a fellow called Alex came into the bar and bought some rum, beer and Coke from me. I wouldn't normally remember it however, I had met this fellow the day before when he came around to look at buying a block of land with a caravan and annex on it over at North Bourke. I actually went with the fellow in his white Toyota Hilux four wheel drive to show him the block. I can remember him coming in very clearly that night. This fellow Alex came in and I'm not sure of the exact conversation, but he ordered a bottle of rum, two bottles of Coke and a dozen stubbies of beer. I added the price up in my head and he didn't have enough money then he said, I'll have a half bottle of rum instead of the full one.' I said, 'The half bottle will bring you back to the money you've got there.' I rang the cost up and he gave me a $20-00 note, one $5-00 note, two $2-00 notes and a bit of silver coin. I gave him his change and he said, 'Thanks Laurie', then left. I remember that while Alex was at the bar there was a woman standing in the doorway and she called out for someone. Alex walked out and at first I thought they were together, but they weren't. One of the other fellows in the bar walked to the door as they left and looked out, then he said something to me and went back to drinking. I haven't seen this Alex fellow since. As I remember he was about 5 foot 10 inches tall, fairly thin with a thin face, he had dark hair and he combed it straight back. I don't really remember what clothes he was wearing, just that it was work type clothing.[26]

On Sunday 22 May, armed with the statements and other information, Godkin and Le Merton checked out of their motel and prepared for the long drive back to Sydney. It was a pleasant autumn day and, with two drivers, they made the trip in a little over nine and a half hours.

# 24

# The sex with a corpse question mark

The charges that Alex Grant faced at Kogarah local court were, as mentioned above, two counts of culpable driving causing death and high-range PCA (prescribed content alcohol). The first two charges under Section 52A(1)(b) of the *Crimes Act 1900* carried penalties of imprisonment for up to ten years. The charge was dangerous driving, substantive matters: dangerous driving occasioning death – a person is guilty of the offence of dangerous driving occasioning death if the vehicle driven by the person is involved in an impact occasioning the death of another person and the driver was, at the time of the impact, driving the vehicle at a speed dangerous to another person or persons. The high-range alcohol charge was made under the *Traffic Act 1909* (New South Wales). High-range PCA applies to drivers with a blood alcohol concentration of over 0.15 grams per 100 millilitres of blood. As we have seen, Grant's blood alcohol content at 9 a.m. the morning after the accident was determined to be 0.159 grams of alcohol per 100 millilitres of blood. It remains unknown what his blood alcohol content may have been any time between midnight and 9 a.m. The maximum penalty for high-range PCA first offences was eighteen months imprisonment and three years disqualification. It is unclear whether Grant's solicitors argued for a first offence given his record of driving under the influence: his first conviction was in Moree in 1980, followed by further convictions for speeding and driving while disqualified in 1981, 1983 and 1986, two months before the accident. If he had been convicted as a second offender high-range PCA, he would have been liable to a penalty of up to two years behind bars and a five-year disqualification. Drink driving offences are the most common dealt with by local courts in New South Wales.

When Grant appeared in court with his solicitor Bill Howes on the morning of 24 May, he was handed an additional charge, one which made the driving charges look like schoolyard clean-up chores. Grant was charged under the *Crimes Act 1900* Section 81(c)(a) with misconduct with regard to corpses. The charge states that any person who indecently interferes with any dead human body shall be liable to imprisonment for two years. Of interest here is the second part to the charge, Section 81(C)(b), which states that any person who improperly interferes with, or offers any indignity to, any dead human body or human remains (whether buried or not), shall be liable to imprisonment for two years. The case that Sergeant Godkin made, with the observations and statements from Constable McKenzie and Detective Ehsman, suggested Cindy's body had been tampered with. There was also an implication earlier in the investigating that there may have been some sexual activity involved – we know this because Clive Pringle was invited to take samples at autopsy from Cindy's body to make such determination. It is curious, therefore, why 81(c)(a) was applied and not 81(c)(b) of the Act. The term 'offer indignity' was in fact used by Quinlivan when describing the charge at a later date. But the charge of offer indignity, or 81(c)(b), was notoriously difficult to prosecute, especially if the defendant pleaded diminished responsibility due to some external agent.

In Grant's case, the defence was to argue that his diminished responsibility was brought about by a large amount of alcohol. Tony Quinlivan was quick to grasp the significance of this. He wrote to Bill Howes on 20 June suggesting that 'the allegation concerning indecent interference with a corpse seems to be capable of being defended by two arguments: firstly – no *mens rea* based on an "O'Connor" defence – too drunk to know what he was doing; secondly – the medical evidence may not justify a finding that the girl was dead at the relevant time'. *Mens rea* is a Latin term meaning a guilty mind or, loosely translated, an intention to commit a crime. There is frequently a requirement to prove *mens rea* before a person can be found guilty. No *mens rea* therefore can be translated as no intention to commit a crime. In Grant's case, Quinlivan was most probably correct, in that Grant may have been too drunk to know what he was doing, yet his early statements in the matter do not appear to prove conclusively that he did not know what he was doing. The onus was on the police to prove Grant committed *actus reus* (the offence) and that he did so intentionally. As we will see, Quinlivan may have jumped the gun in suggesting the charge was defensible under the conditions of no *mens rea* and the O'Connor defence. O'Connor is generally viewed as the most important Australian common law decision on intoxication and whether a defendant was in fact intoxicated to the extent that an *actus reus* was involuntary and thus did not meet the requisite criminal standard of intent.

The O'Connor case came before the High Court of Australia in 1980; *R v O'Connor* (1980) 146 CLR 64. Intoxication is not in itself a defence against punishment for a crime. So it was not sufficient for Quinlivan to argue that his client was too drunk to know what he was doing. The focus for Quinlivan was that the O'Connor case allowed him to argue for a distillation of some of the elements of criminal responsibility that attached to his client. The O'Connor case was also celebrated because it was heard by a High Court which was not in alignment. It was the court on which Lionel Murphy, a former attorney general in the Whitlam government, sat and which was presided over by Sir Garfield Barwick as chief justice.[27] The O'Connor decision ran to forty-four pages. A majority of four to three found that evidence of intoxication should be taken into account when determining whether the prosecution has proved beyond reasonable doubt that a defendant acted voluntarily and intentionally. The court determined that where evidence of intoxication raised any doubt that a defendant had acted voluntarily and intentionally, the defendant should be acquitted. The decision was seen as fundamental to the principle of criminal law that an individual is not guilty unless they acted intentionally and voluntarily.

In the case of Regina v Alexander, Ian Grant there was still some way to go before such a finding might be applied. When Grant attended Kogarah local court on 24 May, the charges against him were adjourned for mention at Bourke local court on 4 July 1988. When a case is adjourned for mention, it usually means that on the adjournment date the case will be mentioned before the court. It does not mean the case will be heard then and it also means there may be continuing matters that require resolution before a hearing date can be set. For Grant's defence lawyers, the matters that required resolution were as set out by Quinlivan in a letter to Howes dated June 20. Quinlivan wrote,

> Mr Grant faces a number of charges and it seems to me that we will not know exactly what charges will be required to be met at committal until the next mention of the matter. I say this because it seems to me that the police cannot proceed simultaneously with the allegations of culpable driving and the 'Section 53' allegations which latter allegations have Mr Grant as a passenger in charge of the relevant motor vehicle! Upon my present instructions it seems to me that genuinely arguable defences are available to Mr Grant in relation to both sets of allegations. That is, in relation to the culpable driving allegations – he was not the driver; in relation to the 'Section 53' allegations – he was not in charge of the motor vehicle.

Quinlivan was more forthright in his assessment of the high-range PCA charge. It may have been a tactic or it may have been on face value that he thought

> The charges relating to P.C.A. and allowing an unlicenced [sic] person to drive do not seem to me to be capable of being defended and I consider that pleas of guilt should be entered at the first available opportunity; any Magistrate should be encouraged to convict in relation to these matters so that it may become possible to argue autrefois[28] convict in relation to either the culpable driving or 'Section 53' allegations.

Quinlivan sought to strengthen his defence of the misconduct charge. He was representing his client as one who might cop the charge of high-range PCA and eighteen months behind bars rather than the alternative of ten years. He was also looking to shore up his client's defences against the misconduct charge. Of course, there were still current the original charges made against Grant at Nyngan, which Quinlivan was referring to when he remarked that Grant could not be guilty of one if he were guilty of the other.

# 25

## The prosecution builds a wonky case

As we know, Grant went to trial in February 1990. For two years, he had the benefit of a seamless defence run by highly competent lawyers acting on his behalf. The cost of funding the defence was substantial. Sources of funding are notoriously difficult to pinpoint. As we have seen earlier, Grant had a benefactor either attached to the business for which he worked or some other independent funding source. Either way, the strength of the defence lay partly in its continuity of resources, both financial and personnel. The prosecution case, in contrast, was fragmented and sloppy. Various individuals took the case forward and in each instance they remained as actors but not in the sense that they were able to drive with any substantive meaning. There was no real ownership of the prosecution case. Ray Godkin was the closest anyone came to making a go of it. Right from the start, it was clear that McKenzie, then Ehsman, then Reid and others who followed were really saying 'whatever'. So a couple of Aboriginals got killed. Whatever. But in all fairness, the system conspired to make them drag their flat feet.

In New South Wales, the police play a substantive role in the prosecution process. At both summary level and indictable offence level, police investigations frame prosecutions. We have seen that the initial charges which were laid by Ehsman occurred after his investigation of the accident scene and interviews with the defendant. We can assume he formed the conclusion that there was sufficient evidence to convict. Even though there is a mechanism which is meant to be independent – the Director of Public Prosecutions – the police are in an invidious position in that they must work in an adversarial capacity to build a case. They have parallel functions – they must at once investigate to determine what happened, while gathering evidence to convict. It is not surprising, therefore, that much of what is gathered does not always appear to be seamless in its delivery. Ehsman, for example, was expected to gather information from the scene, draw conclusions from one of his fellow officers, interview the defendant in an objective fashion because he had not then been charged, and attend the autopsies of two dead teenage girls without forming an opinion as to whether a crime had yet been committed. He was then expected to frame the available information in such a way as to the reasonable guilt or otherwise of the person involved and then to find charges that might fit the crime.

The evidence pointed to the probability that Grant had not been driving yet a statement from him to a police officer required Ehsman to pursue charges on that basis. Even then, when charges have been laid at a police station, they must be presented at court to be assessed by a magistrate to determine their suitability for trial. This is the first hurdle for the police. If they manage to step over it, they are then confronted with additional barriers. In Grant's case, the police were dealing less with a straightforward case of drunken behaviour that caused death and more with a case of differing values in different communities which were located in proximity to each other and which were inexorably intertwined. It was difficult for Ehsman to gather evidence without appearing to act in a manner that might now be considered racially motivated. It was equally difficult to frame charges without appearing to be motivated by tolerance for acts that in other situations and times might go unnoticed.

As Ehsman became tangential to the case, another actor moved in to the lead prosecution role. Sergeant Ray Godkin had not been associated with the early part of the investigation – evidence-gathering and charging – but he was briefed then began further evidence-gathering and on that basis made further charges. There was less pressure on Godkin to act dispassionately because Grant had by then been charged. So Godkin could come into play in a more adversarial way, yet he knew that by adding charges the same court hurdle would need to be cleared again before the charges could be tested. Meanwhile, the defence watched and waited as the police attempted to build their case.

A further difficulty for the police lay in the sense of meaning they may or may not attach to the early stages of a case. We can see that even what seemed to be a simple statement by someone – Grant saying he was, then was not, the driver – complicates matters to the point where sense-making becomes difficult for even the most astute observer. Some would argue that police make sense of a situation by applying known probabilities. This means they may look at a situation and make sense of it by applying values they have developed in their own lives and in the job of policing, which requires them to look at an event through the lens of guilt. In applying values, they form opinions that may underpin the development of meaning. Language and narrative assist in the framing.

In Grant's case, a number of early language and conversational markers were used that could be seen to frame opinions. Mr Baty allegedly said to Grant, 'You've got a couple of dead gins here, mate.' Grant later referred to the girls as 'a couple of Murris' (transcribed as Murrays). There is a further argument that says the police have at their disposal unlimited resources to interview witnesses, take statements, and investigate in as much detail as they like, so that it may be impossible for defence lawyers to examine everything pre-trial. This may be true in high-profile cases which attract news media attention but in isolated towns such as Bourke, police resources are finite. Interestingly for the police in the case in question, it was only the month before the accident that the New South Wales government devised the Director of Public Prosecutions Act which established the office of the Director of Public Prosecutions (DPP). The director was responsible for all indictable prosecutions and for decisions on applications to 'no bill'. The DPP was thus legislatively empowered to prosecute criminal offences. But it took until 1991 for the office to take over prosecutions from the police. Until then, police prosecutors had appeared before judges and magistrates in the supreme court, district courts and local courts. In reality, police prosecutors still prosecute around ninety-five per cent of criminal cases on behalf of the New South Wales Police Force and various other government agencies in court of summary jurisdiction.[29]

While police prosecutors work under stressful conditions and may be in the direct line of fire from defendants, they are frequently not able to get across a brief, so they are disadvantaged right from the start. It is not uncommon for a prosecutor to be handed a brief as he or she is arriving at court. This was not the situation in Grant's case but it goes some way to highlight the fragmentation the police encounter when building their prosecution.

After Godkin had framed charges against Grant, the case went to committal hearing in November 1988. The case was prosecuted by a Sergeant R. Day. Sergeant Day had not been an actor in play before the committal nor is there evidence of his involvement again after the committal. The police case, then, was first carried forward by Ehsman and Reid, who then handed off to Godkin and Le Merton. Godkin handed off to Day at the committal hearing. Godkin continued with evidence-building after the committal hearing. Godkin handed off to a police prosecutor at trial.

New South Wales DPP guidelines for prosecutors state, 'A prosecutor is a "minister of justice". The prosecutor's principal role is to assist the court to arrive at the truth and to do justice between the community and the accused according to law and the dictates of fairness.'[30] It is not coincidental that the word 'community' is used in this context. The prosecution case against Alex Grant did what it could to act inclusively for the affected Bourke community.

# 26

# The crash investigated

For the next few months, the prosecution continued to build a portfolio of statements and other information. It had become evident that there was a conflict between the original charges made at Nyngan and the later charges made at Kogarah. Quinlivan had already foreshadowed a difficulty for the prosecution. Godkin may also have seen the difficulties that lay ahead: he invited Howes and Quinlivan to confer with him before the 4 July mention at Bourke. At issue were the joint charges but equally, the charge of offer indignity played a vital role in determining the prosecution priorities. There was also the matter of the lost time: what transpired between 10 p.m., when Grant bought more grog at the Riverview Hotel, and 4.30 a.m., when Shane Baty and others came upon the vehicle on the Enngonia Road. In this, Grant was most unhelpful. In fact, he was likely considered by the police to be hostile. His information was at best sketchy and he claimed repeatedly that he did not know where they went or how they got there.

Grant was no stranger to alcohol. His record demonstrated a fondness for a few bevvies. So it is highly unlikely, as one who was accustomed to being drunk, that Grant's recall of events was impaired beyond apprehension. He claimed at once to 'have been too drunk and silly at the time', and to 'have blacked out in shock, I don't really know, but there seemed to be a long time after the accident that I can't account for' and 'I don't know if I blacked out or what, there's just too long a blank spot'; 'I remember talking to the girls, I don't know where'; 'It's a bit hazy'; 'I'm not sure if I was knocked out or not'.

Six hours is a long time. If the Hilux left North Bourke a bit after 10 p.m. and drove directly to Enngonia at an average speed of eighty to 100 kilometres an hour, they would have arrived there no later than 11 p.m. If they visited either Mona or Cindy's relatives in Enngonia, that would have surfaced during the police inquiry. There is nothing on record to suggest that any relatives either came forward or were approached to give statements. No one saw the three people in the Hilux from the time they left North Bourke until Shane Baty and others arrived.

The time frame is relevant for a number of reasons. Grant offered a variety of possibilities, none of which seemed plausible. He said variously that when they left North Bourke, Mona drove for no more than twenty minutes, then they stopped while he 'relieved himself' before continuing for a short time before the utility swerved and rolled (Clark interview). He said Mona drove for thirty or forty kilometres, then they stopped and drank some beer before continuing (or turning back) and Mona got up to 100 km/h before throttling back to 70 or 80 km/h then the utility began sliding (Ehsman interview). He said they left North Bourke and drove off to Enngonia and when the 'big girl' pulled off the road twenty kilometres out to turn round, they stopped while he 'had a leak' then he drank a stubbie and a mouthful of rum and the girls drank rum and Coke. They stayed stationary for ten or fifteen minutes before they left and were 'driving along steady' before the vehicle left the road and rolled (Grant statement to Howes). He said they drove some way from North Bourke before 'the older one' asked if she could drive, and she drove about ten or fifteen kilometres before she pulled over and they began drinking the rum and Coke while he had a stubbie. He said he did not drink the rum. Then Mona started driving again and 'the next thing we flipped' (Grant statement to Godkin).

What we do know from the accident scene is that the utility was being driven in a northerly direction and that it crashed sixty-three kilometres from Bourke, or thirty-four kilometres on the southern side of Enngonia. The girls' intent may have been to visit relatives in Enngonia. It was not unknown for such an act to occur and time of night was no barrier to visiting. Grant recalled, though erratically and variously, that the accident happened at 10 p.m., between 12 and 2 a.m., and between 2 and 3 a.m. The more rational of the three is around 11 p.m. Given the medical examiner's report that both girls would not have survived long, it is reasonable to assume that if the accident occurred at around 11 p.m., both Mona and Cindy were dead by midnight. If it happened at midnight, they were dead by 1 a.m.; or an hour after any later possible time. The problem with the accident taking place later than 11 p.m. is the question of what occupied the time of the actors from 10 p.m. when they left North Bourke. As we can see, 11 p.m. gives them time to drive, then stop, then drive again and crash, as Grant first said. That scenario means the girls lay dead on the side of the road for more than four and a half hours before they were found. It is not out of the question that other vehicles travelled the Mitchell Highway that night but in the darkness did not see the ute concealed by the low scrub. Mr Johnson remarked in his statement that a roo shooter he identified as 'Kingy' was the only person he saw that morning. Kingy was driving south of the accident site. He may have driven passed it or he may have emerged from the scrub south of the site. Kingy, whoever he may have been, was never called into the inquiry.

As the girls lay dead, Grant also lay down on the green tarp on the red earth with his arm across Cindy's bare breasts. If the accident happened at 11 p.m., then he appears to have slept soundly until 4.30 a.m. Mr Johnson raised the spectre of carrion coming in to feed on the corpses, thus he and two others remained at the site for a short time until Grant verbally abused them. If they were lying dead on the side of the road for more than four hours, there was no evidence that they had suffered attacks by feral animals.

It is now, and was then, impossible for the police to exhaust all lines of inquiry into the time of the accident, other than having Grant provide details. There is evidence that between the time of the accident and the time of Mr Baty's arrival, Cindy's clothing had been arranged in such a fashion as to expose her body from her neck to her ankles. She did not arrange her clothing herself. And despite Grant's protests that she did do it to herself, it was clear that Cindy had died very soon after being 'removed' from the Hilux, and Grant had spread the tarp and placed her body on it before pulling up her T-shirt and pulling down her tracksuit and underpants. Photographs from the scene also indicate her legs were spread apart. The word 'removed' is used because, again, it was unclear if she was thrown from the ute, as Mona was, or whether Grant dragged her dying body from the passenger side when the ute came to rest. In all probability, Cindy was propelled through the front of the vehicle after the windscreen was smashed in the roll-over.

Thanks to the accuracy of the diagram created by Constable McKenzie at the scene, we know that the utility was out of control for more than 135 metres before it came to rest on its wheels in the table drain. It lost traction with the bitumen and after sixteen metres veered along the dirt shoulder for thirty-two metres, came back to the bitumen for thirty-six metres, veered again onto the shoulder for a further thirty-five metres, then rolled for sixteen metres before coming to rest. Within the roll-over distance of sixteen metres, the windscreen popped, the driver's-side door column was crushed and Mona was thrown fatally from the vehicle. The stabiliser bar behind the cabin was also crushed on the driver's side. A short distance past the windscreen, closer to the scrub line, lay a large metal toolbox. Mona's body lay towards the road four metres from the utility. Four metres beyond Mona's body lay a large auxiliary fuel tank. Cindy's body was spread on the tarp about two metres from the ute. The position of the tarp was crucial to the prosecution and the defence. As was the state of the passenger door. Mr Grant said he dragged Cindy from the passenger side of the vehicle through the door or the window, he was unsure which. Constable McKenzie said he checked the vehicle and he reported that both doors were jammed shut. Photographic evidence, however, showed the passenger door slightly ajar, but it was not clear from the picture whether it could or could not have been opened.

Both the passenger door and the tarp played important roles in establishing the guilt or otherwise of the defendant. Mr Baty and Constable McKenzie stated that the tarp had been spread out neatly by someone and that Cindy's body was lying on it, face upwards, naked from neck to ankle. Grant denied spreading the tarp out and placing Cindy's body on it. He said the tarp fell that way after the crash and that Cindy walked over to it and lay down. He said variously that she pulled her T-shirt up and her track pants down and lay on the tarp suggestively, or that he pulled her from the ute and that was how her clothing came to be in that state. He also said she drank some of his beer and that he had at least two stubbies after the accident. The most plausible explanation is that the defendant was the only occupant not thrown from the vehicle. The vehicle came to rest in the table drain, on its wheels. Mona had been thrown through the front window and had suffered fatal injuries. Cindy had most likely also been thrown through the front window. As she was sitting in the middle of the bench seat, she would have had nothing to hang on to stop her forward trajectory.

If Grant, as he claimed, was sitting in the passenger seat, he may have grabbed hold of the handle above the passenger-side window and thus saved himself from being ejected on impact. The extent of Grant's injuries indicated he was able to extract himself freely from the vehicle. He suffered no severe injuries. The most likely explanation is that both doors, as Constable McKenzie said, were unable to be opened. An impact of such force crushed the driver's side roof. It is inconceivable that either door was serviceable and Constable McKenzie was most likely correct in what he stated. While the door may have appeared to be ajar, as we will see, the hinge mechanism was damaged so that it was unable to be opened. Mona was thrown through the front window and as a result suffered fatal injuries. She lay bleeding from having been scalped. Cindy was also thrown through the front window but her injuries were less externally obvious but more internally serious.

She also died quickly as a result. Grant was knocked sideways, escaping injury when the roof was crushed.

Grant said he checked on both girls and that he thought they were alive. If he checked Mona, even in the dark, he would have known she was dead and that half her head had been torn off. She was also a lot further from the ute and the tarp than Cindy. It was easier to drag Cindy on to the tarp but there is another factor that came into play for Grant. In all his statements, he referred to Mona as the 'big girl' or the 'bigger girl'. Dr Pringle described Mona as an adolescent female Aborigine of short to medium height and of 'plump build'. If, as rumour was allowed at the time to play out, the defendant had a taste for young Aboriginal girls, and was indeed what was known in derogatory terms as a 'gin jockey', then he may have taken a liking to Cindy very early in the evening. Evidence suggests he had met her before. And a witness statement had someone similar to him driving in a white ute with her months earlier. His statements that she came on to him and 'wanted him' were rejected by his barrister as 'sexual fantasies' so it was not unreasonable to speculate that he had indeed laid Cindy on the tarpaulin with the express purpose of having sex with her. The *Australian Urban Dictionary* defines 'gin jockey' as 'a person who has a proclivity towards having sex with Australian aborigines', thus:

Gin Jockey: 'Pack of smokes and a six-pack for a fuck?'
Gin: 'No worries, brudda.'

The fact that Cindy was fifteen and may already have been dead seems not to have bothered the defendant nor to have weighed on his morality.

# 27

# The police make statements

Activity by the police slowed markedly after the mention in Bourke district court on Monday 4 July. Throughout July, no evidence appears to have been gathered and no further statements were taken. It is remarkable that the court system in New South Wales is so overloaded that a case can take months or years to be tested. It was to be a further four months before Grant stood at a committal hearing in Bourke. And it was the middle of August before further statements were made and then not until September and October that the prosecution case gathered its remaining evidence.

The Bourke mention set a committal hearing date of 8 November 1988. By the time of the hearing, it had been eleven months since the accident. As we have already noted, it is unclear where or how Grant spent his time between court appearances. We know that he appeared at Kogarah on Tuesday 24 May and we know he appeared at Bourke on 8 November. His barrister appeared on his behalf before the magistrate in Bourke on 4 July; it was not essential for a defendant to be present for a mention. It was prudent for Grant to remain at large; his presence in Bourke might have inflamed passions.

Between 18 August and 18 October, a period of eight weeks, of six statements taken, three were made by police, one by an important witness to the scene and two by peripheral actors. On 18 August, Constable Richard Le Merton confirmed that he had been with Sergeant Ray Godkin when he interviewed Grant at Hurstville police station in May. Le Merton's statement went to five and a half pages. He had been an observer to the interview but he recollected verbatim. His words need to be compared with those used by Godkin.

Godkin: 'It is my intention to ask you a number of questions about the matter.'

Le Merton: 'Sergeant Godkin said, "It is my intention to ask you a number of questions about the matter."'

Godkin: 'Can you tell me when you first picked the girls up that were involved in the incident?'

Le Merton: 'Sergeant Godkin said, "Can you tell me when you first picked the girls up that were involved in the incident?"'

Godkin: 'Are you able to tell me whether you asked them to get into the vehicle or whether they approached you?'

Le Merton: 'Sergeant Godkin said, "Are you able to tell me whether you asked them to get into the vehicle or whether they approached you?"'

Godkin: 'Can you tell me if anybody in the vehicle was wearing a seatbelt?'

Le Merton: 'Sergeant Godkin said, "Can you tell me if anybody in the vehicle was wearing a seatbelt?"'

Godkin: 'Can you recall how the tarpaulin got to the position it was in beside the utility?'

Le Merton: 'Sergeant Godkin said, "Can you recall how the tarpaulin got to the position it was in beside the utility?"'

Godkin: 'Can you now recall if you at any time interfered with or removed any clothing from the young girl after the accident?'

Le Merton: 'Sergeant Godkin said, "Can you now recall if you at any time interfered with or removed any clothing from the young girl after the accident?"'

Godkin: 'Are you able to tell me how the top part of the young girls [sic] clothing was pulled up below her chin?'

Le Merton: 'Sergeant Godkin said, "Are you able to tell me how the top part of the young girls [sic] clothing was pulled up below her chin?"'

Constable le Merton's statement continued to offer verbatim the contents of the interview between Godkin and Grant. We do not know who witnessed Le Merton's statement, as the signature that appeared at the bottom of each page was illegible and contained no additional typewritten name.

On Sunday 4 September, Texter Johnson gave a statement. Nine months had passed since Tex arrived at the accident scene. He had continued on that day to drive to Quilpie, where he had gone to work. We don't know how long he stayed in Quilpie. By September 1988, however, he was back at North Bourke at Ferguson Farm, where his statement was taken by Constable Le Merton. Ferguson Farm was a large-scale irrigated cotton holding north of the Darling River. Le Merton had gone to Ferguson Farm to take Tex's statement but in 1988 there was no technology that could have assisted Le Merton so he handwrote the statement before returning to Bourke police station, where he transcribed it onto a typewriter. Tex was specific in his recollection to the point of questionability. Tex said among other things that

> there was a body lying on the gravel, face down between the road and the vehicle. The body was clothed in jeans and a dark long sleeved top that was pulled up the back just under the shoulders. The back was bare and it had a cut across the back. The body was cold and purple and it seemed as though it had been dead for a fair while. I went over and saw two more bodies that were lying on a green tarpaulin. There was a body of a young aboriginal girl lying on her back, she had her pants down around her ankles, *but her legs were together*. There was a fellow lying beside the dead girl on her right side, resting on his left side cuddling up to her, with his right arm over her chest near about the centre and I didn't take much notice of the upper part of the girls [sic] clothing. I saw there was a half drunk bottle of beer at his feet. The fellow didn't get up at any stage and he was still lying down when I left. The guy was fully dressed when I saw him.

'But her legs were together' is italicised as it was the changed position of Cindy's legs between the arrival of Mr Johnson and Mr Baty and the arrival of the police from Enngonia that caused the charge of indecent interference to surface. Tex could not have known this unless informed by the police either at the time he gave his statement or sometime before. It is reasonable to assume that Le Merton, at interview, asked Tex about the position of the girl's legs. He may not have coached Tex but we can say with some certainty that he asked whether they were straight or at an angle. What is most interesting, though, is that Tex recalled the position specifically after a nine-month time lapse, yet he said he did not recall looking at the upper part of the girl's body. It might be that Le Merton provided photographic evidence for Tex to consider and that he was then able to reconstruct a more detailed image of the dead girl and the position of her legs.

On Thursday 8 September, Detective Sergeant Patrick Moss of Inverell police visited Peter Hurle at Wee Waa Electrics. Mr Hurle stated, among other things,

> the top metal frame of the driver's side of the seat was bent. The driver's door was sprung and the top of the window frame was bent.[31] I straightened the driver's door. The passenger's side door was open and the lock area was damaged, consistent with some person having forced the lock with a crow bar or similar.

Constable McKenzie had stated that both doors were jammed shut.

On Monday 19 September, Doug Innes of Major Metals provided a one-page typed statement that the passenger side door was in 'good order' at the time it was left. He said, 'an accident involving a forklift which was moving in the yard caused damage to the left hand side of the vehicle'. He added that he had been asked (by someone unidentified by him) to find ignition keys and 'at this point I found I was unable to gain entry so I levered the doors open with a crow bar'. So we have Mr Hurle saying it appeared someone had forced the lock open with a crowbar and Mr Innes conveniently, a few days later, providing a written statement, possibly uninvited by the police, that he had indeed been the culprit who had forced the door open with a 'crow bar'.[32]

A week later, Monday 19 September, Detective Sergeant Moss

made his own statement about his actions concerned with the ute inspection.[33] When Detective Sergeant Moss inspected the utility, as he said in his statement, it had been stripped of all major parts and components. Parts including the driver's door were in the tray of the ute. The passenger door was, he said, 'leaning in the opening of the passenger door'. Detective Moss said

> the cabin of the vehicle showed signs of having been straightened after sustaining extensive damage, consistent with the vehicle having rolled over. The roof, pillars and frame of the cabin appeared to have all been bent at some stage and then straightened. The driver's door was similarly damaged and apparently later straightened. The passenger's door of this vehicle was relatively undamaged, when compared to the remainder of the vehicle. The top of the window frame was buckled, however there was no damage to the skin of the door. The area in the vicinity of the locking mechanism was extensively damaged. The skin had been torn in the area and the mechanism torn appart [sic]. This damage was consistent with having been caused by physical force being applied such as when using a lever or crow bar to force this door open. The damage to the passenger's door was not consistent with it having been sustained during a collision. Inside a shed at 54 Mitchell Street, Wee Waa I saw a roof liner; sun visors; a mat; and dashboard panels. All of these items were covered in a red dusty substance. I made a presumptive test of these items for the presence of blood and obtained a positive result on the roof liner (at nearside front); and the nearside sun visor (on the left side of a label on the visor). Tests gave a negative result on the other items.

Detective Moss's statement was made at Inverell police station. The witness signature was illegible and there was no typed name attached. He too used the term crowbar.

As the police moved slowly and almost blindly forward with their evidence gathering, Grant's lawyers continued their own construction of the case, unencumbered.

# 28

# The police investigate the police

The police at this time were hindered internally: an inquiry into police management structures had been underway for some time[34] and between 1987 and 1991 the political foci of the New South Wales government and the media were on the role of police and the arrest, prosecution and incarceration of Aborigines across the state.[35] The police were to be investigated during that time by a Royal Commission. More importantly for the administration of justice, in 1987, New South Wales police underwent a major restructuring as part of a changing organisational environment resulting from the Lusher Inquiry. The old structure, a vertical hierarchy, was replaced with four regions which took on their own responsibilities for crime, traffic and internal investigations. It was not surprising, then, to see a senior officer from Inverell looking at the ute rather than someone arriving from Sydney. Devolving responsibility to the regions was meant to flatten the structure and remove some or all of the supposed corruption that had existed. But within the system there was a culture that had purportedly been built up over a number of generations. So the problems were not going to go away overnight.

The problems associated with the restructure were exacerbated in many regional areas by the ideology of 'community-based policing' that the government had adopted from recommendation made by its new police commissioner, John Avery. Not only had the reporting and promotion structure altered inexorably but at once the police were expected to operate in an environment where the so-called 'community' had as much power as they did. It is no wonder the prosecution case against Grant moved slowly. The police had been diverted by extraordinary changes to the way they did business. In fact, it would not be beyond the bounds of rational thought to argue they were so occupied with the restructure and the public attention they were receiving that a case such as Grant's was of little consequence to them. It would even be reasonable to speculate that had the event occurred a few years later it would have been prosecuted in a very different way with a very different result.

Meanwhile, on Wednesday 5 October, Bill Howes requested from Bourke District Hospital the medical records for Alex Grant. Two weeks later, a senior clerk, R.J. McAllister, forwarded a photocopy. In 1988, there was no commercial email; there was no document scanning; there was no PDF capability. There was only the Australia Post service.

With enough information to hand and the time of the committal hearing drawing closer, Bill Howes and Tony Quinlivan met with Grant in Sydney on 28 October. Quinlivan had represented Grant at the committal proceedings in Bourke. As Quinlivan noted in correspondence with Howes, Grant was committed to stand trial on all three charges.

In the meantime, Ehsman and Reid had come back into play. On Tuesday 18 October, both men made statements at Bourke police station. Both men continued to be stationed at Bourke but by now Ehsman had been promoted to detective sergeant. Reid's statement was witnessed by Inspector Alan Bassett. At the time of the accident, Bassett had been a senior sergeant.[36] It is unclear who witnessed Ehsman's statement, as the signature is illegible and there is no typed name attached. In describing the event, Ehsman said he arrived at the scene to see a utility with extensive damage to its offside and roof; the roof on the driver's side was crushed onto the top of the driver's seat. He said he saw 'a body of a female aboriginal lying face down on the western table drain between the front of the vehicle and the roadway. I saw that she had a large graze over the entire side of the left of her face, the left ear was missing and there was a large gaping wound from the left eye back to the base of her skull.' Ehsman also said,

> I saw a green canvas tarpaulin spread out on the ground. I saw a body of a female aboriginal lying on her back, her legs were spread apart and she had a pair of dark tracksuit pants pulled down to her ankles, a bra had been pulled down below her breasts and her top was pulled up under her chin. I saw that she was deceased. She had a large cut under her left nostril and an amount of blood on her face. I saw a number of lacerations on her right side and upper arm, also a large gash and lacerations to the area of her right pelvis and hip area.

Detective Ehsman said he examined the scene and saw that the vehicle had extensive damage to the roof, offside panels towards the front, the front of the vehicle and the front nearside panels. He was 'unable to open the doors as they were jammed shut'. Ehsman's statement went on to describe how later he went to Nyngan to interview and charge Grant.

On the same day, Reid corroborated Ehsman's view of the Nyngan events. Reid added that he had observed Grant for the purposes of noting his injuries. He said, "it occurred to me at the time that his injuries were extremely slight considering the injuries sustained by the other two occupants of the vehicle'. Reid's statement was witnessed by Bassett.

On Monday 31 October, two weeks before the committal proceedings, Constable Christopher Clarke provided a statement about his interview with Grant early on the morning of the accident at Bourke Hospital. Clarke's statement was made at Bourke police station. It was witnessed by Detective Reid. The date was typed as 31 October 1989. Clarke's address was noted as Blacktown detectives' office. It is unclear from his statement whether Clarke was at Bourke Hospital with the specific intention of interviewing Grant when he arrived by ambulance the morning after the accident, or whether he was there on other business and coincidentally was able to interview Grant. His statement provides no answer. Clarke said,

Shortly prior to 7.10 am on the morning of 6 December 1987 whilst present at the Bourke District Hospital I had a conversation with other police. I there saw a male person whom I now know to be Alexander Ian Grant, Mitchell Caravan Park, Bourke.

The word 'police' had been circled on a copy of the document in the possession of Tony Quinlivan, who had written a question mark near the circle. Quinlivan may also have been curious about Clarke's presence at the hospital. We must assume Clarke had been in Bourke on other business and that most likely, given the timing, he was at the hospital on other business as well. If so, it was serendipitous for the police that he was able to interview Grant so early after the accident. In his statement, Clarke provided another alternative for where Grant and the girls began their fatal journey. Grant said he had been at the post office and met them there; he said he was ringing a 'partner' in Wee Waa; he said the girls asked for a 'ride home'; he said,

After the accident I got out and one of the girls got out and took off her clothes and said, 'Ya want me?' I said, 'No, we've got a problem here.' I then looked around and there was no traffic and that and I said to myself, 'What the hell, we've got a rolled Toyota here.' She layed [sic] down on the ground and I didn't touch her.

Clarke said he asked Grant, 'The girl who was naked, where was she seated?" He also asked, 'How long after you left Bourke was it that the accident occurred?"

Clarke concluded his statement by noting that he

thence read to Grant the record of the conversation pointing to each word of each question and answer in turn. I then said to Grant, 'Would you mind signing at the end of this record and on the blank lines between each set of question [sic] and answers? Grant then signed at the bottom of the entry and on the previous page. I left the person Grant for a short time where I spoke to Medical Staff who had arrived. I later again spoke to Grant, recovered my notebook and left the Police station. About 10.15am I attended the

Bourke District Hospital Morgue where I inspected the bodies of two deceased females. I recorded information about these two persons and left the Police station.

While Clarke's statement sheds light on a number of points, it also raises a number of questions. Why was Clarke at the hospital? Who were the 'other police' to whom he refers? At what time did he interview Grant? Why was he awaiting medical personnel? What did Clarke do between the time he interviewed Grant and the time he saw Mona and Cindy at the morgue? Why did he say he left the police station rather than left the hospital? Where did he go when he left the hospital? Did he go directly to the police station and write up his report? Why did it take ten months for Clarke to make a statement of his actions?

On Tuesday 8 November, the committal hearing of Alexander Ian Grant took place at Bourke local court. Tony Quinlivan had arrived in town on Sunday afternoon, having driven from Sydney. It is unknown when Grant arrived but it is known that he spent Monday with Quinlivan to prepare his defence. It is most likely he and Bill Howes arrived together. All three spent Monday working through the information they had and talking about the list of witnesses.

Also in town for the hearing were Sergeant Ray Godkin, Constable Ken McKenzie, Dr Clive Pringle, Shane Baty and Tex Johnson. They were all to be called as witnesses for the prosecution. Witnesses are paid expenses by the office of the Director of Public Prosecutions. The scale of expenses is set by the Attorney General's department.

By his actions on Saturday 5 December 1987, Grant had altered inexorably the lives of two families and disrupted the existences of many other individuals. It was time to take account.

# 29

# The Avery alterations

The 1980s proved to be a torrid time for the New South Wales Police Force. They were also years of rapid and at times unsophisticated restructuring and development within the wider areas of justice and the law. Some of the hallmarks of the restructuring remain; others have been less successful both publicly and privately. Some of the early changes to the structure of the police department resulted from an inquiry established by New South Wales Labor Premier Neville Wran.

In 1979, Wran called upon Edwin Lusher, a supreme court judge, to chair a commission of inquiry into police administration. Lusher was born in 1915 and died in 2000. He was a Queen's Counsel when in 1976 Wran invited him to investigate legalising casinos. He recommended legalisation and unsurprisingly, the following year, he was appointed to the bench of the supreme court. When Wran began copping heat about alleged corruption, he took the relatively easy way out and inquired into police administration rather than tackling corruption head on. Allegations of corruption in the police force had been around for a very long time. Various commissioners from the time of Liberal Premier Robin (Bob) Askin had overseen varying degrees and levels of corruption, from police taking bribes to police being known associates of crime syndicates. Representations of corruption were frequently made by media news organisations but at the same time, crime reporters from the other side of the media were keen to argue in favour of police tactics if they got the job done.

The Lusher Inquiry was not designed to 'delve into dark places'[37] so it was structured around closed hearings and questions of police administration rather than corruption. According to Christine Nixon, a former New South Wales assistant commissioner and disgraced Victorian chief commissioner, Lusher recommended 'clever systems that were to improve policing as well as mechanisms designed to keep the politicians and the police at greater distance'. As noted by Nixon and elsewhere, one of the recommendations was the establishment of a police board which was to be independent and to have the power to appoint senior offices and the commissioner. Lusher sought out members of the force who he thought might contribute to the structure of the inquiry. In this, he sought the advice of an inspector named John Avery. Avery was to become commissioner in 1986 – the first to be appointed by the newly created police board. Avery's contribution to the Lusher Inquiry helped establish a different training regime in which cadet officers attended a police academy set up in Goulburn rather than simply being attached to a unit for a few weeks. As a supreme court judge, Lusher commented that corruption can only be treated successfully by assuming it is endemic.[38]

When Avery became commissioner, he took the traditional role of the police and threw it out with the bathwater. His ideas for a new regime came from a master's thesis he earned from Macquarie University.[39] Avery had succumbed to the soft-left approach to society whereby the 'community' was meant to become intimately involved with each other's business. Avery's idea was that the community would work productively with the police to help identify issues that needed fixing. In this, he was ably supported by Nixon, who was appointed and promoted to run the Goulburn academy. The silly idea of community policing was not confined to New South Wales. A similar sweep of softness was afflicting the Western world from London to Toronto to Wellington and on to Sydney and Melbourne. Avery assisted the immediate growth of police studies programs at universities and forced upon society a new methodology for policing: the idea that the police were no longer there to enforce order and to capture crooks, they themselves were to be perpetually scrutinised and reviewed and they were not to take their power for granted. One of Commissioner Avery's strategies was the professional development of police, so they built within themselves an ethic that was framed around integrity. The fact that there were those among the New South Wales police who were corrupt and did corrupt things had been well-known. (Ehsman was named in a later inquiry as one who could be relied upon to 'fit up' a suspect by supplying a gun.) But it had also been how things got done and how New South Wales remained relatively free of major crime.

John Avery was police commissioner from 1984 until 1991. Since the Lusher report in 1981 and Avery's involvement with it, Avery, as commissioner, was instrumental in creating the police board, redeveloping police training, decentralising power (creating four regional commands across New South Wales) and conceptualising community policing. Within this new and yet to be tested framework, extant police officers were required to adapt to the enormous change and at the same time continue to do the job of policing. Not all of Avery's ideas and new policies were grasped enthusiastically. It was well-known in the force that the Lusher recommendations were really set up to break the control and power of the old Criminal Investigation Branch (CIB). Avery's flat structure was the keystone.

Despite the best efforts of the police public relations and media departments, not much had changed within. Devolution of specialised functions occurred in 1988, so that the four regions were more or less in control of their own destinies. The break-up of the old departments, especially the CIB, was seen as a negative by many of the older-school police. The struggle to retain the status quo became the catalyst for the Royal Commission into Police Corruption some years later. The Royal Commission was not inevitable but it did surface at a time when the police were being asked to abandon their old law enforcement approach and to render assistance as a service; thus Avery changed the name from New South Wales Police Force to New South Wales Police Service.[40] At the same time as this was happening – policing across New South Wales being restructured – the New South Wales government in 1989 decided to establish an 'independent' organisation to keep public administration accountable. It was known as the Independent Commission Against Corruption, or ICAC, following the similarly named Hong Kong organisation. At the beginning, ICAC's mandate to investigate and expose corrupt conduct in the New South Wales public sector included the authority to investigate the police service. It goes some way to explaining the authority of the police in that today, ICAC jurisdiction extends to all New South Wales public sector agencies except the police force. Police were not happy about the idea that an independent agency could poke its nose indiscriminately into police business, thus, following the Wood Royal Commission into the New South Wales Police Service in 1996, the Police Integrity Commission was established.

This brief overview is offered so that it might be easier to grasp the significant changes that were occurring at the time of the prosecution of Alex Grant. Criminal investigations had been devolved to four regions and administrative structural changes meant each region was responsible for its own actions rather than looking to a central command for advice and support. It was a provocative time which did not survive its own provocation. The police service reverted to a police force. It is now divided into six regions rather than four and it has three senior executive operations divisions to which they report: field operations, specialist operations and corporate services. The CIB has been reinvented as State Crime Command under a deputy commissioner of field operations who also has responsibilities for the regions. The Western Region is comprised of twelve local area commands, one of which is Darling River based in Bourke. Darling River LAC takes in the towns of Bourke, Brewarrina, Cobar, Enngonia, Nymagee, Nyngan, Wanaaring and Warren – pretty much the same area that was covered under the old structure between 1987 and 1990. Bourke, however, is the only station within the LAC that is open twenty-four hours.

# Part Two

# 30

# The committal hearing

Monday 7 November 1988 dawned hot in Bourke and the rest of western New South Wales. It had been eleven months since the accident and Alexander Ian Grant was once again holed up in the town waiting for something to happen. If he had led a boring existence up until that previous December, since then it had been anything but. He was now in conference with his barrister, Tony Quinlivan, and his solicitor, Bill Howes, in a room at a motel working through the processes that would see him either committed to stand trial or be found not to have a case to answer.

Quinlivan was a very good criminal advocate. He could see in the police case a number of large holes big enough to drive through; holes that ought to see his client free within a few days. Quinlivan, Howes and Grant conferred for much of the day before Quinlivan suggested they break for dinner and a few drinks. Neither Quinlivan nor Howes were familiar with the town but they were cautious in relying on Grant for recommendations. They chose to eat at the motel. Then Quinlivan excused himself and went to bed early. Before he settled down, he rang his wife back in Sydney. He said goodnight to his kids and promised to bring them something.

The following day, Bourke was bathed in bright sunlight and the temperature was already rising through thirty, heading towards thirty-six degrees when the court registrar opened proceedings. There was no air conditioning in Bourke courthouse. In fact, there was not much space for anything other than being at close quarters for the magistrate, the defence, the prosecution, the witnesses, the public and when necessary, the jury. Lawyers were required to work with their clients, before entering the court, in corridors or on the street. It was a courtroom located in the nineteenth century.

Quinlivan parked as close to the court as he could, which was not difficult. There was not much traffic.

Grant took his place with Quinlivan and Howes. On the other side of the court sat the police prosecutor Sergeant Day. Day had arrived in Bourke on Monday and spent some time in conference with Godkin, Ehsman and Reid.

Presiding over the hearing was Rosemary Cater-Smith. Ms Cater-Smith had been a magistrate for four years. She was part of a string of circuit magistrates who travelled throughout New South Wales. Cater-Smith took her place at the bench. Her first question was to Sergeant Day. 'As far as the charges that I have before me are concerned, Sergeant, which matters are you proceeding with today?'

Day replied, 'Hopefully, your papers are marked in accordance with the list, your worship. Matter number one, I seek to proceed. Matters number two and three. Matter number four should stand. It is a summary matter. Matters number thirteen, fourteen and fifteen might stand, your worship. I seek instructions in relation to those. I envisage that those matters – sorry, matters sixteen, seventeen and eighteen – I would envisage those matters may well be withdrawn.'

'Very well then,' replied Ms Cater-Smith.

The prosecution case, therefore, opened with some ambiguity as to which charges were being made against Grant. The list of witnesses, however, went some way to establishing a more solid base. The first witness called was Sergeant Godkin, who was followed by the mothers of the dead girls, Dawn Smith and June Smith, who in turn were followed by Douglas Smith, Lisa Smith, Constable McKenzie, Karen Johnson, Dr Pringle, Shane Baty and Texter Johnson. (We can assume Karen Johnson and Tex Johnson were unrelated. There is nothing to suggest otherwise.)

When asked, Sergeant Godkin provided his name, rank and station. Sergeant Day then suggested to the magistrate that 'apparently the course that can be taken in relation to this witness is that he can utilise his statement for the purpose of giving his evidence and refreshing his memory and that there is no objection to you utilising the same so that you don't have to take notes of the conversation. That might assist.'

Cater-Smith thanked the sergeant, who then asked Godkin to identify his six-page statement of 12 May. He also asked him to identify the statement made by Detective Ludewig and to identify twenty-four pictures taken by Ludewig. He further asked Godkin if he objected to the statements being 'served' on the defence and that he had no objection to it being tendered under Section 48 of the Evidence Act. Day also tendered the statement from Detective Moss, including its pictures. He also tendered the certificate from the Division of Forensic Medicine relating to the parts of the vehicle sent off for testing.

Sergeant Day then showed Godkin the five-page document – the statement from Ehsman, plus the two records of interview, which Godkin said were acceptable. All were tendered as evidence along with the pictures Ehsman had taken at the scene. Warren Hurle's statement was the next to be tendered. A body of evidence was building. The blood sample certificate from Judith Perl was added.

Day attempted levity. 'I tender a statement from Judith Pearl, a consultant pharmacologist, address Vehicle Branch Police Headquarters. That statement is in the form required by Section 48 with the deletion of the date of birth by the look of it – she might be a bit opposed to putting that on there, your worship. But I tender that.' The prosecutor then tendered Le Merton's statement. 'I tender a statement of Richard Trent Le Merton. A Statement of a constable of police attached to the North-West Accident Investigation Squad.'

He then asked Godkin, 'Sergeant, is that a statement, sorry, was Richard Trent Le Merton in your company during the course of this investigation at various stages?'

Godkin replied, 'He was.'

Day concluded, 'Nothing further in chief from this witness, your worship.'

Sergeant Godkin was examined by Tony Quinlivan. The barrister was keen to fragment the police case. He questioned why Godkin had become involved in the case after the defendant had been charged. He questioned what Godkin knew about the conversation Constable McKenzie had had with Grant at the scene. And he raised the possibility that Godkin had not been given an accurate picture of the events.

'It probably was not until after Constable McKenzie had made his written statement on May 6, 1988 that you became aware of the terms of any conversation between Constable McKenzie and Mr Grant?' Quinlivan concluded.

Godkin replied, 'I can't say exactly when he told me. I don't know.'

# 31

# The evidence from Cindy's mother

The next witness was Cindy's mother, Iona Dawn Smith. If the defendant and his team of Sydney lawyers were relying on 'the Bourke defence'[41] they were to be disappointed. Mona and Cindy belonged to a community who knew the value in speaking up for themselves.

Sergeant Day began by asking Mrs Smith questions related to her earlier statement – her name address and her relationship to Jacinta, her pensioner status. It is unclear why the prosecutor needed such information. He asked Mrs Smith if she had last seen her daughter at dinner the night before she died. He got the date wrong. 'Now, is it true that the last time you saw your daughter Jacinta alive was at dinner time on Saturday the 6th December?'

She corrected him, saying it was 5 December.

The prosecutor then asked if she had seen her daughter at the hospital morgue the following day, 6 December. The prosecutor probed for information about Jacinta's whereabouts – had she left town regularly, was she frequently out of her mother's care? He asked about her relationship with her niece, Mona, about the relationship between Jacinta and Mona, its closeness. He asked if either girl had a driver's licence or knew how to drive a motor vehicle. 'Did you know whether or not either Mona or Jacinta had a licence at the time?'

'No.'

'Right, so would you say they didn't?'

At this point, the magistrate interjected, asking, 'She didn't know, is that what you're saying, or they didn't have one?'

Dawn Smith answered directly saying they did not have a licence.

Sergeant Day pursued the matter further, asking whether or not Dawn herself had a licence and a car. 'Right, and what type of vehicle's that?'

'It's a Ford Falcon.'

'Was it an automatic or a manual car?'

'Automatic.'

'Automatic was it? All right.'

Day ended his questioning of Dawn Smith and Quinlivan cross-examined. It was unclear why Dawn Smith had been called first, rather than June Smith, given it was June Smith's daughter Mona who was believed to have been driving.

Under cross-examination, Quinlivan made it clear, asking Dawn Smith a number of questions about her niece Mona's driving ability. In this, he began his tactic to discredit the 'aboriginal statements'. He asked if she was 'absolutely' sure that Mona had never driven, to which she replied no. She had known, however, that Mona had driven around the Reserve a few months earlier – information that Quinlivan extracted with ease.

'You're aware, aren't you, that Mona Smith was driving a motor vehicle around the Reserve a few months before she died, aren't you?'

'I only found that out after the, after the incident, after the girls were gone, I only found out that Jacinta was even driving a vehicle and I didn't even know that.

'That who was driving a vehicle?'

'Both Jacinta and Mona, I didn't know that they was driving a automatic car until after the death of ...'

Quinlivan interrupted her, then changed course. He asked if she had known Mona to go to Enngonia, to which she answered that she did not know. It seemed an absurd answer given Quinlivan's next few questions.

'Do you have relatives living in Enngonia?'

'Yes.'

'On an aboriginal reserve there?'

'Yes.'

'And Mona had friends living in Enngonia?'

'Yes.'

While Quinlivan continued this line of questioning, asking if Mona had or had not gone to Enngonia sometime in the year before she died, Mrs Smith continued to stonewall, saying she did not know.

'So far as you're concerned, Enngonia was a place that Mona may well have gone to from time to time, in the year before her death?'

'She may have and she may have not, I don't know.'

The barrister then sought to discover whether Dawn Smith had known of the girls' whereabouts after lunch on that fateful day. 'What time of the day did you last see Jacinta?

'Around about half past 12, 1 o'clock, I don't exactly know what time it was.

'And you had no idea where she went after that?

'They made their way back down towards the Reserve that way, so I just took it that they was going to the Reserve again. She headed off back down towards Half Case.'[42]

'It wouldn't have been an unusual thing, though, for your daughter and her friends to be out of your company for half a day or during the night time? Or…?

'They got around together and Jacinta was mad on her Granny, what that lives on the Reserve and at the time her Granny was sick, so I allowed her to go down and stayed with her for a couple of weeks or months or whatever time she wanted down there with her, because she was very close to her.'

'But it wouldn't have been unusual for your daughter to not come home for a few days, without you knowing where she was?'

'I always checked up on them. It was the first time, the first night I did not check up on her. That night they went on, on Saturday night but I did go looking for her but I didn't find her. I got as far as Adelaide Street and it's got too dark for me so I couldn't walk to the Reserve.'

Quinlivan's defence took another sharp turn towards discrediting community. 'Do you know Sharon Alice Smith? Of cottage number 13, the Reserve, Bourke?'

'I probably know her but I only know them by their nickname but I don't know their real name. Because they don't use their real name much, they just call them by their nickname.'

'You don't know Sharon Alice Smith to be a cousin of your daughter Jacinta?'

'Yes, I think she is a cousin of Jacinta and Mona.'

As Quinlivan concluded, the prosecutor asked Mrs Smith about Mona's physique – whether or not she was a 'larger' girl. Dawn Smith described Mona as larger than Cindy and taller but not older-looking.

Cindy's mother, Dawn Smith, was retired as a witness. She stepped down from the witness box and walked the few paces to the public gallery, where she took a seat among her family. She wiped her eyes with her handkerchief.

# 32

# Mona's mother takes the stand

The next witness was Mona's mother, June Smith. June gave her address as Cottage 17, the Reserve, and said she performed domestic duties.

In fact, the question asked by Sergeant Day was 'And you perform domestic duties around the house?' to which she answered yes. Day's next questions were equally obtuse and disrespectful in their framing. 'As of December last year, you were the mother of Mona Smith, is that true? And at that time she was approximately sixteen years of age? Had Mona been living with you all her life? And what sort of a relationship did you have with Mona, did you get on well? And did you speak with one another quite often? And Mona, did she spend a lot of time at home and around the Reserve area?'

To all these, June answered politely, yes.

Day then asked one question that required more than a one-word answer before returning to the earlier format. He was interested in establishing the relationship between Mona and Cindy. He asked about Mona's best friend. He asked if Mona could drive a car. He asked if she herself owned a car. He asked if she had known Mona to drive. He asked about the community. 'The community that you live in in the Reserve at Bourke, would you call it a close-knit community?'

'Yes.'

'And do you associate with all the other people who live in the Reserve...?'

'Yes.'

'...there and speak to them?'

'Yes.'

'Have you ever known Mona to try to drive a car?'

'Yes, she tried to drive the blue sedan automatic car but she reversed into a iron peg, so I told her to get out and she never got in it since.'

'You say it was a blue Ford. Did you tell the court whether or not it was an automatic or a manual?'

'It was automatic.'

'Who owned the car, do you know?'

'Yes it was, belonged to Robert Nixon.'

Under cross-examination from Quinlivan, June Smith was immediately taken off-guard. Quinlivan asked her if she could drive an automatic.

June unconsciously lowered her voice in answer.

'Can you drive an automatic car?'

'Who that, me?'

'Yes?'

'No.'

Despite the closeness of the room, the prosecutor and the magistrate found it difficult to hear her.

Quinlivan continued. 'Well, you actually saw an occasion last year, didn't you, where Mona was driving a car?'

'Yes, at the back of my place.'

'You just came out and saw her driving around?'

'She wasn't driving around, she just reversed it.'

'But you've got no idea how long Mona was in the car before she reversed it into the steel peg?'

'No, because the car was parked at the back of the house and she probably was sitting in it.'

Quinlivan moved on to the possibility that Mona had gone to Enngonia at some time without her mother's knowledge. He also pursued the idea that Mona could be gone for long periods of time without her mother's knowledge. Then he asked about Mona's drinking habits. 'Did you know Mona to drink alcohol?'

'Yes, I've heard of her drinking it.'

This was a hard question for Mrs Smith. Again she had lowered her voice so the magistrate had to intervene.

Quinlivan continued along this line. He asked if she approved. He asked if she drank spirits.

'She usually used to drink beer with their friends, but I'd never known her to drink the hot stuff.

'Did you have any idea where your daughter was on the afternoon before she died?'

'No, she…all I know is she left with some friends and went to town.'

Quinlivan did what he said he was going to do: he discredited the Aboriginal evidence. While Dawn Smith spoke briefly of a close-knit community, implying everyone knew everyone and everyone spoke to everyone, she dismantled her own statement by saying she did not know if Sharon was Cindy's cousin. June Smith, in saying she did not know when Cindy had left school, confirmed the shattered image. Similarly, her contribution concerning Mona's drinking habits provided evidence of a less than cohesive community and her comments about Mona and Cindy spending a lot of time wandering around town reinforced the image of the mother being uninterested in her daughter's well-being. So far, Quinlivan had done his job well.

## 33

## The older brother under attack

The next witness was Douglas Smith. The police prosecutor, Sergeant Day, began his questioning of Mr Smith in what can only be described as an unusual manner. As a prosecution witness, it would have seemed reasonable that Day might have sought to underpin Smith's position as credible. In fact, his line of questioning appeared as if he were more interested in discrediting Smith. Doug Smith was Mona's older brother. His sister had been killed less than a year earlier. Day also persisted in referring to Mr Smith by his first name. He had not referred to either Dawn or June by name. One must speculate that Day had a particular mindset when it came to Douglas Smith. Or he may have known Mr Smith in other circumstances. He may have had cause to act as a prosecutor against Mr Smith. Given that he asked Mr Smith if he sometimes went by the name Douglas Shillingsworth, it is fair to say Sergeant Day had done his homework.

He asked how long Mr Smith had lived his present home, but when it came to employment he stated, 'And you're not employed at the moment, Douglas, is that true?' He asked if Mr Smith lived in the same house as his sister Mona and whether he had ever seen her drive a car.

Mr Smith had indeed seen Mona drive Robert Nixon's blue Falcon and he said so.

The prosecutor asked about manual vehicles on the Reserve, to which Mr Smith replied that there were three or four.

Under cross-examination, Mr Smith himself did a good job of fragmenting earlier evidence given by his mother and his aunt. While they had said Mona was driving near the house, Mr Smith said she was a couple of hundred metres away, nearer the road. He said he saw Mona driving. But he said it was not a common sight. He seemed perplexed by the fact she was driving, though he clearly saw her doing so.

Quinlivan asked if he had been present at the time, how far from the site he had been and if he was sure he had seen Mona driving. 'Well, how did all this come about? That Mona was driving the car? What happened?'

'I don't know, she...well, I just come out of the house and I just saw her in the car driving, I don't know how it happened, how she got in or whatever.'

'It would have been a common thing in the Reserve last year for the teenagers in the community to have a go at driving a car?'

'She was the teenager I saw down there drive a car, attempted to drive one. Never seen anyone else. I wouldn't say it was common.'

The barrister circled back to the question of employment and how Mr Smith occupied his time. 'Were you employed at all last year?'

'No.'

'How did you spend your days last year?'

'I used to...just CYSS, CES, running a...I used to make some... I made a bed and that there...just made some...work with wood and that...a bit of carpentry and that's all.'[43]

'But you're not...wouldn't be away from the Reserve during the day?'

'Say about half and half, I suppose, up town and you know.'

Mr Smith again spoke in lower tones, to which the magistrate responded testily. Mr Smith had been asked if he had seen his sister the day before she died. The courtroom was alive to other voices.

Quinlivan shifted back to the drink question. 'Was she drinking when you last saw her?'

'No.'

'Did it appear to you that she had been drinking?'

'No.'

'When you last saw her?'

'No.'

'Did you know your sister to be someone who did drink alcohol?'

'Once or twice I think I might have saw her.'

'Once or twice?'

'Yes.'

'Once or twice last year, or once or twice in her whole life?'

'Last year, in her whole life really.'

That concluded Quinlivan's cross-examination of Mr Smith. Or Mr Shillingsworth, as Day had pointed out to the court. Like most of the Aboriginal youths in Bourke, Mr Smith had spent the year out of work but had taken himself to the CYSS and had busied himself with carpentry. With making things. And his sister had been killed.

# 34

# The girls' aunty Lisa gives evidence

Before the luncheon adjournment, one of the last two Aboriginal witnesses was called. It is unknown why Lisa Edwards and Sharon Smith were not called in sequence. Constable McKenzie was to be interjected between them.

Lisa Edwards took the witness stand and was asked by Sergeant Day if her name was Lisa Patricia Smith. She answered that it was indeed Edwards, to which Day replied, 'Edwards or Smith?'

Lisa replied that it was Edwards.

It is questionable why the police thought her name was Smith.

Day persisted. 'Edwards, right. Was it ever Smith?' to which Lisa Edwards replied that it was not.

Day said, 'Okay then,' but the magistrate had not heard the answer.

Magistrate: 'Did you say yes or no?'

'No,' replied Lisa.

The prosecutor then asked about Ms Edwards' relationship with Mona and Cindy, about whether Mona had gone with a man from the Reserve named Garry Cooke to buy alcohol. He asked if they began drinking in a small blue caravan, after lunch, with a man named David Corn. He asked if they had been drinking all afternoon. 'And is it the case that you were drinking with them from after lunch right up until the night just after it had gone dark?'

'Yes.'

'And just after dark is it right that your mother came up to the... where you were drinking and she belted you with a stick to make you stop drinking?'

'Yes.'

'And is it the case then after that, you picked up the grog that you had left and walked away down to the levy?'

'Yes.'

'Is it the case that you'd been…you sat there at the levy drinking and Cindy dropped a bottle of rum and at that stage you only had about four bottles left?'

'Yes.'

He then asked what state Mona and Cindy had been in when they left after dark to get more grog.

Ms Edwards said she had seen them and they were what she described as 'charged up' – meaning they were not drunk but not sober either.

He asked about Mona's driving ability.

Ms Edwards confirmed she had seen Mona drive at the Reserve and that she had driven the blue Falcon.

Day ended his examination of Lisa Edwards. He had established that Mona could drive and that she had been drinking. Again, if we note that the charges against Grant were drink driving related, one might have assumed Sergeant Day was interested in proving that Mona could not drive and that she had not been drinking.

Lisa remained in the witness stand while she was cross-examined by Quinlivan.

The Sydney barrister was more forthright in his approach. He gave a slick demonstration of big-city professionalism. There was no contest. It was like the television reporter asking a man when he stopped beating his wife. 'When you did see Cindy and Mona, did you normally spend your time drinking?'

'No. We only used to get drunk like on a Wednesday.'

'You used to get drunk on a Wednesday?'

'Yes, on the Wednesday.'

'This was a Saturday, though…?'

'Yes, this was…'

'…that you were…?'

'…a Saturday…'

'…drinking with her?'

'We got drunk. It was a Saturday.'

'Yes. You all got drunk, didn't you?'

'Yes.'

'Because you were drinking from about the middle the day until night time, weren't you?'

'Yes.'

'And Cindy and Mona were drinking for the whole time the same as you were?'

'Yes.'

'And they were drinking beer, weren't they?'

'Yes.'

'And they were drinking some of the rum as well?'

'Yes.'

He then asked about Mona's driving.

Lisa said she had seen Mona driving and that she had seen her get into the car. She said Mona had driven to her grandmother's, Alice Edwards, to collect something, then driven back and left it outside Cottage 13. She had driven from Cottage 17 to Cottage 13 and back again but Quinlivan did not yet ask how far that might have been. Lisa then added that she had once been in the car when Mona drove it.

'You were actually in the car?'

'Yes, I was in the car when she drove the car down to Cottage 13.'

'When was this? When did this happen?'

'Don't remember. Think it was Friday night or Wednesday night.'

'It was at night time, was it?'

'Yes.'

'Had you been drinking?'

'No, we wasn't drinking.'

Then began a long dialogue about who owned the car, where it had been located and, eventually, who Robert Nixon was related to.

If indeed Ms Edwards was telling the truth, Mona had gone into the house and asked Robert Nixon for the keys to the car while June Smith was also in the room. Quinlivan became very frustrated with the witness. He was at a point where the witness was implying that June Smith had known clearly that Mona was and could drive a car. He had for a second time successfully discredited the Aboriginal evidence.

Quinlivan completed his cross-examination. Lisa Edwards left the witness stand and walked from the courthouse with other members of her family. Sergeant Day gathered his papers and he too left the court room. He conferred with other police outside the court before crossing the road and entering the police station where he had lunch. Quinlivan, Howes and Grant left the courthouse and walked around the corner into Oxley Street to find something to eat.

Quinlivan had so far been enormously successful in his tactics. It was clear that the police case was flimsier than he had first thought, but it was a committal hearing, not a trial, and he was pretty sure the magistrate would nonetheless find in favour of committal.

# 35

# The police witness grilled

Magistrates in New South Wales are officers of the state. Elevation to the bench is usually from the bar, where they have acted as advocates on either side, as prosecutors or defenders of criminal and civil proceedings. States in Australia, under a federated system, deal with state laws. There is a three-tier system, with the first being local courts, the second district courts, and the third supreme courts. There are also environmental, industrial and coroner's courts, among others. Magistrates preside over local courts, while judges and registrars preside over district and supreme courts. Local courts are administered by the department of justice and their jurisdictions encompass most criminal and summary prosecutions and civil matters up to a cap of $100,000. Most criminal cases arrive at the court system in New South Wales through the local courts. Magistrates in 1987 were referred to as your worship. Since 2004 they have been referred to as his or her honour. In 1986, magistrates became independent judicial officers under the *Judicial Officers Act 1986*. A little while earlier, in 1985, the Local Courts Act abolished courts of petty sessions by changing the name to local court.

Mrs Cater-Smith had been elevated to the bench four years before Mr Grant's committal hearing. She had been a successful Sydney barrister and was married to a successful police prosecutor.

Ms Cater-Smith came back from lunch ready to hear more witnesses for the prosecution. But before she was able to, Sergeant Day requested permission to tender a statement from Detective Reid. He also tendered statements from Lawrence Barnett and Lloyd Smith.

Sergeant Day had been busy during the lunch adjournment. He called Constable McKenzie to the witness stand.

McKenzie was nervous about giving evidence. And rightly so. He was about to undergo a lengthy session in which the defendant's barrister saw his statements, notebooks and observations as the weakest point in the prosecution's case. He knew what he had seen and he knew what he had heard but he was also cognisant of the fact that charges had altered. He needed to tell it like it was. And the courtroom in reality was nothing like it was portrayed in television police dramas, as most of the witnesses had discovered. In fact, McKenzie was so nervous he frequently answered the question before the prosecutor had finished asking it.

McKenzie gave his name, rank and station. He acknowledged he had prepared a rough sketch of the accident site and that it was contained in the notebook in the prosecutor's possession. It was tendered in evidence and marked exhibit 18. His statement was also tendered and admitted as exhibit 19.

The prosecutor framed his questions around McKenzie's expertise. He asked how long he had been in the police force, about his previous employment as an ambulance officer and his expertise in observing serious motor vehicle accidents.

McKenzie volunteered some unusual information. He told Sergeant Day he did not discover the identities of the girls until some days after the accident.

Day seemed perplexed. He changed tack and asked McKenzie about the photographs from the scene and about the vehicle. 'In your statement, you indicate you made observations of the motor vehicle involved?'

'Yes.'

'Did you observe any blood inside the motor vehicle?'

'No, I didn't detect any bloodstains or any indication of blood whatsoever inside the vehicle at the time I examined it.'

'Just utilising your experience in attending serious motor vehicle accidents, what would you say in relation to the [injuries to the] head occasioned to the girl known as Smith that you saw on the side of the road in relation to perhaps it having happened in the vehicle?'

'I'd say it'd be…'

At this point, Quinlivan objected to the question. McKenzie was being asked to speculate on whether Mona's injuries had occurred inside or outside the ute. He had no way of knowing. Only Grant would have known. And he wasn't telling.

The question was withdrawn.

It was curious that McKenzie frequently answered over the top of Sergeant Day, before Day had completed his questions. It may have been nervousness or more likely McKenzie had in five years not been called to account for statements he had made nor for observations he had made at accident scenes. Day framed McKenzie as one who may have had a lot of experience in this but, on the day, he did not come across that way.

Fortified by his effective tactics earlier in the day, Quinlivan took up his cross-examination. He was to destroy McKenzie's credibility as a witness and as an observer of the scene. McKenzie's testimony, when transcribed from court tapes, took up fifteen pages of typescript.

'Did you make a written note of the injuries that you observed to have been suffered by the deceased girls?'

'No.'

'At any stage?'

'I took a note of descriptions of the deceased as far as their clothing and dimensions et cetera and appearances. But I don't recall making any actual physical notation of their injuries whatsoever. I can remember their injuries but I didn't make any note of them.'

'Did you make any handwritten notes at all?'

'Yes.'

'Of what occurred in your investigations at the scene of the accident?'

'Yes.'

'When did you make those?'

'At the scene of the accident, about, I would say, probably an hour after I'd arrived at the scene while I was waiting for other personnel to arrive.'

Quinlivan drilled deeper, asking when specifically the notes had been made, before the ambulances left, after the detective arrived?

McKenzie gave approximations.

Quinlivan asked where the notes had been made and highlighted the importance of the fact McKenzie had not carried his official notebook with him to the site.

McKenzie's answers were less than satisfactory.

'And whereabouts did you make those handwritten notes?'

'At the scene of the accident.'

'In what sort of document?'

'In a shorthand...a police shorthand notebook that I had with me at the time.'

'Where was your official police notebook?'

'At...back at the police station.'

'Why didn't you take it with you to the scene of the accident?'

'Because at that point in time I'd only just transferred to the station a couple of days prior, and in actual fact I hadn't officially taken up official duties at the station at that point in time...and it was...I was called out at that hour of the morning because my offsider at the police station was off on sick report and I was subsequently caught unawares so to speak and I had that with me in my possession, which I also had used at Dareton prior to going to Enngonia. And I took that with me. I always normally carry a shorthand notebook for quick notation while...while...when I'm travelling around in a police vehicle.'

Quinlivan wanted to know why McKenzie had not gone to the station to collect his notebook before leaving for the scene. He questioned why McKenzie had a shorthand notebook at home but not his official notebook. He moved on to McKenzie's relationship with Grant. He wanted to know when precisely he had asked him his full name, his address, and his employer.

McKenzie was caught.

'When did you first find out the full name of the defendant?'

'When I asked him for his licence.'

'When did you find out his address?'

'Off his licence.'

'What? His licence then revealed that his address was Mitchell Caravan Park, Bourke?'

'No, that's...I'm trying to remember exactly whether that was actually on his licence. I think he did tell me that because he said that he was staying in Bourke. And rather than put the address on at that point in time, I tend to record whether, with most instances, where the person in which I am talking to is actually residing at the time. And that's why I recorded his Mitchell Caravan Park address.'

'Well, no part of your statement where it deals with the conversations you had with the defendant deals with any conversation about his living at Mitchell Caravan Park, Bourke...'

'No.'

'...does it?'

'No.'

'When did you find out that he was employed by Major Metals Excavation? Or did you ever find that out?'

'I...if I remember rightly...I found out some time later on. I think it was there at the police station. When I came in and I was talking to detective Ehsman whilst he, either either just before or just after he'd interviewed the defendant. I remained at the scene for quite some time even after detective Ehsman had left the scene because I was waiting for the tow truck to arrive and there was a lot of events transpired after the defendant had left the scene as well as detective Ehsman. And if I recall correctly, I think it was here at the police station I was told that.'

'And you think detective Ehsman might've told you around about lunch time on December 6th of last year that the defendant was involved in some way with Major Metals Excavations? Is that right?'

'It was here at the police station around that time. Yes.'

It is uncertain whether by 'here' McKenzie meant here as in 'here in Bourke' or that he thought he was in fact in the police station rather than in the courthouse across the road. Most likely he meant here in Bourke.

The barrister then pursued McKenzie from another angle, one of equal value in the dismantling of his evidence and expertise. He questioned the accuracy of McKenzie's conversations with Grant about who was driving. It was unclear if McKenzie had conveyed to Ehsman that Grant had said he was the driver. Quinlivan smashed it. He then asked McKenzie to explain what he meant by Grant being incoherent. And if he had needed to ask him the same questions numerous times, why had he not asked him to repeat his remark about being the driver.

'He was slurred in his speech and appeared incoherent.'

'What do you mean by that: "incoherent"?'

'He had trouble formulating sentences, he had trouble finishing a sentence, he just seemed to have difficulty in saying something that could be legibly understood in the point that he started and finished a sentence.'

'He had difficulty in understanding your questions?'

'I don't think that the difficulty was in the questions, I just feel that he had difficulty in formulating the answers to the questions.'

'Was he giving answers to you that didn't make sense and that you had to ask him to repeat?'

'More like a riddle.'

Magistrate: 'More what?'

'More like a riddle than an answer. He wouldn't give a definite answer. He would tend to start off on something and then change his mind to something else, and then come back to it again. And I would have to ask him to phrase it again.'

'You'd have to concede the possibility, wouldn't you, that when you asked this man whether he was driving the ute, and he said to you, "I wasn't", he wasn't?'

'No, he said, "I was."'

Quinlivan moved on. He asked if McKenzie had covered the body. If Grant's intoxication explained him talking in riddles. If he had tried to open the door of the ute, given that pictures in evidence showed it to be jammed. When the ute had been towed from the police station. About the position of the tarpaulin. All vital components in discrediting McKenzie's capabilities.

'Would you have a look at photograph 7 which is part of exhibit 10? Do you see there on the right-hand extremity of the photograph what appears to be a rolled-up tarpaulin?'

'Yes.'

'That's in fact the position of the tarpaulin after you covered up the body of one of the deceased girls? Isn't it?'

'It'd be…it… I wouldn't say it is exactly the place but it's approximately the place, yes.'

'The object in the middle ground of the photograph on the right hand extremity is certainly the tarpaulin?'

'Yes.'

'And it's certainly not spread out depicting a…'[44]

'No, not there it's not.'

'…body?'

'No.'

'It appears to be the tarpaulin in the position in which you had placed it over the dead girl?'

'No, it's not in the position where I'd…not how I'd placed it over the girl, it's how it was after the girl was removed from the scene.'

'After she was removed from the scene? Are you sure? Are you sure?'

'No, I'm not sure, because when I covered the girl over…if I remember rightly, when I initially covered her over after I arrived at the scene…I didn't…it wasn't all scrunched up like that because there wasn't enough cover to allow that to happen, that…I folded it over her from the side, and made it more like a blanket than just a scrunched-up heap like that.'

'Are you saying that when you tried to use the tarpaulin to cover the girl's dead body, it wasn't quite enough tarpaulin to completely effect the cover of it?'

'There was enough there but the way that's been pulled back it would've been pulled back from over her feet and there wasn't... enough on that side of her, there was only enough on the sides not the length.'

With this, Quinlivan introduced the possibility that McKenzie had made errors of timing in his notebook. McKenzie failed to see how he was being drawn into the vortex until it was too late. His retreat was blocked.

Quinlivan drilled down into detail concerning when Ehsman had arrived, when McKenzie had noted Grant's place of employment and home address. In fact, everything McKenzie said from here on seemed to implicate him in some way as either a poor note-taker or one who had doctored his notebook.

After a continued lengthy examination, Quinlivan somewhat abruptly ceased his cross-examination. He had grilled McKenzie for some time. It had become clear that Quinlivan was searching for a connection, or a collaboration, between the police about the positions of the girls' bodies and whether they might have been moved at some time before they were taken from the scene. He drove hard towards his objective but, as we will see, the magistrate was having none of it.

# 36

## The prosecution changes tactics

As Constable McKenzie left the courthouse, breathing heavily and shaking his head from the encounter, the prosecution switched direction.

Sergeant Day called Karen Johnson to the stand. Karen had been one of the last people to see Mona and Cindy alive. Day asked a series of questions of the teenager, framed in such a way that he appeared either patronising or unfamiliar with reasonable standards when interviewing a minor. Sergeant Day referred to Karen's earlier statement. He asked her where she lived, what her name was and whether she went to school. He asked if she remembered the night Cindy and Mona died.

Karen nodded as she had done in answer to the previous questions.

He asked if she had seen a Toyota Hilux coming up behind them as they walked along Adelaide Street. He asked if the ute had stopped.

'It stopped and then the man opened the door and he asked us if we wanted a lift.'

'What happened then?'

'We said no.'

The magistrate asked for clarity. 'Who said no?'

To which Miss Johnson turned and answered her directly, 'Us, the two of us girls'.

Sergeant Day asked, 'The two of you, that's Betty-Ann and yourself, said no. Right, what happened then?'

'We told him we was going home and then he said, "Do you want a lift home?" and we said no.'

At this point, the magistrate admonished the witness to speak up.

'Can you keep your voice up, I can't hear you. It's no use you giving evidence if you just whisper. You've got to keep your voice up loud, so we can all hear.'[45]

The prosecution continued.

It became clear that Mona and Cindy had arrived while the ute was stopped.

'And then they went over and Mona asked him something and she said, "Will you take us over the levy to see if anyone's coming?" and…'

Again the magistrate intervened, asking where they were wanting to be taken.

Karen repeated, 'Over the levee.

The magistrate responded 'Over? Levee?'

Sergeant Day filled the gap in the magistrate's knowledge.

'Over to the levee to see if anyone was there,' Miss Johnson replied.

Sergeant Day continued. 'Right, what happened then?'

'And then he said yes and then those girls got in and then he went…he didn't go over the levee he went…he turned…Yanda Street.'

Sergeant Day continued. 'Did you notice anything about the man in the truck?'

'I…he had a half a carton with him.'

'Had a half a carton. Did you know what of?'

'No.'

'Did it look like beer?'

'Yes.'

'Half a carton of beer, that's what it looked like to you, is that right?'

'Yes.'

Sergeant Day concluded his examination of Miss Johnson but she was unprepared for the directness of the first few questions from Mr Quinlivan on cross-examination.

It was not a long cross but it was to the point. He asked how well she knew Mona and Cindy; whether she herself had been drinking that night; whether she was drunk that night; and whether Mona and

Cindy seemed 'pretty' drunk. He questioned her accuracy about the time of night at which she had seen Mona and Cindy. 'Did you know Mona and Cindy pretty well?'

'Yes.'

'Last year and when you saw them that night in Adelaide Street, they seemed to you to have been drinking alcohol?'

'Yes.'

'They seemed pretty drunk to you?'

'Yes.'

'Were you pretty drunk yourself?'

'No.'

'Had you been drinking?'

'No.'

'Where were you going?'

'Home.'

'Where had you been?'

'The Reserve.'

'What were you doing there?'

'At my auntie's place.'

'And it was sometime after 8.15 at night that you saw Cindy and Mona?'

'Yes.'

'It might have been as late as 10 o'clock at night?'

'No.'

'Close to 10?'

'No.'

'How much later than 8.15?'

'I think it was about that time.'

'Were you with anybody else?'

'Betty-Ann.'

'Anybody else besides her?'

'No.'

Quinlivan concluded his cross-examination. He sat down and the witness left the stand and went back to sit with her family and friends in the public gallery.

Sergeant Day, changing direction again, called the pathologist Clive Pringle.

## 37

## The pathologist takes the stand

Dr Clive Pringle of Dubbo had made thorough examinations of the bodies of Mona and Cindy Smith two days after the accident. He had travelled from Dubbo to Bourke. Pringle had retired from his regular pathology work in 1984, so it is unclear why he took on the job. Whatever the reason, he did the autopsies and was now, almost a year later, back in Bourke under examination. Indeed, Pringle, when asked, volunteered his occupation as pathologist. He did not reveal that he was retired.

Sergeant Day asked to tender into evidence the reports made by Pringle from the autopsies, which was duly done.

The magistrate, however, had not previously seen the reports. She seemed nonplussed. She asked the sergeant if he expected her to read them there and then.

He replied, 'I wouldn't mind if you read them now, your worship.'

While the magistrate read quickly through the reports, Day had a brief discussion with Pringle in which he asked Pringle to 'go to the conclusion on page four of [Mona Smith's] report, [where] you speak during the course of that conclusion of a period of a short time before death was likely to have occurred. When you speak of a short time, what are you referring to…how long'?

Pringle replied that it was 'maybe within an hour'.

It remains unclear why Day asked immediately about the timing of Mona's death, given the charge of interference was pointed at Grant in relation to Cindy. Nonetheless, when the magistrate finished reading the reports, he continued. 'Within an hour?'

'Hour.'

'Right. You speak of further injuries and complications which would've accelerated her death through the production of severe hypoxia. Now, what sort of shortening of the time she may have been alive would the other observations as far as the injuries that you observed, what other, what is your opinion in relation to the time perhaps it would've taken from that hour that she may have been alive?'

'That'd be very difficult to estimate. The...the...the state of shock which would develop...progressively following the loss of...continuing loss of blood would produce very serious affects generally. Those affects would be compounded by the presence of...of obstruction within the air passages from blood and gastric contents and also by the fact that she had fractured ribs which would've restricted the...her ability to breath properly. And she had...also within the lungs she had haemorrhages in the lungs...a result of tearing of the lungs from the fractures in the ribs. So those would...would accelerate the...the period...would shorten the period considerably.'

The prosecutor asked about the likelihood that Mona would have been conscious, or whether she would have even been able to move, questions upon which Pringle cast considerable doubt.

Again the magistrate intervened – the noise in the courtroom was a constant distraction.

The prosecutor asked about blood loss associated with such a head wound, a question which went some way to explaining why Mona had not moved after the accident and had possibly died very quickly. He then turned his attention to Cindy. He was interested in the possibility that she had remained alive for some time immediately after the accident. Her injuries, the pathologist had reported earlier, were complicated by gastric juices being injected into her air passages and lungs. He now confirmed that she might have lived for an hour or less. He also confirmed that she would have had very little movement and been unable to stand or even get up from the ground.

'Would she be able to sit up, doctor?'

'No.'

'Would she be in extreme pain?'

'Yes.'

'Right. You indicate there in the comment that although death may not have occurred immediately, it would have occurred rapidly and it is most unlikely the deceased was even semi-conscious shortly after the accident. What brings you to the conclusion that she may well have been unconscious, well…almost certainly have been unconscious? Is that because of the…possibly the result of shock as a result of the pain that she would have been experiencing and the injuries that she had just experienced?'

'Yes, the gravity of the injuries are most severe injuries and the shock that would have resulted, that would be adequate to cause her to be unconscious.'

'You speak there of the fashion observed, her clothing being in a certain fashion as observed at the post-mortem examination. Could you remember what state of dress she was in at the time that you first made observations of her prior to the post-mortem examination?'

'Yes. I described that at the beginning of the report. The other garments were arranged above the level of the breasts and the trousers were down around her ankles.'

At this point, Sergeant Day ceased his examination of the pathologist.

Quinlivan took over and kept the focus on Cindy. He asked about the injuries to her back, the abrasions and grazes. He wanted to determine if they had been made by the car or the roadway. He was keen to differentiate the type of grazes to Cindy and the deep head wounds to Mona.

Here, the magistrate asked additional questions, the answers to which it may have been reasonable to assume were included in a briefing document. What it achieved was to allow the defence to continue.

'You said at the end of the report of Jacinta Smith that specimens were taken from the genital area. I suppose they were sent for testing. Did you have anything further to do with that?'

'No, those were given to the scientific officer who attended the post-mortem and they were transferred to the Department of Forensic Biology and I didn't...I haven't seen that report.'

Quinlivan then returned to his cross-examination: 'Would your worship allow me leave just for a moment to readdress myself to that area of the doctor's report in relation to Jacinta Smith? Doctor, would you concede the possibility of Jacinta Smith surviving for say an hour and a half after she suffered her injuries?'

'I think we'd be stretching it really to...to be...you know...going to a length of time like that.'

'It's a very difficult judgement to make, though, isn't it?'

'Yes, it's very difficult and the injuries she had received were really very grave.'

'Not grave enough to take the view that she probably died immediately, though?'

'The trouble with the...this sort of case is that when one sees a person who died from a motor vehicle accident and they're found dead after the accident, you...you don't really know how long they have survived for. I think the death could have occurred very rapidly with her. It need not have been immediate.'

'And I suppose some outer limit can be put on it. I mean, I suppose one can say that she wouldn't have survived for four hours under any stretch of the imagination?'

'No.'

'But no one would be writing to any medical journals about it if the fact was discovered that she in fact survived for two hours. It would not be a totally extraordinary event, would it?'

'No.'

There was no re-examination of the witness by Sergeant Day but again the magistrate seemed curious about something. 'And I don't think you answered directly the question that was asked of you whether she could have died immediately. I know you said it's very difficult to tell but can you be any more specific on that? Is it a possibility or not a possibility?'

'I think it is a possibility. Yes.'

'But whether that was so or not, in your opinion it is most unlikely that she was ever more than semi-conscious?'

'Yes. That's true.' Dr Pringle concluded his testimony.

Two witnesses remained; the men who had first come upon the scene of the accident – Shane Baty and Tex Johnson. The afternoon was drawing to a close as these witnesses gave evidence before the magistrate made her summation.

# 38

## The committal hearing concludes

One must consider that when Shane Baty and Tex Johnson stopped their utes by the side of the road before dawn on Sunday 6 December, when they stepped out and walked towards the scene of what appeared to be a straightforward car crash, they envisaged nothing more than rendering first aid. Most individuals, when confronted by such a scene, have an inbuilt reaction: if at all possible, stop and lend assistance, then get help. Baty and Johnson did just that. They then reported the scene to the police. Now, eleven months later, they were back in Bourke giving evidence at a committal hearing. One of the charges, indecently interfere with a corpse, they most likely had not known existed. They may have never before acted as witnesses in any type of court case. They may have never before given statements to the police – most people live their entire lives without being confronted by such acts. Yet here were Shane and Tex preparing to give evidence for the benefit of the crown in the case against Alex Grant.

It was clear from Shane's chosen words and phrases at the site of the crash that he had a particular way of looking at the society in which he lived. He continued such use during his testimony. Tex, a little older, may have had the same social beliefs but he was less inclined to display them publicly. It is reasonable to assume from their testimonies that neither was truly prepared for what was about to engage them. Both men displayed the outward demeanour that framed life in the outback. They told it how it was and expected to be treated the same way.

Shane preceded Tex into the witness stand. He was asked his name. Day then spelt it for him and he answered by repeating what Day had spelt. This was going to be a long session. He then asked where he lived.

Shane said he used his parent's farm outside Mildura as his address.

Sergeant Day asked with whom he had been travelling (although no other members of the party were ever called to give evidence), what time he had left, what time he came upon the accident scene, and what he did when he arrived.

The time, Mr Baty remarked, was 'piccaninny daylight'.

Sergeant Day asked about the girl he saw on the side of the road. 'And you had a closer look at that person and at that time you saw they were lying face down and in your opinion that person was probably deceased?'

'Yes. The person was dead. There was no doubt about that.'

He then asked Mr Baty if he had looked at the ute and if he had gone over to where there were two other people.

It was here that Mr Baty provided vital evidence about the state of the tarpaulin.

'Now did you walk to the Enngonia side of a white Toyota Hilux ute there of which the roof of the cab had been caved in?'

'Yes, the Hilux was facing back towards Bourke, or the nose of it was facing more towards Bourke, or the road to Bourke anyway, and I walked from that girl…had a bit of a look at the Hilux…just sort of past it…and walked over to where the camp sheet was spread out.'

'Right?'

'And two people were on there.'

'Right. What did you notice about the two people on there?'

'One was male and one was female.'

'Did you know…the camp sheet you said…what was that made of?'

'I didn't really take a close look at it… I suppose calling it a camp sheet… I just took it as canvas or…'

'Right. You've said it was laid out. Could you describe that more fully… What do you mean by laid out?'

'It looked as though it had been sort of spread out, it wasn't something that had been sort of thrown down.'

'Right. Now, did you notice anything about the people lying on it? What position they were in?'

'The girl…aboriginal girl was laying down and the man was long… sort of half draped…had his arm…it would be his right arm because he was lying on his left side across her around about her boob areas… and there. He was fully clothed and she had a white blouse on and she had a pair of panties hanging off her left ankle and there was nothing on below more or less.'

'Nothing below her waist?'

'Well, she had a pair of panties on her ankle.'

The prosecutor asked what Baty did next, whether the man woke. 'What happened then?'

'I said…he said… "Yeah, I'm right." And I said, "You've got two dead gins here," and he said, "No, they're all right."'

'"No, they're all right." What happened then?'

'Then he sort of went back to sleep or passed back out.' Mr Baty described the injuries he saw. 'She was a pretty sort of purply black around her back area. I think it was her back area, I'm too sure [sic].'

Magistrate: 'She was black, did you say? I didn't hear what you said.'

'Purply black…'

Sergeant Day ended his questioning.

Under cross-examination by Quinlivan, Mr Baty appeared to offer the same face-value answers as he had given the prosecution. There had appeared to be no sense that he would embellish or alter his evidence from how he saw the original scene.

It was interesting too that Quinlivan appeared to alter perceptibly his use of language and his inflections. He adjusted to the environment. This was not a Sydney courtroom. He asked about the drive to Enngonia to alert the police, about where the police emerged from, whether he saw them leave. He asked about the man on the tarpaulin.

'Now, when you first saw the man who was lying down with one of these deceased aboriginal girls, he was either asleep or unconscious?'

'Yes.'

'I mean, whilst you were first tending to the girls and checking pulses and such like, there wasn't a stir out of him?'

'No. Like I said, I checked the girl on the side of the road and I walked from there down to where the camp sheet was laid out and I checked over that girl on the camp sheet and while I was checking her over he started to moan as though he was coming to or whatever and... and I started to feel his neck and that and as I said, I stuck my finger in his mouth to check his tongue and all of that.'

Quinlivan asked in detail about the man's state of consciousness, whether he got up off the tarp, and he showed Baty a picture. 'Could I have Exhibit 10 please, your worship? The black and white photographs? Do you remember the girl that was on the camp sheet, that was naked from the waist down? Is that right?'

'Yes, except for the panties.'

'Well, you remember panties as being on one of her ankles, is that right?'

'Yes.'

'I show you a photograph numbered eleven in Exhibit 10. Are you able to recognise a camp sheet that you saw that day as being the covering that appears in this photograph?'

'No. I wouldn't have a clue.'

'What about the clothing that appears to be on this girl's legs, down near her ankles. Seems to be some sort of soft clothing, like a tracksuit bottom?'

'Does, doesn't it?'

'Did you see that when you made your inspection that early morning?'

'No. Not to my actual seeing...from what I've told people...no.'

'Would your view be that the girl shown in photograph 11 just isn't the girl that you saw or you just may be mistaken about the clothing?'

'Well, I'm not mistaken about the clothing. Saying what I've seen, right? That's the girl on the camp sheet, right? And this bloke is supposed to be lying here... I don't know whether it's the same camp sheet or not.'

The magistrate appeared at this point to be unable to hear the witness. The low hum of constant chatter from the public gallery, while not an accepted practice, was a tolerated one in rural Australia.

Quinlivan pointed to the picture. 'This bloke was supposed to be lying here?'

'Yes, that's if that's the same camp sheet and she had her legs straight down, right? And it looked as though to me that she had nothing on below. I don't know whether she had any boots on, but she was naked up here...round here.' (Baty pointed to the photograph.)

'Naked in her genital area?'

'Yes, she had nothing, didn't look like to me that she had any...you know...her pants pulled down or anything. She looked like she was naked from the waist down.'

'Without any clothing at all down near her ankles apart from some panties?'

Mr Baty nodded.

'And her legs were straight?'

'Yes, straight.'

'Not spread?'

'Not spread.'

'Or with one leg straight and one leg...?'

'No...'

'...splayed, just her legs weren't in the way shown in photograph eleven, exhibit 10?'

'The photograph you just showed me? No.'

'In photograph 11 the right leg is...seems to be straight and the left leg is bent and splayed to the left. Is that your recollection of how the body seemed to be when you saw it?'

'No. I just told you. The legs were straight.'

'With no clothes on them at all apart from the panties?'

'That's right.'

'And you're not sure about the shoes?'

'Not sure about the shoes.'

Quinlivan cast a last look at Shane before he stepped down from the witness box. The young pup had said his piece. Now it was time for the big dog.

Texter Leo Johnson took the stand and gave his address as Ferguson Farm, North Bourke, where, as he indicated, he was the farm foreman.

Day asked him some questions about his earlier statement to the police which, when he agreed it was his, was tendered, admitted and marked exhibit 22.

It was not all cut and dried, however. His statement excluded for the benefit of the magistrate and the public gallery the last half of the last sentence in paragraph three. This sentence read, 'The body was cold and purple and it seemed as though it had been dead for a fair while.' The words 'it seemed as though it had been dead for a fair while' were excluded from the committal hearing.

The prosecutor needed to make sure he and Tex were singing from the same hymn book. He asked him about his statement and its accuracy, he asked about the tarp and if it was spread neatly, and about the clothing and if Cindy was naked.

Then Quinlivan began his considered cross-examination. He asked first to see exhibit 10. The magistrate agreed. Quinlivan went through each question again as he had with Shane Baty, only this time they were worded slightly differently. He asked about the man's state of consciousness, about his position relative to the dead girl, about when he began to groan and moan, whether he got up, and about the panties.

'Yeah. Sort of. Yeah. Sort of. Yeah. Something like that. It wasn't just…wasn't them little scanty-looking things.'

'No. Some sort of long-legged pants?'

'Yeah. Looked like to me. Yes.'

'Like a tracksuit or something like that?'

'Something to that effect it could've…yes. Something like that.'

'And that was around both of her ankles?'

'Yes.'

He then asked about the position of the girl's legs, about the time they had left the farm, about how long it took to get to the accident site and whether he left with Mr Baty. 'Now when Mr Baty left the scene, did you leave with him?'

'No. We stayed there because, you know, it was just breaking daylight and you know that crows live on them kangaroos all the time and a person's not going to make much difference to them fellows on daylight.'

There was no re-examination of Mr Johnson by Sergeant Day. The prosecution thus closed its case.

After a brief adjournment, the magistrate asked the defence if there were any submissions. Quinlivan made no submission under either Section 41(2) or 41(6). In reply, the magistrate asked then if such comment meant that Quinlivan could see that there was sufficient evidence for her to bring the matters to trial.

Quinlivan responded, 'Yes. Your worship well understands the controversies in the case but I don't frankly find myself in a position to submit to your worship that your worship ought at this stage form the opinion that a jury probably wouldn't convict. It seems to me to be vacuous for me to submit that now, at this stage.'

Cater-Smith confirmed that Quinlivan meant all three matters – the two charges of culpable driving and the interference.

'Yes. Yes, your worship, although it occurs to me that really before your worship proceeds further there really ought to be a withdrawal of those allegations and charges that have been made in relation to offences which are particularised as arising out of circumstances where my client wasn't the driver of the…of the relevant vehicle. See at this stage there are pending before the court two culpable driving offences obviously based on the fact, on the footing that my client was driving the vehicle and S.53 charges on the basis of which he wasn't the driver

206

of the vehicle. Now, I understand what the police case now is and so does my client and it seems that before your worship ought to commit my client to trial, if that's the view your worship takes about the situation, that there ought to be some withdrawal and disposal by dismissal of the other matters. And there's a third matter as well, I think, in relation to allowing an unlicensed person to drive a vehicle.'

Day stood and addressed the bench. 'I do seek leave to withdraw those,' he replied.

Quinlivan asked if he meant charges 16, 17 and 18.

Day replied, 'That's right.'

Cater-Smith concurred. 'Very well. That's charge cases 16, 17 and 18. Yes, well. I think that that is the proper course in view of what witnesses have said and in view of the evidence that I have heard and I grant you leave to withdraw each of those three charges and they are dismissed."

The police prosecutor had a brain snap. 'I don't think you've got the power to dismiss them. I should just say you've got the power to discharge…'

He was unable to finish as Cater-Smith scowled and interrupted. 'Discharge. Yes.'

A number of over-riding voices threw some confusion into the courtroom as Day replied, 'For that…'

The magistrate cut him down. 'And, well, two of them are indictable matters; the two sets of 53…'

She herself was unable to finish as the prosecutor took his turn: 'That's right. Yes.'

The magistrate corrected her earlier statement and went on, '… matters are indictable matters and the defendant is discharged in respect of each.' She then looked back towards the prosecutor. 'Yes, Sergeant. Did you wish to say anything under section 41(2) or 41(6)?'"

'Well, no, I won't unless you call on me to say something, your worship. I'm quite prepared to if at this stage my submission is that it wouldn't call for me to say anything. I think there's clearly a situation that you would have to find that a jury would be capable of being satisfied without a reasonable doubt.'

With this, the prosecutor took his seat. He shook his head almost imperceptibly. As did the defence counsel. There was a great deal of confusion. It appeared for a fleeting moment that no one controlled the court. Everyone – public, witnesses, lawyers, police defendant, family members – sat silently. They leaned forward to hear the magistrate's words as she summed up and made her decision about the future course of Alex Grant's life. The stillness, for a moment, was palpable.

# 39

# The defendant sent to trial

To those in the public gallery and those who were called as witnesses, the committal hearing of Alexander Ian Grant may have appeared to be complex in its structure and impenetrable in its language. But it was nothing more than a simple struggle by two sides looking to persuade and influence the direction the magistrate might take in handing down her decision. It was a struggle charged with strategy and tactics. The prosecution was required to produce evidence that would satisfy a jury beyond reasonable doubt that the defendant had committed indictable offences within the meaning of the Justices Act. The defence was required to rebut the evidence to show that a jury would not be satisfied that the defendant was guilty. An indictable offence differed at law to a summary offence. A summary offence was a matter heard by a magistrate, and a defendant did not have recourse to a trial with a jury. Summary offences were tried by a judge. No jury. Summary offences might be traffic-related or petty theft. They carried a maximum penalty of two years' imprisonment. An indictable offence was more serious and must be tried by a judge and jury. A plea of not guilty in an indictable offence more or less guaranteed trial by judge and jury. The job of the magistrate in a committal hearing was to determine the facts presented by both sides and to weigh the balance.

Cater-Smith set aside her pen and began her monologue. It held no candle to that of Molly Bloom but it was expansive. 'Well, firstly it's necessary to consider the matter under S41(2) of the Justices Act[46] and there I have to be satisfied...I have to be of the opinion that the evidence is capable of satisfying a jury beyond reasonable doubt that…that the defendant has committed an indictable offence. I have three offences before me: two allegations, namely that on the 6th of December 1987 at Enngonia the defendant drove a motor vehicle whilst he was under the influence of intoxicating liquor, and in that motor vehicle, was one Mona Lisa Smith. She was being conveyed, the vehicle overturned, left the highway and the death of Mona Lisa Smith was occasioned. And another charge in identical terms in which the death of Jacinta Rose Smith was occasioned and a third charge that on the same day, same place, the defendant indecently interfered with a dead human body.

'The evidence at this stage that I am considering, of course, is only the evidence of the prosecution witnesses and I must look at that evidence in the best light. I have heard evidence given by a number of witnesses for the prosecution and I have also before me a number of statements from witnesses that were not required to be called and also a number of certificates and I think firstly I shall look at the certificate that I have before me which is the certificate in relation to the defendant's blood alcohol level. That certificate was tendered and it indicates that the defendant had a blood alcohol level at 0.159 at 9.10 a.m. on the 6th of December 1987. I also have a statement made by a Miss Poole, a pharmacologist, and she considers that reading and she considers it in the light of the time that she was told that this accident occurred and that was at somewhere between 1 a.m. and 2 a.m. on the morning of the 6th December. In her view she indicates that given the defendant's reading at 9.10 a.m., the reading that the defendant would have had at the time of the collision was within the limits of 0.205 and 0.345 and she indicates that the most likely level was 0.260. So clearly, at that time of the morning, the defendant would have been under the influence of intoxicating liquor.

'I've also heard evidence from Constable McKenzie who was the first police officer to attend at the scene and also of Mr Baty and of Mr Johnson who were in fact the first people, as far as the evidence takes it anyhow, to arrive at the scene. And the evidence of Mr Baty and Mr

Johnson was that they arrived somewhere shortly before 5:00am on the morning of 6th December. They saw a body beside…beside the road which I must take was the body of Mona Lisa Smith. Mr Baty formed the opinion that she was dead as did Mr Johnson. Mr Baty then saw two other people lying on a tarpaulin, one aboriginal girl and one man. He spoke to the man. He formed the opinion that the girl was dead and the man he said was asleep or unconscious. After he spoke to him and put his hand in his mouth, he came to and he said that there was a very short conversation. In that conversation he indicated to that man that the two women were dead. The man apparently denied that and said that that was not so. Mr Baty's description of seeing that man and the aboriginal girl was that they were on a tarpaulin, the tarpaulin was quite flat…appeared to have been intentionally laid out in that way and that the man was lying very close to the girl and that he had his arm across her chest area. Mr Johnson gave a similar description of the man and the girl on the tarpaulin. He also described the tarpaulin being laid out in the same manner and he described the man lying beside the girl in the same way. They both said that the girl was naked from the chest to the ankles. The evidence was that she did have some panties…I think was Mr Baty's evidence…on one ankle and Mr Johnson said that she had some tracksuit pants…I think it was on the ankle but both were quite clear that she was naked from the chest to the ankle. They did say however, that as far as they could recollect, her legs were straight and not as shown in a photograph that I have before me as part of exhibit 10. And in that photograph one of her legs is slightly separated from the other, but their evidence was quite clear. Mr Johnson said that the man abused him and following that, he left the scene and both of those two persons then went to the police station at Enngonia.

'As I indicated, Constable McKenzie was the first person to arrive at the scene and when he did arrive he had a conversation with the defendant and he asked the defendant in that conversation who had been the driver of the motor vehicle and the defendant indicated to

211

him that he had and that was the defendant's initial reaction to the question asked of him by the constable. And I think the first reaction of a person is very important and I do place considerable weight on that reaction of the defendant. The constable did say that he was clearly affected by alcohol; well affected, in his view but it does appear that he was able to answer his questions although the constable did say that he spoke in riddles. Exactly why that was is somewhat unclear. Whether I'm to assume it was because or the alcohol I can't say or whether it was because the defendant, in fact, was being less than honest with the constable but that was the observation of Constable McKenzie and shortly after the defendant said to the constable that he was the driver he changed that and indicated that that was not so and that it was the female person who was driving, the deceased female at the front of the vehicle. So, clearly, at that early stage, he did change what he initially said and indicated that it was not him who was the driver of the vehicle.

'Detective Ehsman arrived shortly after, some hour or two I think it was, after Constable McKenzie arrived and he made some observations of the scene. He saw the two bodies that were lying there, he saw the vehicle, he saw the damage to the vehicle and he investigated the accident scene and he indicated, as had Constable McKenzie, that there were tools scattered everywhere and he also noted that there were skid marks. He spoke to the defendant and I have in evidence before me a record of interview dated the 6th of December 1987 and I also have a record of interview dated the 9th of December 1987 and in those records of interview the defendant again indicates that it was not him but it was the girl who was the driver. In the interview of the 6th of December 1987 he indicated, however, that the girl Jacinta Rose Smith was walking around after the accident occurred and in fact he said, in the record of interview, that she made some approach to him along the lines of 'do you really want me?' and to that he replied something again along the lines of 'give us a hand to get the gear on the truck'. And I must say that in the light of the evidence that I have heard from Doctor Pringle that is completely impossible. The doctor having given evidence that it was extremely unlikely that the girl Jacinta Rose Smith was other than semi-conscious and certainly that she would not have been able to walk around after the accident occurred, let alone to give anybody a hand doing anything. The two records of interview are totally at variance with the answers the defendant made to Sergeant Godkin. Sergeant Godkin interviewed the defendant some months later and again asked him for his version of what occurred on that night and the answers that he gave the sergeant on the 11th of May were quite different and the defendant himself acknowledged that that was the situation. When he was asked about the state of Jacinta Rose Smith's clothing he then indicated that the clothes must have come down when he pulled her out of the motor vehicle although in his earlier version he had indicated that she had taken her clothes down herself. Again I might comment – something that would have been quite impossible. So clearly the defendant has been less than honest with the police officers in his account of what occurred on that night and wherever that situation exists one must have grave doubts about what he says to two various people about the occurrences.

'I further have evidence from Detective Reid – he was with Detective Ehsman – he in fact typed the record of interview. And I have evidence from Constable Le Merton and he corroborates it by way of a statement…the evidence that was given by Sergeant Godkin.

'The other evidence that I have relates to Mona Smith's ability to drive a motor vehicle and a group of witnesses gave evidence in that regard. First evidence was given by Mrs Iona Smith who is Jacinta Rose Smith's mother. Evidence was given by Mrs June Smith, by Douglas Smith known as Shillingsood [sic] and by Lisa Edwards. The evidence of those witnesses was as follows. Firstly Mrs Iona Smith indicated that she did not think that Mona Smith could drive a motor vehicle at all. Mrs June Smith, her mother, said that she had seen her drive on one occasion as did Douglas Smith and Lisa Edwards but the account of that occasion…if I am to take it…that it was intended to be… the one occasion…differed considerably between each of those three witnesses. It does seem to me fairly clear that at some stage Mona Smith did drive a motor vehicle and most probably at the Reserve at Bourke and quite possibly that she drove a motor vehicle on more than one occasion. It does seem however that she did not have very extensive experience in driving and I think that I cannot come to any other conclusion but that – from the evidence that was given. Evidence was also given by Carol [sic] Johnson who saw the two girls get in to the motor vehicle which I am being asked to assume was the motor vehicle of the defendant. And I've had evidence from Lloyd Smith who saw the girls at approximately 8:15pm so that it does seem that the girls got into the motor vehicle of the defendant somewhere at approximately 8 or 9 o'clock. I do have further evidence given by Mr Barnett who was the barman at the hotel and he recalls a person by the name of Alex who he recognised – and again I'm being asked to assume was the defendant – come into the hotel at approximately 10.15 p.m. and purchase some rum, some Coke and some beer, so clearly the defendant and the girls were together sometime late on the night of the 5th of December.

'The other evidence that I have relates to the motor vehicle. That is the evidence given by Detective Moss, by Mr Friedman and by Mr Hurle, and that evidence relates to an examination of the motor vehicle. Mr Hurle was the person who bought the wreck and made the parts available to detective Moss. Detective Moss examined the Toyota motor vehicle. He did make some preliminary tests for blood and some of those tests were positive but I then have the certificate of Mr Friedman, the forensic biologist, and he found no blood in the motor vehicle or in three parts of the motor vehicle…I think that was on the sun visors and on the roof. I have the evidence of Doctor Pringle who carried out the post mortem examination on the two girls and as I have already indicated, so far as Jacinta Smith is concerned, he says that it is most unlikely that she was even semi-conscious shortly after the accident. He said that it was very difficult for him to place a time on when death would have occurred. He said that it could have

214

been immediate but it could have been up to some two hours after. But he was quite definite, as I said before, on the fact that she would have been unable to walk and if it is unlikely that she was even semi-conscious then I must say it is also extremely doubtful that she would have been able to disarrange her clothing in the way that has already been described. He further gave evidence that specimens were taken from the genital area and on her left leg and that although he sent away those specimens, he had nothing further to do with those and I do not have before me anything relating to what it was in fact that was found and I can't really say whether anything was found. I just have nothing beyond the evidence that was given by Doctor Pringle in that regard.

'So far as the evidence that he gave relating to Mona Smith was concerned, there the injuries that he observed on Mona Smith were described and again it is difficult to say exactly when death occurred but from his evidence it appears that it would have been fairly shortly after she received the injuries that she died. It is very difficult in a situation such as this to say exactly what the situation was and how the injuries were received, whether inside the motor vehicle or outside the motor vehicle. I have to have evidence before me that at least to the stage sufficient to satisfy S41(2) of the Justices Act, that it was in fact the defendant who was the driver of the motor vehicle in the early hours of the morning of 6 December, and there I must rely on the evidence that was given by Constable McKenzie of the admission that was made by the defendant to him immediately after he was spoken to. And as I've already said, that was in the very early stages, as soon as Constable McKenzie arrived at the scene. I also take into account the different versions that were given by the defendant and there was a version of course given to Constable McKenzie. There was a version given in the record of interviews and then there was another version given to Sergeant Godkin, and I think that I can take all of that into account as some evidence of possible guilt in the matter. I also take into account the fact that Mona Smith, although she may have had some driving experience, clearly had very little driving experience and it does seem most unlikely that the defendant would have let her drive on this particular night, particularly as there was some evidence that that was an unusual course for him – that he usually did not let anybody else drive that motor vehicle – and of course, on that night she also…as was Jacinta Smith…was quite affected by alcohol. On all the evidence that I have before me in respect of those two matters, it does seem that that evidence is capable of satisfying a jury beyond reasonable doubt. So far as the third matter is concerned, there the allegation is that the defendant indecently interfered with a dead human body. Now, there I only have the evidence of Doctor Pringle to guide me so far as the time of death is concerned and so far as the indecent interference is concerned. That also is a little unclear regarding exactly what it was the prosecution are relying on. There is no clear evidence before me of any intercourse or anything of that nature. I must assume that what the prosecution are relying on is the fact that she was completely naked from the chest to the ankles and that it is most likely that her clothes were placed in that position by the defendant. Clearly there was no way the girl herself could have done that. The defendant originally indicated that she did. When he spoke to Sergeant Godkin he said that it had occurred as he dragged her out of the motor vehicle but then that also seemed somewhat unlikely given that her top was pushed upwards and her pants were pulled down around her ankles. It seems to me that I can assume that it was the defendant who did that. I also take account of the fact that the tarpaulin was laid out in the manner that I have described and I further take into account the position in which the defendant was seen with the girl by both Mr Johnson and Mr Baty. He was there seen with his arm across her chest. I do think that I have sufficient evidence that there was some indecent interference at least to the level of S41(2). So far as that interference being with a dead body is concerned, again, I must come back to the evidence of Doctor Pringle who said that death could have occurred immediately. Or perhaps one or two hours later. It does seem to me that perhaps I can make the assumption that death more likely than not occurred early after the accident and that the interference took place after death had occurred. But I'll look at that again under S41(6). At this stage it does seem to me that I have sufficient evidence in respect of that matter to satisfy S41(2) of the Justices Act.'

The magistrate then addressed the defendant directly. 'Accordingly, if you'd stand up please, Mr Grant. You will have an opportunity to give evidence on oath before me and to call evidence but first do you wish to say anything in answer to the charge? You are not obliged to say anything unless you desire but whatever you say will be recorded and may be given against you in evidence at your trial. In addition, you should disregard any promise or threat which may have been made to persuade you to make any admission or confession of your guilt. Now. Do you understand what I've said? You may speak to Mr Quinlivan. Yes. You don't wish to say anything else? Do you desire to give evidence at this stage?'

Alex Grant gave a single-word answer: 'No.'

The magistrate asked if he wished to call any witnesses on his behalf, to which he gave the same answer.

Cater-Smith directed Grant to take his seat. She turned to Quinlivan and asked him if he wished to add anything further.

He answered, 'No, your worship.'

She asked the prosecutor, who indicated he wished to say something further about S41(6). He did so, after which the magistrate turned her attention to further assess the charge of interference with a dead body which, as we know, was under S41(6).

'Well, when considering the matter under S41(6) of the Justices Act, I must commit the defendant for trial unless I am of the opinion that a jury would not be likely to convict him of an indictable offence. It is always difficult where one has no influence than one had when considering the matter under S41(2), but at this stage I must consider the credibility of the witnesses and such matters as the weight to be given to the evidence and the acceptability of the evidence. So far as the credibility of the witnesses is concerned, none of the witnesses who gave evidence here today were substantially shaken. It seemed to me that the evidence that they gave was quite obviously credible evidence and I accept that evidence.

'So far as the weight of the evidence is concerned there again it seemed to me that the evidence that I have before me should be given quite a considerable amount of weight. The only comment that I would make there is that I would have thought that I would have had some results from the tests which were carried out from the samples that were sent by Doctor Pringle. I do not have and of course that leaves that particular aspect somewhat uncertain. It does not lessen the weight that I give to the doctor's evidence but just so far as the medical evidence is concerned I would have liked to have had the result of those tests.

'The matter that concerned me under...when I looked at the evidence in respect of S41(2) of the Justices Act was the question of the time of death of Jacinta Rose Smith. In respect of the allegation that the defendant interfered with a dead human body, certainly there were sexual overtones in the whole of the evidence. Certainly the disarrangement of the clothing led me to the understanding that … that sexual involvement had perhaps taken place, but that is a fairly open question. So far as the defendant's responses to the police officers in that regard was concerned the two stories that he gave to the police officers further added to the thought that I had that clearly he had disarranged the clothing and one could then perhaps assume that it was for an indecent purpose. Further his setting out of the tarpaulin in the manner that has been described also led me to that conclusion.

'The matter that particularly concerned me was the time of death and as I indicated when I considered the matter under S41(2), the evidence of Doctor Pringle in that regard was certainly indefinite, ranging from immediate to up to two hours. Now that I have heard from the prosecutor in that regard, it seems that the prosecution are relying on an act taking place after Mr Grant was seen by both Mr Johnson and Mr Baty, and I do certainly accept the evidence of those two witnesses, that when they came upon the scene – when they saw the body of Jacinta Smith – that that person was then deceased. They were both asked in cross examination regarding the position in which Jacinta Smith's legs were when they saw her, and both did indicate that her legs were straight. I have in evidence Mr Johnson's statement and it is quite clear from that statement that that is how he says the girl's legs were when he saw her. He was shown the photograph that is part of exhibit 10, that does show her legs separated, quite different when one looks at the photograph to the way he described them. And he said that they were not in that position when he saw them. Of course one could postulate that the change in position of her legs came about in some other way. I think perhaps that Mr Quinlivan was getting at that a little when he cross examined Constable McKenzie regarding the covering of the body of Jacinta Smith with the tarpaulin and whether it was possible that he had at that time some how moved her legs. But the constable did not agree that that was so, he merely said that he had covered her, and accordingly I would not postulate further in that regard. But clearly at that time she was dead and her body was in a different position to the position that it was in when it was photographed later that morning. And I do think that that is sufficient for me to be satisfied under S41(6) that there is a likelihood…a tendency that a jury would convict the defendant of that particular indictable offence.

'So far as the other matters are concerned there is nothing further before me than there was before me when I considered the matter under S41(2) and as I indicated when I look at the credibility of the witnesses, the weight and admissibility of the evidence, there is nothing there that would persuade me other than to say that there is a distinct likelihood that a jury would convict the defendant. That being the situation, it is my intention to commit the defendant in respect of all three matters for trial.

Please stand up, Mr Grant. In respect of the three matters that I have before me, the two charges of culpable driving and the charge of indecent interference, you are committed for trial to the district court at such time and place as the director of public prosecutions indicates. You're to be handed a form setting out details of alibi defence[47] and also the provisions of the obtaining of legal aid and without reading that form to you, you are represented and no doubt you will read that form with Mr Quinlivan, who will explain it to you.'

Grant, bewildered, looked to Quinlivan. But Quinlivan was still working the case. The magistrate asked about the question of bail, to which Quinlivan replied, 'Apparently the prosecution's point of view is that it might continue.'

Magistrate: 'Is that so?'

Prosecutor: 'That's so.'

Magistrate: 'Bail to continue in each of the three matters.' Cater-Smith left the court.

The sounds of voices from the public gallery rose so that it was impossible for Quinlivan to hear his client. They too left the court. Family and friends of the deceased poured from the single-storey building onto Oxley Street. They stood around in small groups watching as Quinlivan bundled Grant into a waiting car. As the car moved away, people began shouting, shaking their fists, running into the road. Grant looked out at them, at their faces, at the anger, the hatred. He saw too the mothers of the dead girls standing silently under the shade of a peppercorn tree. Their eyes followed him as he was driven away, south along Richard Street before turning left into Anson to get quickly beyond the town speed zone and onto the Mitchell Highway. Their eyes followed him until the car was out of sight. Committed to stand trial for driving charges and for indecently interfering with one of their babies. They wondered how he had got away with murder.

# 40

# The lawyers build their defence

For the few months following the committal hearing, activity slowed markedly, as it does in any legal case. The continuing compilation of evidence, the analysis of matter relevant to the case, the acquisition of defence support almost ceased until May 1989. It had taken months for Grant's solicitors to acquire a copy of the committal hearing transcript.[48]

In the meantime, Tony Quinlivan had drafted a letter to Picone & Howes which was posted on 11 November, four days after the hearing. Quinlivan provided a clear statement of what had transpired and what was required:

> I represented Mr Grant when his various charges were subjected to committal proceedings in the Local Court at Bourke on November 8th 1988. As you are aware, Mr Grant was committed to stand trial on all three charges. You will appreciate that this came as no surprise; indeed I did not submit against the Magistrate, Ms Cater-Smith, committing Mr Grant. There is only one issue in relation to the culpable driving charges; that is, whether or not Mr Grant was driving the motor vehicle at the relevant time. There is police evidence of an admission in this respect and accordingly committal for trial was inevitable. In relation to the other matter, there was evidence establishing the probability of Jacinta Smith's being dead at about 4.30am when Messrs Baty and Johnson came upon her body, evidence establishing that her breasts had been exposed between that time and when the police arrived at about 5.45am, and no evidence as to anyone other than Mr Grant having been responsible for the indecent interference. Necessarily then, Mr Grant was committed for trial in relation to

the allegation concerning the indecent interference with a corpse. Despite the clear prima facie cases, I think some headway was made towards eventually establishing defences to the charges. In relation to the last offence, whereas I doubt that there will ever be any prospect of disproving the probability of Jacinta Smith being dead when she was subjected to the allegedly indecent interference, the evidence from Messrs Baty and Johnson and from Constable McKenzie with respect to Mr Grant's apparent state of body and mind will not disassist our proposition that if Mr Grant was responsible for the interference then he had no capacity to form the criminal intent to effect it. So far as concerns the culpable driving charges, the evidence of Mr Grant being the driver (apart from the fact that it was his car) comes from the alleged admission to Constable McKenzie and evidence from a group of aboriginals who give evidence to the effect that Mona Smith was not able to drive a manual car. Although I do not believe that the 'aboriginal evidence' will ever be received as reliable, the admission will always be the big problem. However, I think we have gone some way to demonstrating that Constable McKenzie's allegedly corroborating hand-written notes are not, as he would have the Court believe, essentially contemporaneously made. If Constable McKenzie's credit is successfully impugned at trial then there is some prospect of a jury not accepting that the admission was made. Further to this, there is the prospect of the admission being kept out of evidence as a matter of fairness because of the state of Mr Grant. There is also a slim prospect of a jury not being satisfied that Mr Grant actually said that he was the driver, again, by reason of his severe state of intoxication and his incoherence at the time. Realistically though, I think it will be necessary to demonstrate, if it is possible, that Mr Grant probably was not driving, upon the available physical evidence. I refer here to the damage to the motor vehicle, the head injuries to Mona Smith, and the virtual absence of injury to Mr Grant. As soon as a transcript is available I recommend you take advice with respect to what experts should be employed in an effort to prove that both Mr Grant was not driving and Mona Smith was. Further, concerted efforts have to be made in an attempt to obtain evidence that Mona Smith was actually capable of driving. I look forward to advising in due course with respect to the engaging of appropriate experts and to further advising with respect to the evidential requirements of the case for trial.

Picone & Howes sent Quinlivan a copy of the committal transcript on 11 May 1989 with the addition of a paragraph seeking advice about the appropriateness of approaching an expert 'who may be able to assist us as to how the accident occurred and which way the vehicle rolled'. We might assume the solicitors exhausted all avenues in this regard, as no expert surfaced. Included with that correspondence was an information sheet titled 'Information to be Ascertained from the Defence', which was required to be filed at the Dubbo courthouse. The information sheet included requests for when witnesses may have been unavailable; the need for interpreters; whether fresh evidence had surfaced; whether the accused was fit to plead; whether a no bill application had been made; whether there was a chance the accused might change his plea; whether the defendant would be disadvantaged if the trial was not listed within the next twelve months; whether there were any special factors which should be taken into account when listing the matter.

By early June, the charge relating to high-range PCA was adjourned. Grant was living somewhere in Sydney, most likely in the southern suburbs, possibly in Bexley, at an address he had earlier given to police. He had some months to consider his position. We will see that before the trial in February 1990 he managed to get an acquaintance, a woman he was presumed to have then been in a relationship with, to write a reference letter on his behalf. But between June 1989 and February 1990 when he went to trial, there is some evidence that Grant found work in Sydney. In fact, by October 1989, there is hard evidence that he sought work as a taxi driver. His application was refused, however, because he had convictions recorded against him and charges pending.

On 18 September, Grant's solicitors informed Quinlivan that the matters had been listed for call-over on Friday 6 October at 10 a.m., in the district court at Sydney. A call-over occurs when a defence has been filed. It is an administrative procedure to make sure the matter is ready for trial and that parties have complied with a court's directions. It is heard before the trial judge.

Picone & Howes had received from the criminal listing directorate of the district court in Dubbo on 11 August the proposed draft indictment. The draft indictment read,

Alexander Ian Grant: on 6th December 1987, at Enngonia in the State of New South Wales, did drive a motor utility, whilst under the influence of intoxicating liquor, when through the said motor vehicle in which one Mona Lisa Smith was being conveyed, overturning, the death of the said Mona Lisa Smith was occasioned (Section 52A(1)(b)). And further, on 6th December 1987, at Enngonia in the State of New South Wales did drive a motor vehicle utility, whilst under the influence of intoxicating liquor, when through the said motor vehicle in which one Jacinta Rose Smith was being conveyed, overturning, the death of Jacinta Rose Smith was occasioned (Section 52A(1)(b)). And further, on 6th December, 1987, At Enngonia in the State of New South Wales, did offer indignity to a dead human body (Section 81C).

They then received from the same criminal listing directorate, on 12 September, notice of the listing for call-over with an additional notification that the case was listed for hearing at Bourke on 23 October. Bill Howes wrote immediately to Quinlivan with advice that they needed to inform the court that they were not ready for the hearing to commence. Howes indicated that the advice they had was 'contrary to the advices [sic] given to the writer by phone, they had placed the matter in the October sittings'. The schedule for Bourke court on 23 October included charges of maliciously inflicting actual bodily harm with intent to have intercourse; sexual intercourse without consent; maliciously inflicting grievous bodily harm; conspiring to pervert the course of justice; common assault and use offensive language; threatening injury to prevent lawful apprehension; assault; using an offensive weapon with intent to prevent lawful apprehension, possessing an unlicensed pistol, assault; escaping from lawful custody and assaulting an officer in the execution of duty; and manslaughter.[49] All of the cases on that day, with the exception of Grant's and two others, were represented by the Western Aboriginal Legal Service (WALS).[50]

The notice from the district court indicated that the call-over required information to be provided to the judge: the name of the crown (prosecutor) instructed in the matter; whether the matter was ready to proceed; the crown's estimate as to the duration of the trail; whether all witnesses were available during the sittings; and whether there were any issues that needed to be determined prior to the trial. It indicated the defendant did not need to attend the call-over if his solicitor was appearing on his behalf. Bill Howes attended the call-over and successfully argued for a later trial date. He argued that Mr Quinlivan was not available on the date proposed. The trial date was pushed out to 1 February 1990.

An additional three months was enormously important for the defence team; in the minds of Quinlivan and Howes was the prospect of presenting a case to the crown solicitor that would see the interference charge dropped. Their strategy was simple; get the crown solicitor to agree to ask the attorney general to 'no bill' the charge. A successful no bill application meant the charge would 'go away'. At the time of the accident and, following that, the charging and prosecuting of the defendant, the law in New South Wales was such that a prima facie test was all that was needed to prosecute.[51] Rozenes argues two fundamental considerations are now required: is the evidence sufficient to justify a prosecution and is a prosecution required in the public interest? The public interest test in the 1980s was something that had not been part of the social narrative other than inside the academies. Had it been, there is most likely no doubt that prosecution would have occurred and, more importantly, that the charge of offer indignity would not have been no billed. As it was, other important social vectors intersected, so that the defendant found himself at a time where his luck held.

We will return to the coalescing of events as they affected the decision of the attorney general, John Dowd, to uphold the no bill application.

# 41

## The no bill tactic

Two years had passed since the deaths and deprivations visited on Mona and Cindy on the Enngonia Road. Yet inexplicably the defence claimed they were unprepared for court. It must have seemed inconceivable to the families of the dead girls that the justice system appeared to favour the defendant.

Then, as now, justice moved slowly. The system in which charging and prosecution overlapped was cumbersome. The burden of proof lay with the prosecution. In the years between 1987 and 1990, political interference was running high in New South Wales as politicians struggled to restructure the police force and the judicial system. The objective was simple – eliminate the Protestant/Masonic power base within the justice system. At the time, there appeared on the surface to be no additional hidden play, yet over time the ascendancy and injection into New South Wales party politics of the Catholic Church deserves some investigation, which is outside the scope of this work.

It is not unreasonable, however, to argue that the internecine strife that was being wrought combined with other social factors to assist the attorney general in his decision to no bill the interference charge. So now there were two parallel strategies being presented by the defence. The first was the tactic to appeal to the solicitor-general to seek to no bill the interference charge. The second was to mount a defence against the charge of culpable driving – to argue Grant was not driving and, indeed, Constable McKenzie may have misheard him the morning of the accident when he said he was driving.

As we have seen, the matter was listed for call-over on Friday 9

October 1989. Mr Howes attended the Downing Centre court in Sydney, asked the district court judge Neil Newton for a later trial date, and presented other documents relevant to the case. His request was granted. Three days later, Grant was refused an application for a taxi driver's licence. This is an interesting aside as, in a handwritten statement three months later, Grant claimed he let his driver's licence expire in November 1989, a month after the taxi licence was refused.

On Wednesday 18 October, Howes received notification from the solicitor for public prosecutions that the prosecution intended to call an additional witness; Warwick Jay Hayes, the forensic analyst who had examined Cindy's clothing. Then things went quiet for a while. The tension was released.[52]

It was late December, almost Christmas, before Quinlivan and Howes conferred with Grant on the content of the no bill application. A compelling draft ensued. The draft application was addressed to the attorney general, John Dowd. A covering letter was addressed to the crown prosecutor, Terry Wolfe, under Tony Quinlivan's signature.

Dear Terry

You will recall that on December 14th 1989 I spoke with you about this matter. I had called you for the purpose of proposing that there ought to be separate trials of the 'culpable driving' and 'corpse' issues. It seemed to me that a fair trial of the culpable driving issues would be seriously prejudiced by having heard with them the material relevant only to the charge of offering an indignity to a dead human body. During the course of our discussion you invited me urgently to prepare and submit for your attention a 'No Bill' application in relation to the 'corpse' issue. With this letter you should also be in receipt of such application under the hand of my instructing solicitor. I understand that on or about January 22, 1990 you will be in a position to communicate the result of the No Bill application; I look forward to hearing from you then. Should the application not be successful, then I will maintain on my client's behalf the separate trial proposition mentioned above. Should the crown not concede the desirability of separate trials, then the Court will be moved for appropriate directions before the commencement of any trial at Bourke on January 29th, 1990.

We can see, before we look closely at the no bill application, that a conversation had occurred between the crown prosecutor and the defence barrister. We can also see from the language of the correspondence that the crown prosecutor may have had some concerns with the 'corpse' issue, as Quinlivan described it, as it related to a part of the state which had very recently, historically speaking, been subjected to violent demonstrations and 'riots' by Aborigines against the police and service providers in Bourke and surrounding towns. The Brewarrina riot of October 1987 had not faded from memory; in fact, the police had inflamed the issue when allegations and a video recording surfaced of police attending a party in 1989 wearing black face paint and nooses around their necks. One was heard to say, 'I'm Lloyd Boney' before holding up a noose. In 1992, ABC television news ran the video footage with New South Wales Premier Nick Greiner stating that the police had responsibilities while on the job and off duty. Earlier in April 1989, an Aboriginal man named David Gundy had been killed in a police raid on a property in Redfern, New South Wales. Special weapons and tactical operations police had been searching for another man when Gundy was accidentally killed. The issue of police and Aboriginal relations was then something the crown prosecutor must have considered very carefully when he spoke with Quinlivan. Otherwise, Wolfe was expected to make his recommendation on the basis of a conversation with the defence barrister and a seven-page outline of the case written by the defence. Whether or not the prosecution made representations to Wolfe to reject the application is unknown. What he received from the defence was the following, addressed to the honourable the attorney-general, John Dowd:

We are the solicitors acting for the abovenamed accused. Mr Grant will stand trial in the District Court at Bourke on January 29th

1990. We have been advised that the crown presently proposes to indict Mr Grant on two charges of culpable driving and a charge of offering indignity to a dead human body (Section 81C Crimes Act 1900). We write to respectfully submit that you ought direct that no further proceedings be taken against the accused in relation to the Section 81C matter. On December 6th, 1987 Jacinta Smith died from injuries sustained in a motor vehicle accident at Enngonia. The Section 81C allegation relates to the late Jacinta Smith, and, as the crown case is understood, the relevant 'indignity' is said to be the moving of her T-shirt and exposing of her chest; of course, the allegation is that this occurred after she died. This application is made on two bases. Firstly, that there is no evidence capable of proving beyond reasonable doubt that Jacinta Smith was dead at the time her T-shirt was removed. Secondly, that the inferences available to be drawn from the accused's intoxication are such that a reasonable jury, properly instructed, would not be satisfied beyond reasonable doubt that if the T-shirt was moved by the accused, he did it voluntarily. The only evidence as to when the motor vehicle accident happened, comes from the accused himself in the course of various records of interview and statements to police. Though the crown would be circumspect as to the reliability of the accused in his versions, not least because of his intoxicated state, there seems no reason to suppose the accused was consciously misleading when he offered approximate times of the accident, shortly after police investigations commenced. The necessity to rely on the accused's timing of the accident is noted, for instance, in some of the crown's preparation of its case – expert pharmacological evidence as to the accused's probable blood/alcohol level at the time of the accident is obtained from Dr Judith Perl on the assumption that the accident happened when the accused said it happened. The accused has said the accident happened between about 1.00 a.m. and 3.00 a.m. on December 6th, 1987. In the Record of Interview on December 6th, 1987 (Q.27) the accused said the accident happened 'about 1 or 2 o'clock, I don't know, I don't know'. Earlier in his statement to Constable Clarke as to when the accident happened the accused said 'I don't know, I can't honestly say about 2 o'clock, 3 o'clock I don't know I can't confirm it, it was around, let me think, I'd be telling lies if I said, it could have been 1 o'clock, 2 o'clock, I don't know, it could have been later'. Circumstantial evidence as to the likely time of the accident does not assist in finding a more accurate estimate of the time of the accident. Mr Barnett's statement has him selling alcohol to the accused at about 10:00 p.m. on December 5th 1987. The accident happened about 63 kilometres from Bourke. But the journey was apparently interrupted by ' ...the toilet...a smoke...a yarn' (see Record of Interview, December 6th 1987 Q.17). Between about 4.30 a.m. and 4.50 a.m. on December 6th, 1987 Messrs Baty and Johnson came upon the aftermath of the accident. It is Mr Baty's evidence of the upper part of Jacinta Smith's body then being covered which provides the evidence of her chest being exposed thereafter, or so it was when Constable McKenzie arrived at 5.45 a.m. Mr Baty had contacted Constable McKenzie by 5.15 a.m., about 25 minutes after leaving the accident scene (see Constable McKenzie's statement and Committal Transcript p.59.10). So he left the accident scene about 4.50 a.m. Mr. Johnson left about 5.00 a.m. (see Committal Transcript p.66.5). In our submission, no admissible evidence proves beyond reasonable doubt that Jacinta Smith was dead about 5.00 a.m., at about which time the T-shirt may have been moved. (We assume here, for the benefit of the crown case, that Mr Baty's observation that Jacinta Smith was wearing a buttoned-up white blouse (see his statement and Committal Transcript p.58.8) may be excused as a mistake not affecting the reliability of his evidence that the upper part of the body was covered by clothing. Certainly, the lay impression of Messrs Baty and Johnson was that Jacinta Smith was dead – indeed, at first, Mr Baty believed the accused was dead (Committal Transcript p.60.6) – but this will not prove the necessary element of Jacinta Smith's death. The only admissible relevant evidence providing a timing of Jacinta Smith's death is that of Dr Pringle. His relevant evidence during the committal proceedings is this – 'The trouble with this sort of case is that when one sees a person who died from a motor vehicle accident and they're found dead after the accident you ... don't really know how long they've survived for. I think the death could have occurred very rapidly with her, it need not have been immediate' (Committal Transcript pp. 55.10-56.1). The doctor gave further evidence that it would not be regarded as scientifically extraordinary if Jacinta Smith had lived for two hours after she sustained her injuries (Committal Transcript p. 56. 3) (The doctor's evidence that 'you really don't know how long they've survived for' demonstrates the Section 81C charge be proved by the crown; the evidence does not prove beyond reasonable doubt that Jacinta Smith was dead at about 5.00 a.m., between two and four hours after the accident happened, on such evidence as there is to that event. If the crown were to rely upon the state of undress of Jacinta Smith's lower body as evidence relevant to the Section 81C charge, then such occurred before 4.30 a.m. and again, the evidence is incapable of proving Jacinta Smith was then dead. If the crown were to rely upon the possible change in position of Jacinta Smith's legs between about 5.00 a.m. and 5.45 a.m. then, as earlier submitted, the evidence is not capable of proving beyond reasonable doubt that Jacinta Smith was dead at about 5.00 a.m. and indeed, the evidence concerning the change in position of Jacinta Smith's legs is consistent with her then being alive.

The second basis for this application relates to the accused's intoxication at about the time of the accident, and at about 5.00a.m. on December 6th 1987, the probably relevant time of his allegedly offering any indignity to Jacinta Smith's body. Quite apart from the inferences that flow from Dr Perl's scientific evidence of the accused's advanced intoxication, Constable McKenzie's evidence of the accused's general incoherence at about 6.00 a.m. (Committal Transcript p. 37.5) and Mr Baty's and Mr Johnson's evidence of the accused soporific state between about 4.30 a.m. and 5.00 a.m. all goes to disenable the crown from proving beyond reasonable doubt that any form of alleged interference with Jacinta Smith's clothes or body was voluntarily undertaken by the accused. When Mr Baty left the accused he said '…he sort of went back to sleep or passed back out' (Committal Transcript p.59.3). The accused's own evidence of his condition before and after Messrs Baty and Johnson appeared was that he was 'blacked out' (see Record of Interview December 9th, 1987, Q.27 and Q. 28). On the two submitted bases, we very respectfully anticipate that you will direct that no further proceedings be taken against the accused in relation to the Section 81C matter.

# 42

# The O'Connor defence

As we have seen from the application to have the charge of interference no billed, the defence relied upon the probability that Cindy could have still been alive when her breasts were exposed. The defence did not draw attention to the fact that her tracksuit pants had also been interfered with, exposing her stomach, genitals and legs. It touched lightly upon the idea that her legs had been moved but it did not dwell on the statements that presented evidence that her legs changed position between when she was observed by Baty and Johnson and the time when McKenzie arrived at the scene. The evidence, the defence argued, was incapable of proving beyond reasonable doubt that Cindy was dead at the time. The second basis for the application related to Grant's state of intoxication and thus, the overarching theme of the defence presented by O'Connor to the High Court of Australia in June 1980.[53]

In their forty-two-page decision Barwick C.J., Gibbs, Stephen, Mason, Murphy, Aickin and Wilson J.J., made it clear that the case was complex and in its complexity it opened many avenues for behaviour that would not normally be accepted within a structured, well-functioning society. As Chief Justice Barwick explained, Mr O'Connor was indicted by the Supreme Court of Victoria on two counts: one of stealing (*Crimes Act 1958* (Vict.), as amended, s.72), the other, under s.17 of that Act, of wounding with intent to resist arrest. He was acquitted of the charges by the jury but found guilty of an alternative charge made available by s.423 of that Act. That section provided that where on the trial of any person for any felony except murder or manslaughter the presentment indictment or information alleges that the defendant did wound or did cause grievous bodily harm to any person and the jury are satisfied that the defendant is guilty of the wounding or of inflicting the grievous bodily harm charged in such presentment indictment or information but are not satisfied that the defendant is guilty of the felony charged they may acquit him of such felony and find him guilty of unlawfully wounding or of inflicting grievous bodily harm (as the case may be); and he shall be liable to punishment accordingly.

The circumstances of the case were that the respondent was observed by a neighbour pilfering a car owned by an officer of the Victoria police. The car was standing outside the block of flats in which the officer lived. A neighbour alerted the officer to what was going on. By the time the officer reached his car, O'Connor had removed from it a map holder and a knife. The officer, having identified himself to O'Connor, asked him why he took the map holder. O'Connor ran away. The officer ran after him, caught up with him and arrested him. During the course of his arrest, the respondent opened the blade of the knife he had taken from the car and, seemingly in an endeavour to resist, stabbed the constable. At the time, O'Connor said, 'I don't know anything, I wasn't there.' At his trial, O'Connor gave evidence that he had been taking a particular drug and also drinking alcohol during a substantial part of the day of the occurrence and that he had no recollection of what had occurred that day with the officer or with the officer's car. His only recollection was of placing his foot in an open door of a white car. According to medical evidence called on his behalf, the drug O'Connor claimed to have been taking was hallucinatory and in association with alcohol could have rendered him incapable of reasoning and of forming an intent to steal or to wound. The acts attributed to O'Connor were consistent with the effects of the hallucinogenic drug. The trial judge instructed the jury that they could take into account the evidence as to the respondent's intoxicated condition when considering the charges of theft and of wounding to resist arrest, but that they could not take that evidence into consideration when considering the alternative charge of unlawful wounding. The judge founded this direction on the reasons given by the House of Lords, London, in *Director of Public Prosecutions v. Majewski* (1977) AC 44.

O'Connor appealed to the Court of Criminal Appeal of Victoria. That court was not prepared to accept the views expressed in Majewski. Basing themselves largely on views expressed by Garfield Barwick in *Ryan v. The Queen* (1967) 121 CLR 205, the Victorian Criminal Appeal Court allowed O'Connor's appeal and entered a verdict of acquittal on the alternative charge. O'Connor was discharged.

The Solicitor-General for Victoria, appearing in support of an application for special leave, pressed on the court the views of their lordships in Majewski's case. He submitted that O'Connor's evidence of self-induced intoxication was irrelevant to the consideration by the jury of the charge of unlawful wounding. He claimed that such evidence was inadmissible on the trial of a charge of a crime which did not require that the act charged should have been done to achieve a particular purpose, that is to say, where the charge was not of a crime, as he said, of 'specific intent'. The solicitor-general explanation was that voluntary intoxication whether by alcohol or by another drug or by a combination of drugs is irrelevant in the case of a crime described as a crime of only 'basic intent' on the basis that the voluntary ingestion of the alcohol or self-administration of another drug by an accused precludes him asserting or endeavouring to establish that the acts performed whilst so intoxicated were involuntary acts, that is, unaccompanied by an exercise of his will, or that he had not had an intent to do the act charged. The solicitor-general said that the voluntary nature of the ingestion or administration of the alcohol or other drug renders all the acts of a criminal nature done during the resulting intoxicated state voluntary acts for relevant purposes: and that the intention to do the criminal act whilst so intoxicated must be unchallengeably presumed. Thus, the voluntary taking of the alcohol and drugs to the point of intoxication satisfied the requirements of the relevant *mens rea*.

An alternative explanation of the submission given by the solicitor-general was that while criminal responsibility did not ordinarily attach to an involuntary act or to an act done without the requisite intent, self-induced intoxication constitutes an exception from the general rule, an exception based on 'public policy'.

O'Connor's counsel submitted that the High Court ought not to adopted the reasoning and conclusion of the House of Lords; that it should have declared the common law in accordance with recognised principles, namely, that no person can be convicted of doing a criminal act which that person had not voluntarily done and that no person can be convicted of any crime unless the proscribed act was done by that person with the actual intent appropriate to the commission of the particular crime. He submitted that there was no basis in the common law for presuming an act to be voluntary beyond challenge or for presuming unchallengeably that an accused had the actual intent necessary to constitute the crime.

Chief Justice Barwick was concerned that the application by O'Connor's counsel raised a 'fundamental question of grave import'. He added, in what today may seem a somewhat archaic aside, that the High Court of Australia was now 'the final arbiter of what is the common law in Australia'. In this, Barwick was reflecting on the then recent dismantling of the avenue of appeal to the Privy Council in England if a High Court decision did not fall in favour of an applicant. That avenue had been cut off by the Whitlam government. In 1980, when O'Connor was being handed down, it remained a contentious issue. Barwick added,

> In days before the common law fundamentals of criminal liability with which we are now familiar had been educed and declared, it was said that drunkenness was no defence to or excuse for the commission of crime: indeed, it might be an exacerbation of the

offence. This formulation still retains some currency. The use of the words defence and excuse suggests that the saying is based on the idea that drunkenness might furnish a defence to or excuse for an offence otherwise established. But proof of a state of intoxication, whether self-induced or not, so far from constituting itself a matter of defence or excuse, is at most merely part of the totality of the evidence which may raise a reasonable doubt as to the existence of essential elements of criminal responsibility.[54]

In his consideration of O'Connor, Barwick opined that

the conviction is of unlawful wounding. But the physical act which supported it was the stabbing with a knife. Doubtless, such an act would be likely to wound. But in relation to intent, it is important, none the less, I think, to distinguish between an intent to use the knife and an intent to wound. In a sense, wounding as a result of the stabbing: perhaps an immediate result. I have taken a minimal position in relation to intent and say that at the least an intent to do the physical act involved in the crime charged is indispensable to criminal responsibility.

Barwick's opinion is directly relevant to the argument put by Quinlivan and Howes on behalf of Alex Grant. The charge was offer indignity but the physical act which supported it was the moving of Cindy's clothing and the positioning of her legs. If we insert Barwick's words, then, 'doubtless, such an act was likely to offer indignity in itself. But in relation to intent it was important to distinguish between an intent to arrange the clothing and an intent to offer indignity (or to consider some other sexual encounter)'. Barwick also remarked that

the distinction between basic intent and specific intent becomes less logically attractive if the view is taken that the basic intent must extend both to the physical act and to its immediate consequence. To add an additional consequence to the *actus reus* scarce warrants a distinction between the two types of crime in relation to the quality and extent of the intent, the *mens rea*, required in the one and that required in the other.

Barwick speculated further that the House of Lords decision[55] may have rested on the idea of public policy – of safeguarding citizens and maintaining social order.

It is important to grasp the significance of the term 'social order' so that we may enhance our understanding of the prosecution case against Mr Grant and of how Mr Quinlivan arrived at a decision to invoke the O'Connor defence. It also goes some way to explaining the thinking of the attorney-general John Dowd in consenting to no bill the charge. The government of New South Wales has never been able to create an effective policy of social order in towns such as Bourke. Governments may have been willing but the lack of ability is keenly demonstrated, as we have seen above, by comparative analysis of the number of police stationed in Bourke with numbers in similar-sized towns across the state. Social order has eluded governments of all political types.

When Barwick wrote of social order occurring in England due to public policy, his meaning of social order applied to how it ought to have been exercised in the public sphere as defined by European social theory. This, of course, was a long way from the reality of Bourke and the other so-called 'aboriginal towns' of north-western New South Wales for all of the twentieth century. Barwick and the other High Court judges were not working in the real world. They were handing down decisions based upon constitutional proscription. Even Lionel Murphy, the former Whitlam government attorney-general, was constrained, though he had many left-of-centre supporters keen to display him publicly as the voice of the people.

Barwick further speculated that the House wanted to treat the 'wantonness' of intoxication as a form of recklessness or wickedness of mind which satisfied the requirement of *mens rea*. It may be that Mr Grant had no *mens rea* – no guilty mind, or no intention to commit a prohibited act. Alternatively, it might be assumed that his state of intoxication on Saturday 5 December 1987 was such that in the sequence of physical acts undertaken by him – picking up teenage girls in the street at night; buying alcohol for them at the North Bourke hotel at 10 p.m.; allowing an unlicensed teenager to drive his vehicle; exposing the breasts and genitals of a fifteen-year-old (dead or alive) all add up to the possibility of demonstrating intent to commit an act or acts which lie outside the framework of social order and well within the framework of *mens rea*.

# 43

# The ordinary life story

Television provides an almost infinite variety of criminal, courtroom and victim dramas. The production houses of the United Kingdom and the United States of America seem almost pathologically intrigued by the state of crime, especially violent crime and violent death. Forensic analysis and microscopic investigation into evidence invariably lead to charges and convictions and the reinforcement of right versus wrong where right wins. Only rarely do those charged with televisual crimes escape a custodial sentence, as it is referred to. The televisual justice system is a thing of great beauty.

As we have seen, however, the real world is very different. It took more than two years for Grant to come to trial. Even then, the date was changed twice to accommodate the defence. The prosecution was taking witness statements in the days before the trial – Kevin Harper, the police officer on duty at Enngonia on the morning of the accident, was interviewed at Gulargambone police station on Monday 29 January 1990 – three days before the trial. One day before the trial, Wednesday 31 January, ambulance officer Ron Willoughby gave a statement about his inspection of the accident site. Ambulance officer Kelvin Brennan was located at Armidale ambulance station. He too gave a statement. Neither Harper, Brennan, nor Willoughby had been subjected to interviews nor asked to provide statements at an earlier time. Willoughby's statement was witnessed by Richard Le Merton. No witness signature appeared on Harper's statement. Brennan's was witnessed by a Constable Phillip O'Toole at Armidale police station.

A week and a half earlier, in a vain attempt to prove himself of good character, Grant had got his girlfriend to write a short letter on his behalf and also to write one from her perspective about him. The handwritten letters, in neat, cursive script stated,

I Alexander Ian Grant was born in Hamilton, New Zealand, on the 22/9/47. I went to Fairfield College in Hamilton. I left college at the age of 15 and went to work on my uncles [sic] sheep farm milking cows, until I was 18. I then started driving trucks, buses and taxis. I married a farm girl but we got divorced 4 years later. I then moved to Auckland and was earthmoving for 61/2 years, before coming to Australia in 1977. I worked on Groote Eyland for 2 years before I went to work in Moree, and Wee Waa, on the cotton irrigation. I then became a partner in an Excavation business for some 3 1/2 years, until the accident. I sold out of the partnership as a result of this as I knew I couldn't handle the business. At the time I was drinking to [sic] much but I did not realize or wouldn't listen. On coming to Sydney I went to the A. A. and that made me sit up and take notice of the problems of alchol [sic] and something I couldn't believe. Now I use public transport for work and I don't worry about driving any more. In fact I have not renewed my license [sic] since it expired in November 1989.

The second letter read,

To Whom It May Concern

I am living in a de facto relationship with Mr Alexander Ian Grant, whom I have known for the past 20 years. After the death of my sons [sic] father in New Zealand I came to Australia for a holiday with a friend of mine. I met Mr Grant while I was here. We started going out together and after awhile we decided to live in a de facto relationship. I returned to New Zealand and packed up everything in my house and had it sent over on a boat. We have been together for 18 months and he has never once driven a car after drinking alchol [sic]. We both always travel on Public transport. We have discussed his accident on several occassions [sic] and my honest opinion is that I find it very hard to believe that he was driving when this accident occurred. Even when he drank alchol [sic] in New Zealand I never seen him drive a vehicle after. I have found him to be a very kind and honest person and he has said to me over and over again that he was not driving the vehicle when his accident occured [sic], I must say that I do believe he is telling the truth. There is absolutely no doubt in my mind about this.

Yours sincerely

Linda Jane Windsor

The letters remained in the possession of Mr Quinlivan. They were not tendered as evidence at the trial.

In the same week, the registrar at the district court criminal registry responded to the no bill application with a three-paragraph statement that read,

I advise you that the Director of Public Prosecutions decided on 23rd January, 1990 not to proceed further against the accused in respect of the above charge. Please note that the remainder of the charges still pending against the accused, are to proceed to trial. Please inform the Criminal Listing Directorate accordingly.

The letter was dated 24 January. It was signed on behalf of the Director of Public Prosecutions. There was great relief in the defence camp. It was now a simple matter for Quinlivan to convince the trial jury of the evidence that Grant could not have been driving the vehicle at the time of the accident – that they ought to be persuaded beyond reasonable doubt.

On Wednesday 31 January, Grant, Quinlivan and Howes made their way back to Bourke. Ehsman and Le Merton were already there, as was Terry Wolfe the crown prosecutor. Godkin however, was not. Sergeant Godkin had since left the police for a community role – he was then president of the Australian Commonwealth Games Cycling Association which, at that very time, was competing in Auckland, New Zealand. In what appeared to be a last-ditch effort to present a strong prosecution case, Godkin was called back to Australia for the trial by none other than police commissioner John Avery.[56]

# 44

# The end game

Family and friends of the dead girls packed the public spaces of the court house in Bourke on Thursday 1 February 1990. Their expectations were high. They had not been informed directly of the result of the no bill application. Indeed, they had not known such a thing existed or was even possible. Their world consisted of summary justice – being caught and charged by the police with traffic offences and petty crime, hauled up before a magistrate and convicted. A large number of people in the court that day could have been identified as summary offenders who had appeared before a magistrate, charged and been sent to prison for a maximum of two years. Others had been charged and fined, though it was more usual than not that the offenders were unable to pay the fines. A small number knew the consequences of indictable offences – they held positive expectations that Grant would be charged. They were unprepared for the weakness of the prosecution case. They were unprepared for the fact that Grant was not being tried for the offer indignity to a dead human body charge.

On 8 February, after six days before district court judge Neil Newton, the jury handed down a verdict of not guilty. His honour discharged the jury and the accused. Messrs Grant, Quinlivan and Howes required a police escort from the courthouse. They knew the drill. It was a warm Thursday evening. Daylight saving. They drove quickly onto the Mitchell Highway.

The ghosts of the teenage cousins, Mona Smith and Cindy Smith, lay still and silent by the side of the road.

# Author's note

This is not a remarkable story. It did not alter history nor change society. It is the story of two teenaged Aboriginal girls who lived and died in the remote outback Australian town of Bourke. Both girls died in tragic and violent circumstances. There was no international media coverage, no protest marches and no global social media screaming for justice.

When I met Tony Quinlivan towards the end of summer 1990, we discussed his defence of his client against multiple charges relating to the violent and bloody deaths of Mona and Cindy. Tony talked in detail about the event and about the outcome – particularly the committal hearing and the trial. He spoke of his use of a defence that had recently been successfully appealed at the High Court. He recounted his opinion of the police case; how they had altered various charges; how they had gone about the gathering of evidence. His story was absorbing, though ultimately difficult for me to follow as I was not trained in the law. I met with him on a number of occasions. I then set the project aside.

It was not until October 2014 that I fulfilled a long-held promise to myself, to Cindy and Mona and to Tony. I went to Bourke, following the road Tony and others had taken in the years between the crash in December 1987, and the trial in February 1990. I drove to Orange, where I had lunch with Mark and Linda Filmer, with whom I have been friends for more than twenty years. Mark is one of the best journalists I have known. He is insightful, highly intelligent and honest. As we talked about the journey to Bourke and the reason for it, he listened intently. He then fossicked in his library and turned up a copy of a book entitled *The Shearer's Tale* by a lawyer named Tom Molomby. Mark said he thought it would resonate and provide structure, given what I was attempting. As usual, he was right. I read Molomby's book and it did indeed assist me to develop a structure.

In Bourke, I looked at sites and scenes that had become real in my imagination. I visited the library and the local newspaper office. I drove around the Reserve, around the levee, and out to Enngonia. I inspected the crash site as closely as possible, using the sketch plan drawn by Ken McKenzie. I sat in the courthouse and I walked along the streets where Cindy and Mona walked before that fateful night. I looked for the pubs where the accused consumed thirty drinks before he met Cindy and Mona on the street. Some things had changed in Bourke in the intervening years but overall it remained pretty much as it was in December 1987. It was a town full of despair and deprivation.

At Bourke cemetery, I could find no evidence of the graves that may have marked the resting places of the girls. There is a large stone monument in the cemetery in memory of eye surgeon Fred Hollows. Overall, the cemetery is in disrepair.

I did not feel confident, nor that it would be acceptable, to make approaches or appeals to Cindy or Mona's relatives, even if it were possible to find them. I was in unfamiliar territory professionally and culturally and I did not wish to cause grief. I spent time in and around Bourke then drove east through Brewarrina, Wee Waa and Walgett.

There is nothing remarkable in the story itself. Nor is there anything significant about the actors in the event – the girls, the man charged with their deaths, the police, the defence lawyers, the court. I have attempted to frame the event as nothing more than it was – a sad, brief encounter between three people that left two of them dead and the third defending himself against some nasty charges. It had not let go of me and it took me a quarter of a century before I was able to write Cindy and Mona's story.

I did not write their story with hope in mind. It is a story of despair from beginning to end. If there is any hope, it is that their story will reach a wider audience. Their lives were lost in tragic circumstances but their story is now told. Tony Quinlivan gave me their story. I owed him. And I owed Mona and Cindy.

# Notes

1. Enngonia Police station was a small single-storey dwelling in the middle of town. It was one of three permanent buildings, which included the primary school and the pub, which was more like a demountable school building itself than a pub. There were a few houses scattered along the highway. The police residence adjoined the station.

2. In flood, the waters of the Darling River cover a large part of northern and western New South Wales. In the monotone of flat landscape between its source near Brewarrina and its mouth at Wentworth, there are few obstacles capable of holding back its vastness over its 1,472-kilometre length. Such is the flat open plain of its existence that early builders of roads, railways and towns used levees and embankments to keep agriculture and industry flowing when the Darling flooded. The Mitchell Highway between Bourke and the Queensland border is one such road. It is banked high along its length with culverts regularly placed and table drains on either side with batters of twenty degrees. The Mitchell Highway between Bourke and Enngonia runs flat and at times straight. It is not as straight as the section between Nyngan and Bourke but the stretch on which the accident occurred on the night of 6 December was straight for three kilometres south to Bourke and two kilometres north to Enngonia. The weather was clear. The vehicle in which Alex Grant was travelling with Mona and Cindy Smith left the roadway sometime between midnight and 2 a.m. on Sunday 6 December. Deep gouge marks on the bitumen indicate that the vehicle swerved across the road, then, in an attempt to correct, swerved in the other direction, was uncontrolled and rolled a number of times along the table drain on the western side of the road. It came to a halt in scrub, on its wheels, a couple of hundred metres on. Gear from the utility was strewn along the side of the road.

3. There were few commercial buildings and no houses of more than a single storey in Bourke in 1987. Houses were constructed of timber, asbestos

245

cement and corrugated iron. Some of the older colonial buildings were made of brick. The newspaper office, which was located in a residential area, was built of stone and brick. The older houses on the Reserve were constructed of asbestos cement and corrugated iron.

4. In NSW, beers are sold in different-sized glasses, with a standard drink defined as ten grams of alcohol. A full-strength beer in a 'middy' glass is 1.1 standard drinks or 285ml, which is ten fluid ounces. Middies and schooners are the main glass sizes in NSW, in which a schooner is fifteen fluid ounces, or 425ml. A schooner of full-strength beer is equivalent to 1.6 standard drinks.

5. As an aside, the *Sydney Morning Herald* of 23 August 1950 reported the town of Bourke had been cut off by a flood in the Darling that reached a height of forty five feet eleven inches above its normal level. The railway line built above the flood level was the only access.

6. The Act has since been amended. Recent statistics show that 14.5% of suspended sentences are for driving while disqualified and 3.2% for high-range PCA (Brignell & Poletti 2003).

7. Grant's criminal history record indicated that on 20 January 20 1988, six weeks after the fatal accident, he was charged with exceeding the speed limit by more than fifteen kilometres an hour. He was fined $50. It is unknown whose vehicle he was driving or where the offence took place. Two weeks later, Grant received a warning letter from the Roads and Traffic Authority in relation to speeding offences of October 1986 and January 1988.

8. For the full text of the letter, see chapter 43.

9. Clarke's notes show the word 'Grant' written in capital letters throughout the interview.

10. A few months earlier, on 15 August, Sergeant Reid had been directly involved in a riot in the nearby town of Brewarrina following the funeral of local Aboriginal man Lloyd James Boney, who had been found hanged in a police cell in Brewarrina on 6 August.

11. Bourke is now part of what is known as the Darling River Local Area Command, or LAC. It has three police at the rank of inspector with different geographic responsibilities. One inspector is responsible for

Bourke, another is responsible for Brewarrina, Enngonia and Wanaaring, and the third is responsible for Nyngan, Cobar, Warren and Nymagee.

12. Wootten 1991.

13. In 1987, the Bourke Golf Club housed a bar, a restaurant and a good quality sand-green eighteen-hole golf course rated par 72. It was the preserve of the service providers. It no longer has a trading licence nor a restaurant and is known now as the Darling River Golf Club. Back then, however, it was the province of the coppers, white business owners and public servants. Aborigines were generally not allowed in. There may have been one or two who appeared to be more white than black and who may have played golf. They would have been the exceptions.

14. Pringle reported,

> Both labia were swollen, the right more than the left. There was no sign of injury to either of the swollen labia nor were there any signs of injury to the labia minors or in the vestibula about the lower end of the vagina. The pubic hairs appeared dry and separate and showed no signs of being matted together. The external genitalia in general appeared relatively dry. Swabbings were taken from 1) the labia majora, the labia minora and the vestibule and 2) from the lower part of the vagina. On the front and inner aspect of the lower part of the left thigh, on the inside of the left knee and on the front and inner side of the left leg as well as on the inner aspect of the right leg just below the knee there were several areas of dried material some oval and others irregular in outline which had a glistening surface when viewed obliquely in good light. Photographs were taken of these areas and an attempt was made to sample this material with swabs moistened with sterile normal saline; two such swabbings were taken from the left thigh. As these areas were being sampled with the saline moistened swabs there was no sign of this material become sticky as it was moistened. A large piece of skin bearing some of this dried material on it was removed and divided into two parts; one was placed in a sterile dry container for forensic biological examination and the other was placed in formal saline for microscopic examination.
>
> Extensive sheets of abrasions were present on the front and side of

the left half of the trunk and over the right half of the back and buttock and the upper half approximately of the back of the right thigh. These areas generally appeared dark and haemorrhagic. Photographs were taken of them. On the front of the right half of the trunk the abrasions were in two parts; one 18cm long and up to 5cm wide, extended from the upper part of the chest above the breast to the level of the top of the iliac crest. The other commenced on the outer aspect of the upper part of the hip where it was 11cm wide; it extended forwards almost horizontally for a distance of 19cm onto the interior abdominal wall in the right lower quadrant of the abdomen. On the left side of the back of the body the abrasions covered an area 54cm long and were in two parts, separated by a strip of skin, about 10-15cm wide, above and below the posterior part of the iliac crest. The upper of these two areas was up to 18cm wide and extended from the lower scapular area to the loin. Several ragged splits were present in the skin here and were roughly parallel with the spine; subcutaneous fat was visible in the depths of a few of these splits. The lower of these areas was up to 12cm wide and extended from the upper part of the right buttock to about the middle of the thigh. Several parallel scratches close together and running in the same direction as the long axis of the body were present in this abrasion.

A dark haemorrhagic abrasion 9 x 5cm was present on the outer side of the lower part of the right arm. A scratch 9cm long ran upwards from it towards the shoulder. Below it on the back and outer side of the elbow and forearm there were several smaller dark abrasions and scratches. A dark haemorrhagic abrasion with a hard dried surface about 9cm long and 2cm wide was present over the left frontal eminence; its outer end was 2cm above the outer end of the eyebrow. It sloped upward towards the middle of the forehead and ended 4cm above the inner half of the eyebrow. An area of bruising was present over the right cheek and a ragged triangular shaped laceration about 2cm across was present at the junction of the left nostril with the face. No fractures were detected in the bones of the skull face or jaw. Several small slightly brown abrasions with dried hard surfaces were distributed across the neck — one over the lower part of the right sterno-mastoid, two in much the same position over the left sterno-mastoid and one in the supraclavicular are close to the outer end of the left clavicle. No fractures were detected in the bones of the limbs.

15. Further, Pringle stated,

Within the abdomen and pelvis the following were observed: A large amount of blood was present in the peritoneal cavity. The liver had two very deep tears into its right lobe posteriorly and several superficial tears in its convex outer surface. The left lobe of the liver was undamaged. There was a fracture of the pelvis anteriorly on the left side through the superior pubic ramus. On the right side the sacro iliac joint had been disrupted and was completely disarticulated — the fingers could be inserted through the sprung joint as far as the posterior surface of the sacrum. A few sharp pieces of bones stuck out from the ilium immediately adjacent to the joint.

The urinary bladder was ruptured – its internal surface was exposed through the tear anteriorly involving its full length. There was heavy bleeding into the extra-peritoneal and retropubic tissues of the pelvis. This bleeding appeared to be in continuity with a haematoma in the right labium majus and the area of lividity-like discolouration in the lower abdomen immediately above the pubic area, in the inguinal regions and in the inner aspects of the upper parts of the thigh.

The right psoas major muscle on the posterior abdominal wall had ruptured above the pelvis and there was heavy bleeding into the retroperitoneal tissues on the posterior abdominal wall, more on the right that on the left side. The right kidney was obscured by heavy bleeding into the tissues around it but it was not torn or otherwise damaged; the right suprarenal gland had been disrupted by haemorrhage. The left kidney, ureter and suprarenal gland were normal.

The stomach contained a small amount of dark grey green thick fluid material with a faintly alcoholic smell. It appeared normal as did also the duodenum and the small and large intestines. The appendix was present.

The upper part of the vagina in the pelvis was opened so that access both for visual inspection and for swabbing of its interior could be gained. No fluid resembling semen or cervical mucus was seen. A swabbing was however taken from this part of the vagina for examination for seminal material.

The remaining abdominal and pelvic organs were normal. No fractures were seen in the lumbar spine.

Within the chest which included the structures in the neck the following was seen:

There were no fractures in the cervical spine. The pharynx, larynx, trachea and major bronchi contained gastric material; similar material was subsequently found in the air passages within the tissues of both lungs. The thyroid gland was normal.

A small amount of blood was found in the right plural cavity. There were no fractures in the ribs and sternum or in the thoracic spine. The diaphragm was intact and normal.

A small haematoma was present in the upper lobe of the right lung. Haemorrhages were present in both lungs, more on the right than on the left side.

About 5 to 10 mls of clear fluid was present in the pericardial sac. The heart and major blood vessels were normal.

The esophagus was normal.

On reflecting the scalp from the skull haemorrhages were seen in the scalp and on the surface of the skull over a wider area than that occupied by the abrasion seen externally over the left frontal eminence. No intracranial haemorrhages were seen after the skull was opened.

There were no fractures in the vault or base of the skull.

The brain appeared normal.

The following organs were reserved for examination by the Government Analytical Laboratories: Blood, femoral vein, for alcohol estimation; Blood, cardiac, for alcohol estimation; Pericardial fluid, for alcohol estimation; The liver; The stomach and its contents; Bile

The following specimens were reserved for examination by the Division of Forensic Medicine:

In one container: Heart 1 piece, Lung 2 pieces, liver 1 piece, kidney 1 piece

In a second container: Skin from left leg with dried material on it.

The following specimens were reserved for examination by the

Department of Forensic Biology:

    Swabbing vulva (1)

    Swabbing lower vagina (1)

    Swabbing upper vagina (1)

    Swabbing dried material left thigh (2)

    Skin – left leg with dried material on it.

Pringle then commented on his observations,

The deceased died as a result of multiple internal injuries sustained in a motor vehicle accident in which she was reported to be one of two passengers in the vehicle.

The injuries sustained were:

1. Fracture of the pelvis, disarticulation of the right sacra iliac joint and rupture of the urinary bladder.

2. Rupture of the right psoas major muscle.

3. Rupture of the liver.

4. Haemorrhages into the lung.

These injuries were complicated by aspiration of gastric contents into the major air passages and the lungs and were accompanied by considerable internal bleeding. Although death may not have occurred immediately it would have occurred rapidly and it is most unlikely that the deceased was even semiconscious shortly after the accident. The injuries sustained by the deceased would have prevented her walking even if sufficiently conscious to want to do so, and she would not have been able to arrange her clothing in the fashion observed at the post mortem examination which according to the information provided to me by the police was the same as at the scene of the accident.

The observations made at the post mortem examination did not provide evidence that sexual interference with the deceased at the scene of the accident had taken place. Several specimens have been taken from the genital area and from the dried material on the deceased's left leg to clarify the point.

16. Pringle stated,

She was dressed in black tracksuit pants, a navy blue windcheater with white band, red topped football socks (also striped white and blue), running shoes and bikini type panties. Burrs, other grass seeds and particles were present on the external surface of her clothes and socks. Heavy bleeding had occurred over her face and neck and had soaked into the top of her windcheater. The bleeding had come from a massive scalp laceration which commenced just behind the outer end of the left eyebrow and ended on the back of her head near the external occipital protuberance in the midline. The scalp below the laceration had been torn away from the side of the skull and formed a flap which hung loosely outwards. Above the laceration the scalp was firmly adherent to the skull. The left ear had been torn off and in its place there was a large ragged laceration on the side of the head. A large area of the bone of the vault of the skull was exposed in the floor of this wound as well as the extensively torn and mangled temporalis muscle and damaged blood vessels. No fractures were evident in the bone exposed nor could any be felt anywhere in the skull, face or jaw.

On the right side of the head and face there was a large dark haemorrhagic abrasion with a dried hard surface 12 x 6cm approximately which occupied the forehead for a few centimetres above the outer half of the eyebrow and most of the space below the eye and the ear; it extended down into the upper part of the side of the face and onto the cheek below the right eye. Closely related to the wound on the left side of the head there was an extensive dark haemorrhagic abrasion with a hard, and in places, round surface on the side and back of the neck which extended from the vicinity of the ragged wound (where the left ear had been), across the supraclavicular area and onto the front, top and back of the shoulder. This abrasion did not reach the outer side of the shoulder.

Across the back on the lower scapular area there were 6 to 8 broad scratch like marks with dark red dried surfaces; these markings were up to 8cm long and 1/2cm wide, were roughly parallel with one another and sloped downwards from the right to the left side of the body.

On the left buttock there was an abrasion like that seen on the left side of the neck, etc; it was about 6cm long and 2cm wide; its direction was much the same as that of the scratches described on the back, i.e. it sloped downwards and outwards towards the outer side of the hip. A dark haemorrhagic abrasion 5 x 1/2cm was present about the middle of the left upper arm on its antero lateral aspect. An extensive area of bruising occupied roughly the middle one third of the outer part of the front of the left thigh. Within this area of bruising there were two scratches parallel with one another each about 12cm long and 1.5cm apart. A small moist haemorrhagic abrasion 2-3cm in diameter was present on the left calf and a surgical dressing was present on some blister like lesions on the top of her left foot.

No fractures were detected in the bones of the limbs or trunk.

The external genitalia and pubic hair were normal.

17. Pringle stated,

On reflecting the intact scalp covering the right side of the skull as well as a narrow strip to the left of the midline running antero-posteriorly haemorrhages were present in the scalp at various levels as well as on the surface of the skull. No fractures were detected in the vault of the skull nor were any intercranial haemorrhages seen after the skull had been opened. The brain appeared normal. No fractures were seen in the base of the skull. The upper two cervical vertebrae felt normal to examination with a finger introduced through the foramen magnum into the upper part of the spinal canal in the neck. Within the chest which included the structures in the neck the following was observed.

No fracture was detected in the spine in the neck.

Considerable bleeding had occurred around the right subclavian vessels, the right common carotid artery and for a short distance around the external and internal carotid arteries. This perivascular bleeding was continuous with bleeding in the chest around the arch of the aorta and the upper half of the descending aorta and also extended around the major bronchi and pulmonary arteries as far as the roots of the lungs. No tear was found in a major blood vessel in the areas so affected to account for this bleeding. The pharynx and larynx contained fluid blood and gastric contents as did also the trachea and major bronchi. These structures were otherwise normal.

About 500 mls of fluid blood was present in the right plural cavity.

On the right side of the back of the chest a few centimetres from the side of the spine the 8th to 11th ribs inclusive were broken in a line roughly parallel with the spine; the jagged ends of these broken ribs projected slightly into the pleural cavity through tears in the overlying parietal pleura. No fractures were present in the spine or the left ribs or in the sternum. The left pleural cavity did not contain free fluid or blood. The diaphragm on both sides was intact and normal.

In the right lung there were two deep ragged tears on the inferior aspect of its lower lobe, a haematoma about 4cm across in its upper lobe and small areas of bleeding scattered throughout the remainder of this lung. The left lung was very dark, almost haemorrhagic in appearance. Within both lungs the larger air passages contained blood and thick fluid with a sour smell of gastric contents.

About 10 mls of slightly blood-tinged fluid was present in the pericardial sac. The heart and major blood vessels were normal apart from the perivascular bleeding already described.

Within the abdomen and pelvis the following was observed:

No free fluid or blood was present in the peritoneal cavity. None of the abdominal or pelvic organs showed evidence of injury. No fractures were evident in the lumbar spine or in the pelvis.

The liver was pale and in patches looked to be fatty; it was otherwise normal.

The stomach contained solid partly digested food but very little fluid; it appeared normal and its contents smelled faintly of alcohol. The remainder of the abdominal and pelvic organs were normal.

On completing the autopsy, Dr Pringle reserved a number of specimens for examination both by the government analyst and by the division of forensic medicine. They included blood from the femoral vein and the heart, plus pericardial fluid for alcohol estimation; blood for general chemical examination from the right pleural cavity; the liver, the stomach and its contents, bile and urine. Given the injuries to the girl Dr Pringle appeared unsurprised that an adequate amount of blood could not be obtained from the heart, and that 'barely sufficient was available for the alcohol estimation'. He sent off for examination a piece of her heart, two pieces of her right lung, a piece of liver and a piece of kidney. He also sent off two pieces of cerebrum. In his comments at the end of his report, Dr Pringle noted that such traumatic scalping as Mona had endured she would have died quickly.

> The post mortem findings indicate that the deceased had died as a consequence of the injuries she had received in a motor vehicle accident in which she is reported to have been the driver. Her massive scalp wound – partial avulsion of the scalp, i.e. traumatic scalping – would have caused considerable blood loss. There was an extensive abrasion on the opposite side of her head and face which would suggest that the head was subjected to considerable traumatic violence and that the deceased would very likely have been semiconscious or unconscious as a result. The combination of these circumstances would have been sufficient to bring about her death in a short time but there were also other injuries and complications which would have accelerated her death through the production of severe hypoxia; these were haemorrhages into the lung associated with lacerations in the right lung, the presence of blood and aspirated vomitus in the air passages in the lungs and fractured ribs which would have restricted her breathing.

18. Cuneen, C., 1997, 'Community Conferencing and the Fiction of Indigenous Control', *Australian and New Zealand Journal of Criminology*, Vol. 30 No # 292–311.

19. Ibid.

20. Grant told Baty and Johnson on their arrival at the scene that both he and the girls were all okay and to leave them alone.

21. Mulurulu Station is approximately 730 kilometres from Sydney. Its nearest town is Ivanhoe, ninety-seven kilometres away. Mulurulu Station address is via Mildura but Mildura is across the border in Victoria; Dareton is back across the Murray River in NSW.

22. It may seem unimportant but the identification of a vehicle and its year of manufacture are usually well-known quantities to people who live in the Australian bush.

23. In July 1997, a major restructure of the NSW Police Service resulted

in the expansion of four regions into eleven. The North West Region and its associated commands such as the Accident Investigation Squad were abolished. Earlier, in 1990 the *Police Regulation Act (1899)* was repealed, a consequence being the dissolution of the Police Force of NSW and the Police Department. In its place came the New South Wales Police Service which, from 1 July 1990 had the aim of 'the police and the community working together to establish a safer environment by reducing violence, crime and fear'. In 2002, it changed its name to New South Wales Police and again in 2007 it reverted to its historical name, New South Wales Police Force. The love affair with the community had ended in tears.

24. The blue Falcon was owned by June's boyfriend Robert Nixon. It is worth noting that during the investigation and trial, the fathers of the dead girls did not appear. Their whereabouts remain unknown.

25. The Oxley Club Sharon spoke of was the RSL Club. It is no longer in existence. As to the rodeo, there is no record of a rodeo taking place in Bourke in November or December 1987. It may have been a local event, unlike the national events that take place in nearby towns such as Coonamble or the Barwon River Rodeo that is an annual event in nearby Brewarrina on Easter Saturday.

26. With this, Mr Barnett provided some important pieces of information for the police. The description of the man, though it was not recorded as being the description of Alex Grant, was enough to recognise it was him. Coupled with the name and the type of alcohol he had purchased, it was clear the man in the Riverview Hotel at 10 p.m. on Saturday 5 December was Alex Grant. Of equal interest was the mystery woman at the door. Barnett's recollection was that the woman was not accompanying Grant yet he was unable to say for certain given that the other patron returned to the bar. Mona or Cindy or both may have followed Grant as far as the door of the bar. Barnett did not provide a description of the woman.

27. In Australian constitutional history, Sir Garfield Barwick was celebrated as the adviser from whom Sir John Kerr – the Governor-General who had felt it necessary to 'sack' the Whitlam government – had taken constitutional advice.

28. *Autrefois* is a French word which has become part of criminal law terminology. It is a complex mechanism whereby an accused cannot be

tried for a crime because the record shows he or she had already been subjected to trial for the same conduct. If the previous trial resulted in conviction, the defendant can plead *autrefois* convict. In America, the action is known as double jeopardy. It has been made popular in television programs where an accused cannot be convicted of a crime a second time.

29. NSW Police Force 2015.

30. Department of Public Prosecutions 2003.

31. By 'sprung', Mr Hurle most likely meant the door had been opened beyond its normal operation, thus bending the hinges or the mounting. It would have resulted in the door being forward of its normal opening position.

32. The use of the term 'crowbar' by both men is a little unusual. It may be that crowbar was used as a term for a short piece of bent steel but more widely, in industrial language, the term 'pinch bar' was used. It is hard to believe that two men living in regional Australia in a small town would use the popular rather than the accepted term.

33. The 1985 Toyota Hilux owned by Major Metals was the fourth generation of Japanese utility sold around the world. Production of the model took place between 1984 and 1988. It was a front-engine rear-wheel-drive four-wheel-drive that came as either a two-door or a four-door. Engine sizes ranged between 1.6-litre petrol and 2.4-litre diesel turbo with a 4/5 speed manual or 3/4 speed automatic transmission. The model owned by Major Metals had 62kW of power. By way of comparison, a 2015 model had a 2.4-litre turbo diesel engine with power output of 126kW. In the space of a generation, technology had doubled the power output of the vehicle.

34. Lusher Inquiry 1981.

35. Finnane in Dixon.

36. By 1989, Bassett had risen to the rank of chief inspector and he had come to the attention of NSW Independent MP John Hatton. Hatton named Bassett in parliament, charging him with being complicit in racist actions within the Bourke command. An investigation was carried out and Bassett was subsequently transferred to Newcastle.

37. Nixon, C., *Fair Cop*, p. 51.

38. Whitton, E., ICAC submission 2014.

39. At the same time that Avery was studying part-time at Macquarie, the Rev. Fred Nile was undertaking studies in politics with Dr Meredith Bergmann. Nile was at the time a controversial figure in NSW politics and went on to hold the balance of power in the NSW Legislative Council. Bergmann too aspired to be more than an academic and became a Labor member of the Upper House and ultimately its president.

40. It has since reverted, but it does not acknowledge that the change back means the service idea failed. Indeed, one need only watch one or two police crime dramas on television to know that the idea of providing a service has led to a diminution of respect for police, especially in a multicultural society where non-English speaking communities value enforcement rather than service.

41. The Bourke Defence had been coined some years earlier by solicitors working for the Aboriginal Legal Service. In essence, it was tactical: there was a strong prospect that if a court appearance were delayed, a witness might not appear.

42. Half Case was the local name for the grocery store. It is now an IGA supermarket.

43. CYSS was Community Youth Support Services; CES was the Commonwealth Employment Service.

44. It was impossible to hear the remainder of the questions for the loudness of other voices in the courtroom.

45. One must wonder how much instruction a teenaged witness may have been given in court procedures before entering the witness stand. It seemed to be assumed that all witnesses would demonstrate fearlessness when confronted by the court. It may have even been assumed that an Aboriginal teenage girl would have such capacity.

46. In 2001, the *Justices Act 1902* was repealed and replaced with the Justices Legislation Repeal and Amendment Act; the Criminal Procedure Amendment (Justices and Local Courts) Act; and the Crimes (Local Courts Appeal and Review) Act. According to the parliamentary secretary at the time, the Hon. Ian MacDonald, the 1902 Justices Act was 'a complex, disjointed, procedure-oriented and difficult to understand piece of

legislation'. In 2014, MacDonald was charged by the NSW Independent Commission Against Corruption with misconduct in public office. His case went before the local court.

47. An alibi defence is a defence based upon information that a defendant was not at the scene of a crime when the crime occurred. The success of an alibi defence rests on the ability of alibi witnesses to undergo cross-examination by a prosecution.

48. The transcript itself had been typed up at Bathurst at the District Court Criminal Registry on 30 November 1988 from original recordings made at the hearing at Bourke. Six transcription typists certified that the transcript was a correct transcript of the depositions sound-recorded at Bourke. Sound recordings of hearings and trials are held for a certain time and then destroyed. If there is no transcript of a hearing, or if the hearing has not been heard in public, then access to such transcripts is restricted to parties to a case. The hearing transcript, when finalised, was sent to the Dubbo office of the solicitor for public prosecutions.

49. The penultimate charge of escaping from lawful custody and assaulting an officer in the execution of duty was made against Daniel James Booth, one of the witnesses in Mr Grant's case.

50. The WALS is now known as ALS NSW/ACT. It is an Aboriginal community organisation giving information and referral, and legal advice and court representation to Aboriginal and Torres Strait Islander men, women and children across NSW and the ACT.

51. Rozenes, M., *Prosecutorial Discretion in Australia Today* (undated).

52. It was to be another eight weeks before activity resumed, at which time subpoenas were issued on the registrar, Nyngan local court, to produce the court file pertaining to the charges against Grant listed at Nyngan Local Court on 16 December 1987; and the Commissioner of Police for five items, including Ehsman's notebook, the incident report, the official notebook of Constable McKenzie, the plan of the accident site and the occurrence pad from Bourke police station. A subpoena was also issued on the Roads and Traffic Authority for production of all documents and history of the driver's licence issued to Mr Grant.

53. *The Queen v. O'Connor (1980)* 146 CLR 64 2.6.1908.

54. In the Majewski case in England in 1977, Robert Stefan Majewski was convicted in a Crown court of assaults occasioning actual bodily harm and of assaults of a police constable in the execution of his duty. The charges arose out of a drunken brawl in a public house and a subsequent incident at a police station. At his trial, Majewski gave evidence that when the assaults were committed he had been taking a mixture of drugs and a fair amount of alcohol, none under medical advice. As a result, he said he did not know what he was doing on the evening in question and had no recollection of the incidents to which the charges related. The trial judge was not impressed. He raised the issue of intent and its relationship to drug and alcohol use. In directing the jury, he said,

> where an offence does not require a specific intent (any intention, for example, to cause grievous bodily harm as certain offences do or offences such as theft requiring an intention of dishonesty) where no such intention is, as it were, a constituent part of the offence, then if a man has induced in himself a state in which he is under the influence of drink and drugs then that state is no defence. Indeed, in every single case in this indictment the allegation is one of assault. That does not require the proof by the prosecution of any specific intention and therefore the fact that [the defendant] may have taken drink and drugs is irrelevant provided that you are satisfied that the state which he was in as a result of those drink and drugs or a combination of both was self-induced because, so that you can understand this, what the law really says is that, if a person disables himself by his own conduct, by the taking of drink and drugs, from having powers of comprehension as to what is going on or his powers of self-control, he cannot then turn round and say: 'I am not responsible for what I did' because he put himself into that position in the first place. That is the logic of it but the practical effect of it, members of the jury, is this, that upon my direction in law you can ignore the subject of drink and drugs as being in any way a defence to any one or more of the counts in this indictment.

55. The House found in the Majewski case that self-induced intoxication was irrelevant if tendered solely to raise a doubt about the presence of

intention to do the physical act involved in the crime. The act of an accused was to have been incontestably presumed to have been voluntary and to have been done with an intent to do the physical act involved in the crime.

56. Godkin was at the cycle track in Auckland when he received a telex that read,

Tuesday January 30 1990 1:00pm Nemesis 12:45hrs 30/01/90 To New Zealand. Bourke message No. 90/03 12:45hrs 30/01/90 Please have your police attend the commonwealth games cycling track in Auckland and locate Mr Raymond George Godkin, president of the Australian commonwealth games association and president of the cycling team. Request ex-sen/sgt Godkin contact the Bourke police station on (068) 72-2555 as soon as possible and if after 6.00pm E.S.T. to contact Enngonia police on (068) 74-7555, in relation to the trial of Alexander Ian Grant charged 'culpable driving cause death'. The crown prosecutor Terry Wolfe requires his attendance at the trial and arrangements need to be made to book air travel for him if he requires it. Crown stresses this matter is of utmost urgency. Avery Commissioner. Officer in Charge: Const 1/C Le-Merton. Authority C/Insp Bassett. Station of origin: Bourke police station. Station telephone number: (068) 72-2555.

www.ingramcontent.com/pod-product-compliance
Lightning Source LLC
Chambersburg PA
CBHW030240030426
42336CB00009B/184